CliffsNotes®

Praxis II®:
Elementary Education
(0011, 0012, 0014) Test Prep

by

Jocelyn L. Paris, M.Ed.
and Judy L. Paris, M.Ed.

WILEY
Wiley Publishing, Inc.

About the Authors

Jocelyn has had a colorful and enriching life centered on teaching. She graduated with a B.A. from the University of Arizona and obtained her Master's in Elementary Education at Northern Arizona University. She has taught preschool through high school age students ranging in all abilities from severe to profound mentally retarded to deaf to gifted to emotionally and behaviorally challenged. Jocelyn has taught in a multitude of settings as well: public school, charter school, residential school for the deaf and blind, private school, and Montessori school. She also is author of *Idioms*, published by Butte Publications, Inc. Jocelyn loves to coach sports and has coached basketball, volleyball, and soccer for elementary through high school varsity teams. One of her true passions lies with Camp Abilities, a fundamentally appropriate sports camp for the Visually Impaired. She has been involved in these camps for the past six years in Arizona, New York, and Alaska.

For more than 35 years, **Judy** has been professionally involved in the field of education as a teacher, a special education director, a superintendent, a consultant, an author, and a mentor and currently serves as adjunct faculty at several universities. She holds degrees and certifications in special education, early childhood education, elementary education, and educational leadership/administration. She has presented a paper at Oxford and was named Teacher of the Year. Although retired from public education, she currently creates plays for young children, develops college courses and exams, teaches in summer enrichment camps, conducts professional development workshops, and writes educational materials. It is because of her desire for all children to be allowed to learn through discovery, to be offered a variety of educational opportunities, and to experience the world around that has led to her newest endeavor of developing a children's museum for her community.

Authors' Acknowledgments

To Chip for always being in my back pocket; to Mabel for greeting me each day with a smile and kisses; to Haley for PB&J sammies; to Justin and Andrea for keeping me updated on the weather; to Gram and Gramp for coupons and jokes; to Mom and Dad for supporting and loving me; and to my students for keeping me young, making me old, listening to my stories, educating me, laughing at my jokes, and renewing my faith in the future. — Jocelyn L. Paris

To the most amazing educator I know, who awakes each day to instill knowledge in our youth, who yearns for a beautiful tomorrow, who strives to support the unfortunate, and who will make an enormous difference to future generations....my Jocelyn. —Judy L. Paris

Publisher's Acknowledgments

Editorial

Project Editor: Kelly D. Henthorne

Acquisitions Editor: Greg Tubach

Composition

Proofreader: Leeann Harney

Wiley Publishing, Inc. Composition Services

CliffsNotes® Praxis II®: Elementary Education (0011, 0012, 0014) Test Prep

Published by:
Wiley Publishing, Inc.
111 River Street
Hoboken, NJ 07030-5774
www.wiley.com

Copyright © 2009 Wiley, Hoboken, NJ

Published by Wiley, Hoboken, NJ
Published simultaneously in Canada

Library of Congress Cataloging-in-Publication Data

Paris, Jocelyn L., 1977-
  CliffsNotes Praxis II : elementary education (0011, 0012, 0014) test prep /
by Jocelyn L. Paris and Judy L. Paris.
    p. cm.
  ISBN-13: 978-0-470-25956-6
  1. Education, Elementary--United States--Examinations--Study guides. 2.
Teaching--United States--Examinations--Study guides. 3. National teacher
examinations--United States--Study guides. I. Paris, Judy L., 1950- II.
LB1762.P37 2008
  370.76--dc22

                        2008046682

For general information on our other products and services or to obtain technical support, please contact our Customer Care Department within the U.S. at 800-762-2974, outside the U.S. at 317-572-3993, or fax 317-572-4002.

Wiley also publishes its books in a variety of electronic formats. Some content that appears in print may not be available in electronic books. For more information about Wiley products, please visit our web site at www.wiley.com.

Table of Contents

PART II: PRACTICE EXAMINATIONS WITH ANSWER EXPLANATIONS

Introduction

Although teaching is a rewarding profession, it is also a difficult one. Consistent re-evaluation of teaching methods and ever-changing social attitudes toward education are always affecting the education profession. If you have made it this far, you know that teaching requires you to consistently increase your knowledge of the field. The Praxis exam is just one way to ensure that you have the core subject knowledge you will be teaching as well as the professional knowledge (curriculum, instruction, and assessment) needed in this profession. Because you want to become the best teacher you can be, you have decided to study for the Praxis examinations. All good teachers prepare and do their homework.

Pat yourself on the back as you have chosen an excellent study guide that will help you prepare for the Praxis II exam and will be useful in your elementary classroom for years to come. You are in the final stage toward the acquisition of your teaching certification/license. The elementary Praxis II exams are focused on broad content knowledge, instructional theories, strategies and methods, as well as a general understanding of elementary students. Ensuring that you are successful on the Praxis II elementary exams is a positive move for your career.

Effective educators utilize content knowledge and apply principles to classroom structure, behavior management, curriculum design, and assessments. Educators should seek current information on policies, research, and strategies. Joining professional organizations, reading research studies, taking university courses, attending professional development trainings, and subscribing to professional journals will help educators to improve student programs.

Children in elementary schools possess individual strengths and specific needs. It is the educator's role to address both in an appropriate manner so that all children may learn and develop into capable citizens. Teachers must be creative, flexible, and confident as they work in educational settings providing activities to students who possess a wide range of abilities. Working with elementary students can be stimulating yet demanding.

Getting Started

Whether you are a recent college graduate or an experienced teacher, taking the Praxis II exam meets certain state certification requirements. The final score on the exam will reflect what you have gained from teacher preparation courses and from utilizing current teaching practices in the classroom. To prepare for the actual exam, you may also want to review college texts, conduct Internet research, or visit the library.

Remember that the practice exams offered in this guide will provide you with information about the format and types of questions on the Praxis II elementary exams. The content and questions in the practice exams and on the actual exams may differ in both substance and difficulty. After completing a practice exam in this guide, use the answers and detailed explanations for further study on these specific topics.

Format of the Exam

Each Praxis II exam provided in this guide is designed to help individuals evaluate general content knowledge regarding the teaching of elementary students. Each of the elementary exams included here are slightly different in composition. Two of the exams are comprised of a set of *multiple-choice questions*, although the number of questions varies. One exam includes *essay exercises* that require more detailed narrative answers. All of the exam questions are based on instructional situations, issues surrounding curriculum or assessment, or broad content knowledge pertinent to the education of elementary students.

Three general topics are related to the elementary education Praxis II exams included in this study guide, and each has an accompanying practice test. The specific code numbers and titles are listed here.

#0014	Elementary Education: Content Knowledge
#0011	Elementary Education: Curriculum, Instruction, and Assessment
#0012	Elementary Education: Content Area Exercises

Multiple-Choice Questions

Multiple-choice questions include a **stem** (statement) and four answer choices, the correct answer being the **key.** The stem may be written in one of these formats: *question, statement, fill-in-the-blank,* or *least/except choices*. The four answer choices that follow the stem are identified by letter selections "A", "B", "C" and "D". The three **distractors** may be related to the correct answer, but select only the best possible answer.

The multiple-choice questions are designed to test total knowledge of the subject material regarding elementary education. These questions are factually written, so think carefully when making final answer selections.

In both the practice test and the actual exam, some of the multiple-choice questions may be based on a scenario that resembles an actual classroom situation. Read the brief excerpt and think about how the posed questions should be answered in reference to the information provided. Consider what an educator should do if placed in this particular circumstance.

Multiple-Choice Format and Strategy

To answer discrete multiple-choice questions correctly, strong reading skills are necessary. Reading with care to understand the basic premise of the question while remaining confident in the knowledge of the area tested is essential. The exam questions reflect the *best practices* used in elementary education.

Prior to answering questions on the practice or actual exam, read and then reread each question. Think about your selection before looking at the list of answer options. Check to see whether your selection is listed in the four choices, which makes finding the best answer an easier task. If the information in the question is unknown, look at all of the options and use the process of elimination. Remove any choices that seem impossible or not probable, as that may help in selecting a correct answer from fewer choices.

Types of multiple-choice formats:

Fill-in-the-Blank or Complete the Statement

This type of question offers information through a partial sentence that must be completed using one of the posed options. Select the best option to complete the sentence, using facts and data about elementary education.

Question/Statement or Which of the Following?

This type of question asks a short question or delivers a statement that must be answered by selecting one of the four options provided. The most frequently used question type on multiple-choice exams is the question that begins with "Which of the following ...." To answer these, read the question carefully and think about all the options, choosing the one that BEST suits the question.

Least/Not/Except

This type of question requires the selection of an answer that is incorrect, or least likely to be correct. These questions place a negative slant on the outcome of the answer, so be careful when selecting the appropriate response. These questions require an examinee to decide which of the three options are correct answers, and then to eliminate those to determine the incorrect answer. One strategy to use is to restate the question in a positive way in order to select the three correct answers, thereby leaving the fourth choice as the answer.

For example:

> *Which of the following is NOT included on ...*
>
> *Which is the LEAST likely ...*
>
> *All of the following are true EXCEPT ...*
>
> *Which choice is NOT a component of ...*

The multiple-choice questions termed with "Least," "Not," or "Except" are included on the Praxis exams, but samples are **not** included in this guide on the practice exams, so examinees will study only the correct information in preparing for the Praxis II exam. These questions on the actual exam can be tricky, so use caution.

Essay Writing 101

An essay is defined as a short piece of writing on a specific topic or subject. In an essay, the writer must present his views clearly, concisely, and succinctly. It should contain an introduction, body, and conclusion as well as have well-supported opinions.

Essays should be well thought out in argument and content. The content provided must be supported by specific details with a clearly defined purpose. There are specific steps to use when writing an essay.

- *Analysis*—Clearly define the aims of the essay, include reasons, and give evidence/facts.
- *Main Point*—Pinpoint your main points and add supporting details.
- *Outline*—Sketch out the essay, jot down key points and map out the structure of your arguments.
- *Introduction*—Grab the reader's attention, set up the issue, and lead into your argument. In a short essay (less than 1000 words), after grabbing the reader's attention, begin describing a specific, concrete situation.
- *Body*—This is the crux of the essay where the writer focuses upon the argument or information in detail and presents clear ideas and opinions.
- *Conclusion*—Use wrap-up sentences to conclude the essay. Restate or summarize the main point(s) in a fresh and rephrased manner in order to leave the reader with a memorable impression.

Essay Questions

An essay exercise poses a complex problem related to elementary education in which the examinee must develop a written answer. Each of the essay questions given relates to one of the four main subject areas, or it may pertain to integrated subjects. The questions focus on instructional approaches, methods or strategies, solving problems, achieving goals, outlining curriculum, or addressing assessment.

Answers must be written in a test answer booklet provided at the testing center. The essay answers will be scored using a pre-determined, standardized grading rubric. Because the questions are not known prior to the exam, examinees must be careful to pace their writing while attending to the responses with all the necessary information.

Several strategies helpful to examinees for essay questions on the Praxis II exam follow:

- Read the question you must answer prior to reading the rest of the information given.
- Engage in reading the essay question information by taking notes to help with your answer.
- Outline the ideas and content that is important to writing an essay answer.
- Think about the necessary details and focus on the accuracy of the answer.
- Develop a clear and concise narrative response specific to the situation.
- Review the response to be sure all points were answered.

It is very important for examinees to write clear, concise, complete answers and watch for questions that have more than one part, requiring multiple responses. If an essay answer is written in too simple a format, the answer may not receive full credit. The Praxis II exam that includes essay questions in this study guide is Elementary Education: Content Area Exercises (0012).

Time Frame

The amount of time allowed for taking each elementary Praxis II exam is based on the specific format of the test. For the three exams listed in this guide, examinees are allotted 2 hours to answer between 110 and 120 multiple-choice questions and 2 hours to answer 4 essay questions.

The specific exams, the number of questions, the format, and the time limits are listed:

Content Knowledge	120 MC Questions	2 hours
Curriculum, Instruction, and Assessment	110 MC Questions	2 hours
Content Area Exercises	4 Essay Questions	2 hours

Examinees should practice pacing themselves prior to taking the actual exam. They should consider the time arrangement on the practice exams. When taking the actual Praxis II exam, examinees need time to read each question, to consider each answer, and to review all of the final answers before submitting the test for a score. When writing an essay answer, examinees need time to read the question, consider the formation of a narrative answer, take the time to write the answer, and finally review the answer.

When faced with multiple-choice questions, examinees must think about all of the possibilities and select the most appropriate response. If an examinee is unsure of the correct response for a multiple-choice question, she should still answer the question as there is no penalty for guessing exam answers. On the essay questions, examinees should make every attempt to develop a thorough and thoughtful response in a narrative format.

Content of the Exam

Each of the specific elementary tests in this guide are comprised of content categories, and the actual Praxis II exams assess an examinee's understanding of the concepts and the applications of the concepts related to these specific content categories.

This general list outlines the broad topics, the number of questions, and the percentage of the final score dedicated to that section for each exam.

Elementary Education: Content Knowledge

Language Arts	30	25%
Mathematics	30	25%
Social Studies	30	25%
Science	30	25%

Elementary Education: Curriculum, Instruction, and Assessment

Reading and Language Arts Curriculum, Instruction, and Assessment	38	35%
Mathematics Curriculum, Instruction, and Assessment	22	20%
Science Curriculum, Instruction, and Assessment	11	10%
Social Studies Curriculum, Instruction, and Assessment	11	10%
Arts and Physical Education Curriculum, Instruction, and Assessment	11	10%
General Information About Curriculum, Instruction, and Assessment	17	15%

Elementary Education: Content Area Exercises

Reading/Language Arts	1	25%
Mathematics	1	25%
Science or Social Studies	1	25%
Interdisciplinary Instruction	1	25%

Frequently Asked Questions

Examinees generally have questions prior to taking a Praxis II exam, and the following questions are presented as those most commonly posed. However, if you need further assistance, contact the Educational Testing Services at www.ets.org/praxis or call 800-772-9476.

Q. What are the Elementary Education Praxis II exams about?

A. The Praxis II exams have been developed by the Educational Testing Service (ETS) to measure an individual's knowledge in specific topics related to elementary education. These include general education practices to measure the knowledge of prospective teachers. Many states require these examinations in order to complete the certification or licensure process for professional practice. Some professional organizations also may require the completion of a Praxis exam for membership.

Q. How should an examinee register for a Praxis II exam?

A. Most individuals find that registering online is quick and easy. Contact the Educational Testing Services on their Web site or at the telephone number listed previously. Registration may be completed any time prior to taking the test, but it is recommended that registration be completed 1–3 months ahead of the testing date.

Q. What if an examinee misses the registration period for the preferred test date?

A. Late registration is allowed, but there may be a fee added for late registration. Examinees should hurry to be situated for the correct exam and obtain a seat at the test location. Check specific information about late registration on the ETS Web site.

Q. Can the registration date be changed if needed?

A. Contact ETS as soon as possible if a conflict or problem arises with confirmed registration dates. ETS should be able to help with scheduling issues or changes to the existing registration, but remember, a fee may be incurred.

Q. Which states require the Elementary Education Praxis II exams for certification?

A. Some states use certification tests developed by the state or by a separate testing company, and these states do not require the use of the Praxis II exams. Contact the specific department of education to find out which exams are required in each state of interest. Ask about the scores considered as passing, since acceptable scores differ in each state. If an examinee has already taken the exam in one state and is moving to another state, he should ask whether the current score will be accepted. Most states will allow the transfer of a score as long as it meets the required passing score in that state and the score is recent.

On the ETS Web site (www.ets.org/praxis/states) examinees may access specific requirements by clicking on the name of that state. However, it is highly recommended to speak with someone at the state department of education, since regulations sometimes change before Web sites do.

Q. How does an examinee know which exam should be taken?

A. States mandating Praxis II exams for certification or licensure differ on the required test. Research these requirements by contacting the department of education in the particular state. The teacher certification office should have the information needed to select the correct exam or the combination of exams.

Q. What is considered a passing score for teacher certification?

A. The teacher certification office at the department of education in each state should provide the score considered acceptable for passing. Contact this office in the specific state to find out which score is adequate for teacher certification.

Q. When can examinees expect to receive the scores?

A. ETS attempts a quick return of scores, so expect the scores to be delivered in four to six weeks, pending no major holidays. A list of dates is available on the ETS Web site, as well as an informational guide to interpret the score received.

Q. For an individual with a disability, are accommodations allowed?

A. Yes. For individuals with disabilities there is a process to apply for accommodations. Information on accommodations is available in the Praxis II test registration booklet, or on the ETS Web site.

Q. What should examinees plan to bring to the exam site on the date of the test?

A. Examinees need to bring the following:

- Identification that includes name, a photo, and signature
- An alternative identification that includes the same (optional but recommended)
- Proof of registration
- Several #2 pencils and an eraser
- Ink pens for essay answers (some exams)
- Watch (optional but recommended)
- Extra clothing (optional but temperatures may vary)

Q. How can examinees best prepare to take a Praxis II Exam?

A. Using this study guide should help improve the chances of passing a Praxis II Elementary exam. Understanding the test format, taking the practice exams, and reviewing the contents of the study guide should reinforce an examinee's base of knowledge.

Using this Study Guide

CliffsNotes Praxis II: Elementary Education includes several supports to help guide examinees.

- **General Curriculum Introduction and Overview Section**: A section that includes information which supports all subject areas of elementary education. This section outlines learning theories and guidelines for developing curriculum, preparing lessons, managing the classroom, and implementing assessments.

- **Content Area Information**: A comprehensive section for each subject area should be used to study the specific content categories described in the exam (0014). The headings are a guide to select topics to study. Following the basic content portion is a section devoted to the curriculum, instruction, and assessment for the specific subject area (0011) and a content exercise (0012). These sections should be the focus of intense study. These are broken into four major subjects: language arts, mathematics, science, and social studies.

- **Final Thoughts and Tips:** A review of the test-taking strategies is provided with tips for test preparation to aid in achieving exam success.

- **Practice Exams:** A sample full-length test is provided for each of the three separate topics in elementary education. These tests are offered as a guide regarding the content and format of the actual Praxis II exam. In addition to the exams are the answers with detailed justifications for the correct answer. This is an added study tool.

Elementary Education: Content Knowledge (0014)

The Praxis II Content Knowledge examination for elementary education is a comprehensive and detailed investigation of the core information that an examinee possesses pertaining to the topics covered: language arts, mathematics, social studies, and science. This multiple-choice test was constructed to assess the base knowledge of individuals who plan to teach at the elementary level.

Examinees should plan on a two-hour exam of the content categories that comprise the four main subjects in an elementary classroom. The information in this exam is based on the content that is included in curricula for elementary children at all grade levels. Whether an individual plans to teach 2nd grade or 5th grade, all elementary subject matter must be understood.

This guide provides in-depth content for exam 0014 divided by the four main subject areas, but it is not inclusive of the entire breadth of the content available for all grade levels. After reviewing and studying the content available in this guide, if you feel that further study is necessary, refer to subject areas on the Internet or utilize library information or college texts.

Examinees should review the description of the content in the following list, along with the percentages and number of questions, to determine the areas that may need the most concentrated study. When taking the actual exam, the questions are situated in the test booklet according to each subject area. A scientific or four-function calculator is permitted for use on this exam.

The Praxis II Elementary Education: Content Knowledge 0014 is divided as follows:

Language Arts	30 questions	25% of the test
	Understanding Literature	30%
	Text Structures and Organization for Reading and Writing	5%
	Literacy Acquisition and Reading Instruction	30%
	Language in Writing	25%
	Communication Skills	10%
Mathematics	**30 questions**	**25% of the test**
	Critical Thinking	none given
	Number Sense and Numeration	31%
	Algebraic Concepts	23%
	Informal Geometry and Measurement	23%
	Data Organization and Interpretation	23%

Social Studies	30 questions	25% of the test
	Geography	15%
	World History	10%
	United States History	25%
	Political Science	20%
	Anthropology, Sociology, Psychology	15%
	Economics	15%
Science	30 questions	25% of the test
	Earth Science	25%
	Life Science	25%
	Physical Science	25%
	Science in Personal and Social Perspectives	10%
	History and the Nature of Science	5-10%
	Unifying Processes	5-10%

As an examinee, you will notice this exam covers a vast array of information on these four topics. It may seem difficult to know what to study, although the outline given of the percentages will provide a good start in preparing for the amount of test questions that will be included on the exam in certain topic areas. On the actual exam, there may be diagrams, charts, equations, story problems, definitions, readings, poetry, or examples of items used in a classroom. Examinees will want to make sure they study the broad content of these subject areas and concentrate on the specific areas where they feel they may lack knowledge.

A practice exam for #0014 is found at the end of this guide and should help with further study. The answers are not only provided, but a general explanation is also available. Use the practice exam to help in deciding the areas to study and the depth of your studies.

No matter what you study for this exam, the amount of information you retain will be invaluable to your career as a teacher. Innumerable times, students ask for information about the subjects or topics being studied, and it is a wise teacher who is able to provide the details and facts to answer student questions.

Curriculum, Instruction, and Assessment (0011)

The Praxis II exam 0011 is a broad-based set of materials that covers the common subjects taught in elementary education. In a multiple-choice format, this two-hour exam includes 110 questions centered on language arts, mathematics, science, social studies, fine arts, and physical education. The questions are related to curriculum planning, instructional design, and the assessment of students.

The breakdown of the Content Categories for the Curricuum, Instruction, and Assessment exam is as follows:

Reading and Language Arts	38 Questions	35%
Mathematics	22 Questions	20%

Science	11 Questions	10%
Social Studies	11 Questions	10%
Arts and Physical Education	11 Questions	10%
General Information	17 Questions	15%

The material included in this section pertains primarily to the general information of curriculum, instruction, and assessment, but this information may also be applied directly to specific elementary topics or subject areas (science, math, language arts, social studies, and integrated subjects). There is a content-specific section under each subject area in this guide to also study for the 0011 exam.

Examinees should be knowledgeable in all subject areas, as well as with the general aspects of the educational process. Review of previously learned concepts, an understanding of the educational practices, and the ability to apply those concepts and practices will enable the examinee to acquire a satisfactory score on the Praxis II. Remember as you study that to enhance the academic process educators should do the following:

- Acknowledge the theories of development and learning, incorporating them into a personal philosophy.
- Gain knowledge about the core subjects at the elementary level.
- Design and plan effective instruction that encompasses all learners.
- Encourage students to be active participants in creating the learning environment, activities, and experiences.
- Promote learning opportunities that allow students to interact with adults and work cooperatively with others.
- Utilize multiple instructional strategies and a variety of methods.
- Provide adequate materials and developmentally appropriate activities and experiences.
- Instill the use of critical thinking skills, problem-solving skills, and decision-making skills in daily activities.
- Manage behaviors through positive situations, modeling, and training.

Curriculum, instruction, and assessment are the critical elements of educational programming in all subject areas.

> Curriculum is *what* is taught.
> Instruction is *how* it is taught.
> Assessment examines *whether* it was taught and how well it was learned.

Knowledge and Understanding of Human Development

In order to adequately and effectively educate children, teachers must be knowledgeable about the stages and theories related to human development. There are long-standing thoughts about human development and contemporary ideas focused on current research and observation. Educators should review the content of the concepts of human development to better understand how children evolve in the early stages. This review will aid teachers in creating a positive classroom environment and incorporating the theories of learning into instructional delivery.

Constructivism

A popular early theory of human development, constructivism implies that learning evolves and becomes more complex and more complete over time as individuals build upon prior knowledge. Piaget was instrumental in describing that children develop by constructing or building knowledge based on what is already known. He believed that disequilibrium, equilibrium, and assimilation (and sometimes accommodation) are steps in the process of constructing knowledge.

The two principles of this theory are as follows:

> Learning is an individualized process; students learn different things from the same experience.
> Learners must be active in the learning process.

Zone of Proximal Development (Vygotsky)

This theory was defined by the Russian psychologist Lev Vygotsky. His theory was based on the idea that when children have assistance with learning, they can do more collaboratively than by themselves. He described the **zone of proximal development** as the difference between what a child can do on her own and what that child can do with assistance, either from adults or peers. Vygotsky believed that children who interact and work with others perceive things differently, and this collaboration facilitates movement into this zone where certain learning processes occur.

Bronfenbrenner Ecological Model

The child is at the center of an integrated system that functions interactively within itself and may be diagrammed using four concentric circles.

- Microsystem: the child, the environment, and those people or entities with whom the child directly interacts—family, school, and neighborhood
- Mesosystem: interactions of the people with each other in the child's environment; not directly affecting the child
- Exosystem: the broader community in which the child lives; the extended family, friends of family, and social services
- Macrosystem: the attitudes, ideologies (laws, values), customs of the culture in which the child lives

Maslow's Hierarchy of Needs

Abraham Maslow created a hierarchy on which one may observe the more sophisticated needs of an individual at the top levels of the hierarchy. He believed that basic needs must be met for a child to grow and develop; the most basic needs being those that are physiological (air, food, water, rest, shelter). As those needs are met, a child may advance up the steps of the various levels to the top where the child develops into her potential and becomes the best she can be. If all the needs on this hierarchy are met, the child will have the ability to seek knowledge, learn, and develop appropriately. The following is the hierarchy from bottom to top:

- Level I: basic needs; exploration, manipulation, physiological needs
- Level II: security, protection, safety
- Level III: closeness and love
- Level IV: esteem and self-esteem
- Level V: self-actualization

Psychosocial Theory of Development

Erikson identified eight stages of human development, each thought to influence the next stage in the developmental process.

1. Trust vs. Mistrust
2. Autonomy vs. Shame and doubt
3. Initiative vs. Guilt
4. Industry vs. Inferiority
5. Identity vs. Role confusion
6. Intimacy vs. Isolation
7. Generativity vs. Stagnation
8. Integrity vs. Despair

Domains of Learning

Five specific areas of development are referred to as the early **domains of learning**, and educators generally address these domains in the early childhood years to be sure a student is developing appropriately across all sectors. These domains affect one another as a child develops, and instruction should support these domains, providing the child with a strong foundation of learning.

The five domains, which are briefly summarized in this section, include the following:

- Cognitive Domain
- Language/Communication Domain
- Physical/Motor Domain
- Social-Emotional Domain
- Self-Help/Adaptive Domain

Cognitive Domain

The Cognitive domain is the most critical domain as mental skills are essential for the development of all other domains throughout a lifetime. This domain focuses on the primary mental skills such as thinking and reasoning. Other mental skills include remembering, problem solving, decision making, naming, recognizing, making generalizations, understanding cause-and-effect relationships, and analyzing perceptions.

The theorists who most closely concentrated their philosophy on this domain include

- Skinner, Behavioral Learning Theory
- Piaget, Cognitive Development Theory

Language/Communication Domain

Communication and language are very important in life, and this is a critical domain of development. Language, the systematic use of sounds, signs, or written symbols for the purpose of communication or expression, must become meaningful to children, and they must acquire skills using language structures, pattern combinations, gestures, facial expressions, early literacy, and expressive and receptive language in order to develop in this area. The skills of this domain are acquired based on a child's environment and experiences. Early literacy development is a child's first introduction to reading and writing. Children must be exposed to activities that stimulate oral language and listening in order for them to acquire reading and writing skills.

Physical-Motor Domain

Children interact with their environment in very physical ways. The motor domain is the first to develop as children begin moving, and they continue to collect large amounts of data through this domain of learning throughout their lives. The motor domain includes gross motor (large muscles), fine motor (small muscles), sensory-integration (tactile, vestibular, and proprioception), and perceptual (coordination of muscles and movement). The theories formed by Gesell, Piaget, Ayres, and Kephart apply to the physical-motor domain of learning.

Social-Emotional Domain

Emotions are an expression of feelings that reflect needs and desires. If their basic needs are met, a bond forms with the caregiver, which permits other social relationships to emerge and more complex emotions to evolve. Children gain social skills through many interactive experiences in their daily lives. This strengthens their perception of self-esteem, self-confidence, and self-competence.

Other factors influence the proper development of this domain. The cognitive and language domains affect and are affected by the development of the social-emotional domain. The establishment of an effective and age-appropriate environment is also a critical component to a child's developmental stages.

Theories related to the social-emotional domain include Maslow's Humanism Theory, Skinner's Behaviorism Theory, Erikson's Psychosocial Theory, Bandura's Social Learning Theory, and Gardner's Multiple Intelligences Theory.

Self-Help/Adaptive Behavior Domain

Adaptive behaviors, self-help, or personal skills necessary throughout a lifetime are generally acquired during daily routines influenced by parental involvement. Adaptive behaviors are based on the child's age and level of development, as well as the cultural mores of the family (preferences, beliefs, and values). When children master these competencies, they strengthen their self-esteem and develop a sense of independence.

Pedagogy/Learning Theories

Educational pedagogy is the academic or scholarly influence on the act of learning. Theories are the foundation of educational principles and help to define educational practices and instructional delivery models. Understanding how individuals learn will aid educators in their development of unit and lesson plans that address all learners. Numerous theories are related to learning, but only a few broad-based theories have been selected for description in this section. Examinees most likely studied many pedagogical aspects of education and instruction in their coursework. It is not important whether an individual agrees with all the possible theories, but rather that the individual understands and can apply those approaches that are most appropriate for the students being served.

Educators should evaluate their personal philosophy about how children learn, and this philosophy is generally based on existing learning theories. Learning theories can be guidelines on how to deliver instruction to students. Educators know that not every theory works for or relates to every student and his needs. Students are uniquely individual, so the approaches used to address their learning needs should be based on researched information.

Cognitive

Based on Piaget's work and Gestalt psychology, this theory reflects the internal mental processes that are used to acquire knowledge. These processes include problem solving, memory, and language. This theory describes how people understand, analyze, and solve problems.

Cognitive theorists believe that students acquire new information and skills based on prior knowledge. Instruction under this theory must be delivered at the appropriate level or stage of student development and guided in the environment so students may develop an application of the learned skills. Motivational activities will enhance and encourage learning. Instructional application includes learning styles, metacognition, peer tutoring, scaffolded instruction, and behavioral temperaments.

Behavioral

The behavioral theory describes a systematic approach to learning and instruction and is based on the work of Skinner. He believed that learning is a function of the changes in behaviors and the responses to these events. The primary components emphasize the effectiveness of explicit teaching and direct instruction and incorporate the ABC model of instruction (A = antecedent or stimulus; B = target behavior or response; C = consequences or reinforcement). The focus is on measurable learning behaviors that can be observed and documented.

Developmental Theory

This theory emphasizes the natural progression of growth, focusing on the sequence of the developmental stages of cognitive abilities. According to this approach, the key concept to learning suggests that a level of maturity or *readiness* must be reached; when children mature, they naturally begin to learn.

Psychodynamic

This pedagogical approach is based on the premise that human behavior and human relationships are shaped by conscious and unconscious influences. It has been determined that an individual's personality and his reactions to situations are the result of interactions in the mind, the genetic constitution, emotions, and the environment. These factors affect a person's behavior and mental state. Therefore, the psychodynamic theory is the study of human behavior based on motivation and the functional significance of emotions created through the research of Brucke, Jung, and Freud.

Sociological

The social learning theory was constructed by Bandura, who discovered that children learn through their observations of others. According to this approach, educators would be wise to model and demonstrate learning activities and key concepts, so children may observe what they need to learn.

Ecological

This theory focuses on the social experiences and family background and culture that impact a student's development and future academic success. Individuals develop within their personal environments, facing various situations and interactions. These influences from the home, the school, and the community affect how well the student will achieve, and his academic success is related to these past and present experiences.

Eclectic

The eclectic approach to learning promotes the combination of various pedagogical practices to better meet the academic needs of the students. Professionals may select components from the different theoretical approaches to design instruction. Some approaches work better for certain types of students in different environments for various age groups. This type of approach offers the educator a theoretical approach based on his personal philosophy and the ability to change the approach based on the evolving needs of students.

Multiple Intelligences Theory

Howard Gardner introduced this theory of multiple intelligences, each comprised of distinguishing features. This theory has impact on the instructional presentation in classrooms, as individuals possess a range of intelligences, which include not only academic aspects, but other talents and skills. He believed that individuals possess all of the intelligences, yet some are at a higher and more noticeable level. He emphasized that educators should teach to the set of intelligences in order to address the needs and capabilities of all students in a classroom. This theory offers a method of diverse instruction. The nine intelligences are as follows:

- **verbal**—The ability to express oneself orally or in writing and may have the ability to master other languages. The most emphasized intelligence in classrooms, verbal intelligence includes instruction through lecture and textbooks.
- **logical**—The intelligence of logic, reasoning, and problem solving, logical intelligence promotes sequential and orderly instruction and structured environments. Instruction conforms to teacher-directed activities.
- **visual**—The intelligence that enables individuals to use spatial reasoning (use of charts, maps, illustrations, puzzles, and so on) to grasp ideas and solutions to problems prior to explaining them or applying them.
- **musical**—The ability to use patterns, sounds, and rhythms to make sense of the environment. Musical intelligence is not a sole auditory intelligence and includes the study and instruction of mathematics.
- **intrapersonal**—This intelligence focuses on the affective reasoning, which includes feelings, values, and attitudes and promotes meaningful learning.

- **interpersonal**—This area supports interactions with other individuals in the learning process, such as cooperative groups, and interactive whole group instruction, in order to make more sense of the information.
- **kinesthetic**—Interacting with the physical environment defines this area of intelligence, and it encourages activities that utilize fine and gross motor skills, such as learning centers, science experiments, drama-based lessons, and hands-on learning experiences.
- **naturalist**—This intelligence includes skills such as classification and categorization, which are used in the fields of biology, anatomy, zoology, and geology.
- **existential**—A broad-based intelligence, the existential intelligence encompasses aesthetics, philosophy, and religion and permits students to understand their relationship to the world with skills such as summarization and synthesizing.

Theories of learning styles include the following:

- Visual, auditory, kinesthetic (Bandler-Grinder)
- Left-right cerebral, left-right limbic brain dominance (Herrmann)
- Physical, psychological, sociological, emotional, environmental (Dunn and Dunn)
- Concrete random and sequential, abstract random and sequential (Gregorc-Butler)
- 4-MAT system that includes "if, why, how, what"

Curriculum

Curriculum is a designed plan for learning that requires purposeful preparation by the teacher who will organize and manage the learning situation, impart the core content knowledge, and promote the development of skills expected for the learners. Planning, effectiveness, and addressing learner differences all affect the quality of the curriculum. Curriculum is a process that includes the knowledge that is to be transmitted to the students and the outcomes or products to be assessed.

Curriculum is influenced by several factors, and these must be considered when planning and implementing a curriculum at the elementary level. These factors include society values, content standards, accountability systems, research studies, community expectations, culture and language of learners, and the diversity of learning styles.

Components

The framework of curriculum is according to individual states and the standards that are presented for each grade level. These standards encompass the knowledge and skills to guide implementation of the curriculum.

Every curriculum is designed with a set of critical components that should include

- Vision statement/introduction
- Content expectations/standards
- Pedagogy/teaching practices
- Assessment
- Instructional strategies/learning activities
- Differentiated instruction techniques
- Goals and objectives
- Grouping and pacing plans
- Products and materials
- Resources/technology use
- Extension activities
- Closure and follow-up

Purpose

A curriculum should meet the needs of the learners and provide

- Varied opportunities to gain core knowledge
- Assorted activities to apply the learned knowledge
- Methods to integrate the various subjects and disciplines
- Strategies for addressing diverse learners
- Activities that are motivating and challenging
- Assessments that promote continued learning

Design

A curriculum plan, usually created in a chart format encompassing a range of academic goals, instructional objectives, specific skills, and so on, is organized according to the successive levels at which each are taught. The instructional plan can be established when the teacher considers the content of the subject, the levels of the students, and the curriculum goals. The teacher designs the plan and develops the educational activities that are meaningful to the students to enhance their success.

Scope and sequence is a vital design component of the curriculum and essential to the whole school plan as well as the planning of individual teachers in developing learning sequences. The scope and sequence is an outline of the topics and skills to be taught at each grade level. **Scope** includes those decisions about what information and activities are significant and manageable. Consideration of **sequence** includes decisions about what is necessary to include for the sequential development of skills and concepts of the content.

Instructional Objectives

Objectives should identify a learning outcome and be consistent with the overall broad-based goals of the curriculum or subject area. The purpose of an objective is to provide individuals an understanding of the desired instructional outcomes and to identify what an educator intends for the learner to know at the end of the unit or lesson. Each objective should be stated in measurable, precise terms and include three components: targeted audience, the behavior that is expected of the learner, and the conditions under which the learner must demonstrate knowledge.

Implementing Standards

Under the federal law, No Child Left Behind (NCLB), schools were required to reflect standards-based instruction in their educational programs. Each state has now established a set of standards for the subject areas taught at each grade level. National organizations have also developed standards they believe are critical to the effective learning of all children across the country.

When educators use and apply standards, they should ensure that the standards are

- Rigorous, manageable, and developmentally appropriate
- Focused on the academic subjects and core curriculum
- Leveled so students may complete work and perform in diverse ways
- Written clearly for all parties to understand

Integrated Curriculum

An integrated or interdisciplinary curriculum is one that builds upon knowledge across various subjects. It allows learners to explore a common theme that incorporates more than one area of study. Teachers may present more meaningful experiences and link concepts in unique and creative ways. Students may pursue the study of a specific topic that provides learning activities related to mathematics, art, social studies, science, language arts, music, and so on, thus offering skill development and knowledge acquisition by linking subjects in a more authentic manner. An integrated curriculum includes a combination of topics and subjects, varied resources, thematic units, flexible schedules, a multitude of instructional activities that link concepts, and variations in assessments. This approach has been determined to improve academic achievement, instill motivation and interest, and promote lifelong learning for students.

Types of Planning

Teachers plan in different manners and according to the requirements set forth by their state, their district, and their school. Some teachers must provide comprehensive, detailed plans that align with the school curriculum, the district competencies, and the state standards. Some teachers may be able to provide general plans with broad objectives and abbreviated activities. Either way, educators must become efficient and effective planners in order to meet the goals of the institution and the goals for the learner. Three types of planning are used: long-range planning, daily planning, and individual planning.

- **Long-range planning** includes those plans necessary for the year, the semester, the quarter, or the month. Teachers must be aware of the expectations and competencies created in the district and incorporate the standards in these plans, predicting where the students should be by the end of the selected time period. In long-range planning, the plans are generally broken into units or themes, and teachers must also consider the standardized testing needs that will arise.
- **Daily planning** comprises the regular everyday plans used in the classroom. For elementary teachers, this means covering the standards and objectives outlined in the unit plan for all subjects and may require that the teacher create plans for certain electives (art, physical education, music, and so on) or develop an integrated instructional approach.
- **Individual planning** is necessary when teachers are faced with diverse student needs, such as students who are gifted or talented, or those placed in special education. Special accommodations or curriculum modifications may be necessary for all of these students, and teachers must make plans for including these students in the general education plans.

Materials

Curriculum materials are educational resources, selected according to the subject, content, and grade level, which provide students with instructional experiences and activities to meet curriculum objectives and learner goals. They are essential to instruction and meeting the academic needs of all students. Curriculum materials may be commercially made, teacher made, or student created, or found on the Internet, in libraries, museums, or other community institutions.

Materials should be provided for all curricular areas taught and, whenever possible, cross over multiple subjects for integration of topics and content. Several points should be considered when teachers select curriculum materials.

- Examine the instructional situation to determine the best use and type.
- Choose materials that are appropriate for both the learners and the subject/topic.
- Keep materials in working order, safe, and easy to handle or manage.
- Make all materials accessible to learners or in close proximity to the classroom.
- Train learners on guidelines for the use and for return to specific locations.

Examples of curriculum materials include games, posters, collections, models, transparencies, kits, textbooks, computer programs, manipulatives, art supplies, music materials, video or sound recordings, puppets, and educational toys.

Environments

Creating a viable environment conducive to active learning takes planning and preparation, but when done well, it is a positive preventive strategy. The classroom climate fosters student achievement, and teachers should collaborate with their students to adopt a code of conduct, create classroom procedures, and improve room arrangements to include them in the learning process.

Instruction

Effective classroom instruction depends on planning, which is a systematic and organized way to develop lessons and activities for the learners. Designing instruction supports the teacher in the classroom and helps the teacher visualize the whole picture. Educators must know themselves, their philosophy, their teaching style, and the learners in order to plan the appropriate instruction.

Three purposes for the process of instructional design are as follows:

1. Identifies the outcomes of the instruction and for the learners
2. Guides the development of content through a scope and sequence
3. Establishes the assessment plan to gauge instructional effectiveness

The process of designing and preparing for instruction includes

1. Define the instructional goals (general statements of expectations and outcomes)
2. Perform an instructional analysis (identification of the learning steps to reach goals)
3. Distinguish present knowledge, skill, and behavior levels of students (the focus of instruction)
4. Identify performance objectives (specific statements of learner outcomes)
5. Choose instructional methods (strategies and techniques to impart knowledge and content based on objectives and outcomes)
6. Gather instructional materials (based on methodologies and learners but may be changed as instruction occurs)
7. Conduct formative evaluation (ongoing assessment to alter instruction based on learner needs)
8. Conduct summative evaluation (at the end of instruction to verify effectiveness of teaching and how well learner achieved objectives)

Principles

Research studies collaboratively identify the fundamentals of effective instruction as

- High expectations for learners
- Active engagement of students
- Thematic unit instruction
- Interactive cross-age tutors
- Cooperative learning activities
- Teacher effectiveness

General Models of Instruction

The type of model selected for instruction should be based on the learners, the content to be delivered, and the teacher's abilities. The following are some of the models known, and each may have select variations. Specific models, which are more commonly used, are further defined in this section.

Model	Creator	Benefits	Limitations
Brain-based	Brooks	• Allows natural flow of learning according to function of the brain • Promotes environment, content lessons, and student involvement as factors of learning	• Takes time to manage and implement for diverse learners • Teachers should be familiar with brain research and human development, including stages of learning

Model	Creator	Benefits	Limitations
Cognitive-constructivist	Piaget	• Stimulates critical thinking skills • Allows students' independent learning	• Requires teacher to be knowledgeable about subject and proper modeling
Cooperative learning	Johnson	• Easy integration of multiple intelligence and learning style theories • Focuses on social and academic goals • Useful for any content or subject • Improves academic achievement	• Difficult for some types of students • Additional time needed for planning and monitoring • May need to instruct on social skills
Conceptual-expository learning	Ausubel	• Helps when presenting abstract concepts • Emphasizes deductive reasoning • Higher level of thinking	• Teacher directed • Concepts may be too advanced for learners
Delineator approach	Gregorc	• Teaches students using both concrete and abstract perceptual qualities • Helps students learn to create sequential order	• Some students may have difficulty with concrete level
Direct instruction	Hunter	• Improves academic achievement • Supports learners with varied needs • Structured for sequential learners	• Some teachers may not follow the steps carefully or review information or monitor students accurately
Discovery learning	Bruner	• Improves learners' interest/motivation • Promotes inductive reasoning, intuitive thinking, and critical thinking skills • Allows students to be actively, independently engaged	• May not offer benefits to lower- or higher-level learners • Questions the effect on achievement
Inquiry learning (inductive)	Taba	• Motivational and meaningful for learners • Develops problem-solving and critical-thinking skills • Encourages use of scientific methods • Acknowledges that learning requires interaction between the learner and the data	• Takes more time than most models • Limited effect on academic achievement • Some students have problems with the step of application of information
Mastery learning ("all children can learn")	Bloom	• Allows individual time for acquiring knowledge • Process continues after assessment • Remediation implemented as needed	• Students may feel intimidated or overwhelmed by repeated concepts • Students may be at uniquely different levels of learning • Requires time and patience of teacher and ability to monitor all students effectively
Multiple intelligences	Gardner	• Addresses the various types of intelligence • Allows students to be successful in all lessons	• Requires time of teacher to identify strengths of individuals
Traditional approach		• Follows standardized scope and sequence in textbook, written assignments, and exams • Sets milestones and accomplishments • Grading rubric established	• Does not address individual learning styles or specific teaching style • Promotes artificial learning of information and concepts • Teacher-directed without much active learner involvement

Constructivist Approach

A child-centered approach in which a student is actively involved in directing her own learning. It bases the new concepts and delivery of information on a learner's previous knowledge. A student is motivated by the process and learns through inquiry and practice. It is the experiential learning that promotes a thorough understanding and an application of what is learned.

Cooperative Learning

In the Cooperative Learning Model, Johnson and Johnson identified five elements:

- **Positive interdependence**—Students understand that success is linked to other students and their success, knowing that each must contribute effort for the entire group to be successful.
- **Promotive interaction**—Students support one another by sharing resources, encouraging one another's efforts and contributions, solving problems together, and checking for understanding.
- **Accountability**—Students realize that each member in the group is responsible for learning the material so the group may achieve the final goal.
- **Interaction**—Students know that interpersonal skills must be used to be successful, which include effective communication, problem solving, decision making, building rapport, compromise, and cooperation.
- **Group processing**—The group assesses their ability to function and acquisition of knowledge, which may include on-task behaviors, goals met, cooperative efforts, and feedback on data.

Madeline Hunter's Direct Instruction

Hunter's model includes instructional sequence steps for any subject area and any grade level. Her model focuses on direct instruction and a systematic instructional method requiring the educator to have a grasp of the subject at a level of mastery. It places instructional theory into practice.

Direct instruction is the technique used when the teacher very specifically provides support for curricular topics. Use of this approach demonstrates instruction that proceeds in steps to accommodate students' understanding of the information and materials with the primary outcome being successful participation of students as active learners. Review of previous concepts and monitoring of student learning are important components in this approach.

Hunter's Essential Elements of Instruction	
Standards-expectations objectives	Identifies what students will be able to do as a result of this lesson
Anticipatory set	Opening activity that prepares students for the upcoming lesson—a "hook"
Instruction • Input • Modeling • Check for understanding	What the teacher must do to present lesson—deliver concepts, provide information, knowledge, or develop skills
Guided practice	How the teacher helps students to do the work of new tasks
Closure	How the teacher helps students to summarize new information and gain skills
Independent practice	Student opportunities to practice new learning or apply skills

Teaching Practice of Explicit Instruction

Explicit instruction is a well-developed and designed systematic instructional approach used for all elementary school content areas: reading, mathematics, language arts, social studies, sciences, physical education, and the fine arts. Explicit instruction is synonymous with direct instruction (Madeline Hunter Model), which is based on the behavior theory.

This approach promotes the use of materials and activities that give students structure and support in the learning process with a focus on the academic tasks to be learned. Each step toward goal attainment is taught to students and includes modeling, positive feedback, and practice opportunities. The environment must accommodate learning and be organized so students may work toward predetermined skills. The teacher is in control of the lessons, the environment, and the materials, while allowing proper time for instruction, student practice, and performance. Students are provided feedback and are expected to gain mastery before moving to the next skill level.

Bloom's Taxonomy

Benjamin Bloom and John Carroll created the Mastery Teaching Model in 1971 with a focus on defining objectives in terms of measurable outcomes. After instruction occurs, students are assessed, and the areas of concern are readdressed. They believed this process had a positive effect on student achievement and self-concept. Bloom then developed a taxonomy for categorizing learning structures in educational settings, which incorporated specific questions to obtain the various levels. This is a well-known process used in elementary education programs to guide instruction.

Level	Skill	Verbs		Questions
Knowledge (find out) (remember)	• Observe and recall information • Know dates, events, places • Know major ideas/concepts • Remember previous material	Define List Show Describe Label Collect Observe Listen	Identify Name Match Locate	Who? What? When? Where?
Comprehension (understand)	• Understand information • Interpret facts, contrast, compare • Grasp the meaning of material • Explain and summarize • Predict outcomes and effects (trends)	Discuss Restate Predict Give Associate	Define Explain Reports Review Estimate Express Chart Summarize	Why? How?
Application (use)	• Use information • Ability to use methods, concepts, theories, in new situations • Apply rules, laws, methods, theories • Solve problems using appropriate techniques	Apply Demonstrate Illustrate Show Solve Examine Modify	Relate Classify Compute Operate Use Employ Interpret	Apply
Analysis (take apart)	• Recognize patterns • Organize parts • Implications • Identify components • Conclude and clarify	Analyze Order Connect Arrange Divide Infer Compare	Explain Distinguish Sort Test Criticize Calculate	Diagram How? What?

(continued)

Level	Skill	Verbs		Questions
Synthesis (create new)	• Arrange things in a new way • Generalize from given facts • Relate knowledge from various areas • Predict and draw conclusions	Compile Combine Create Design Invent Compose	Produce Collect Manage Assemble Develop Formulate	What if?
Evaluation (judge)	• Assess the validity and value of ideas/theories • Make choices based upon reasoning and valid arguments • Verify the value of data and evidence • Recognize bias and subjectivity	Evaluate Value Measure Decide Justify Criticize	Contrast Debate Support Rank Convince Select	Why? Why not?

Differentiated Instruction

Differentiated instruction is an educational strategy used to ensure that all students will acquire information and learn regardless of their individual abilities, strengths, interests, and needs. It incorporates student-centered instruction, and a variety of strategies to achieve outcomes for all learners. Using the approach of differentiated instruction focuses on the various learning styles of all students to ensure that instruction is appropriate for individuals through educational activities, class tasks, student groupings, and assessment.

When using differentiated instruction, educators vary the content offered, the process of presentation, and the product that is the end result of the instruction. Instruction may be delivered using various learning formats: whole class, small groups, and individuals. Acquiring the skills of using differentiated instruction takes time and practice, as it is a learned skill. Effectively and efficiently being able to address various learners, plan for the appropriate instructional practices, monitor the goals and outcomes, utilize consistent assessment of instruction, and implement proper delivery is considered mastery of this strategy.

Guided Instruction

This approach to instruction is a combination of the teacher-centered and student-centered approaches, which allows the teacher to balance these based on the students' needs. Teachers can guide the direction of the instruction, facilitating the learning process while students are then provided with time for practice and application of what is learned.

Instructional Formats

Instructional formats, which describe the manner in which instruction is delivered, vary according to the type of students and their needs, the teacher preferences, and the subjects or content to be learned. These formats may include the use of motivational acts, modeling, drill and practice, demonstration, corrective feedback, and reinforcements. These formats may be used with either individual students or small groups of students.

Some of the formats that are most often used include

- **Co-teaching**—when two teachers actively share the teaching of all students
- **Peer tutoring**—when educators employ strategies that include same-age and cross-age peers to tutor other students
- **Collaboration**—when teachers with diverse expertise work together to enhance the education of students
- **Cooperative learning**—when educators implement classroom situations that promote learning among students through cooperation, not competition

Methods/Strategies

The strategies and methods selected for the classroom must support the learners and their needs, while encouraging independence, generalization of skills, and application of knowledge. Most strategies are backed by empirical research, although some strategies will work with certain groups of individuals, and some are better for particular subject areas.

Strategies are the skills or techniques used to assist a student in accessing and learning through the curriculum. Empirical evidence suggests that all students benefit from good quality strategies implemented daily. Educators must ensure that the strategies are well-designed and chosen with emphasis on the learners' needs and abilities so knowledge will be transferred and applied.

Many proven instructional practices are effective at the elementary level. Educators should turn to the research-based methods/strategies that demonstrate proven effectiveness for elementary age students. The principles to consider when choosing a strategy include structured instruction, opportunities for practice, comprehensiveness, and whether it fosters independence.

Some of the beneficial instructional strategies/methods are explained in this section.

Developmentally Appropriate Practices

Utilizing developmentally appropriate practices is to consider the level at which a student is presently functioning when creating curriculum, addressing standards, and developing instructional activities. Classroom teachers who follow the concept of developmentally appropriate practices take into account the various stages of human development and sequentially follow the ability levels of the students in order to progressively develop those skills at a higher level. The activities and practices evolve according to student developmental levels.

The purpose of using developmentally appropriate practices is to meet the needs of all learners in a suitable environment in the best possible manner. Educators must consider the age of the students, ability and skill levels, interests, cultural backgrounds, and social behaviors when creating curriculum activities and then build upon these various events to enhance learning according to each student's development.

Sometimes state standards are not at the appropriate level to impose developmentally appropriate practices, so the educator must work at establishing suitable activities and addressing the instructional needs of the students. In order to create an environment that promotes developmentally appropriate practices, teachers should integrate the standards in the curriculum, provide adequate materials and equipment, participate in ongoing training, and use effective communication with parents.

Integration Strategies

There are many ways to integrate across the curriculum as well as many reasons why this is so beneficial to students. Strategic integration is an instructional design component, which combines essential information in ways that result in new and more complex knowledge. The strategic integration of curriculum content aids students in learning to use and apply specific knowledge beyond the classroom. Characteristics of strategic instruction include the following:

- Design offers opportunities to integrate several big ideas.
- Content learned must be applicable to multiple contexts.
- Complex concepts and facts should be integrated once mastered.

Scaffolded Instruction

Scaffolding is a teaching strategy that provides a temporary support or guidance to the learner who is not ready to perform a task independently. This strategy may be in the form of steps, tasks, materials, and personal support during initial learning that reduces the task complexity by structuring it into manageable chunks to increase successful task completion. It allows needed support in the beginning, then gradually decreases the teacher participation as the student becomes more competent, and ends with independent practice as the student masters the skill. The degree of scaffolding changes with the abilities of the learner, the goals of instruction, and the complexities of the task. Gradual and planned removal of the scaffolds occur as the learner becomes more successful and independent in task completion. Thus, the purpose of scaffolding is to allow all students to become successful in independent activities.

Two types of scaffolded instruction are verbal and procedural.

In **verbal instruction,** the teacher uses prompting, questioning, and further explanations to encourage students to move into higher levels. For example, paraphrasing, think alouds, reinforcement, modeling, and appropriate speech.

In **procedural instruction,** specific instructional techniques such as the following are used:

- Instructional framework-specific teaching, modeling, and practice of the skill with others as well as expectations for independent application
- One-on-one teaching and modeling
- Small group instruction in which a more experienced student practices or models a newly learned skill with a less experienced one
- Grouping or partnering in which teachers place students who are more experienced in a topic with those who are less experienced

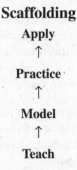

Scaffolding

Apply

↑

Practice

↑

Model

↑

Teach

An example of scaffolded instruction is **reciprocal teaching.** Through dialogue between the teacher and student, learning is guided with the teacher helping to shape learning opportunities and conducting ongoing assessments. (Especially effective in teaching reading comprehension skills such as: summarizing, asking questions, clarifying, and predicting.)

Cooperative Learning

This is a technique of grouping students used to assist them with learning activities in a student-centered environment to keep them actively engaged. Students must utilize positive interdependence, individual accountability, interactions with others, and equal participation. Cooperative teaming includes partnering, triads, small grouping, and whole group.

Following are examples of pairing strategy:

- **Think-Pair-Share**—Teacher poses a question or topic to the students and allows them time to think before discussion; partners talk about the question or topic and then share their answers and discussions with the class.
- **Round Robin Recall**—Students are divided into small groups, and each member must recall all they know about a topic or subject presented in a set amount of time.

Grouping Model

Independent Work

↑

Partners

↑

Small Group

↑

Whole Class

Questioning Strategies

An important skill that teachers should develop is the technique of asking a question and waiting for an answer. When referring to Bloom's taxonomy, questions to students may begin at the **knowledge** level and proceed through to the higher order of thinking skills at the **evaluation** level to better assess student gains. At the first level, the questions are based on the information just learned, while at the final level, questions are based on critical thinking and application of content. For example,

> Knowledge: Define the ...
>
> Application: How would you use the ...?
>
> Evaluation: Decide which method ... and compare ...

Task Analysis

Using the method of **task analysis** helps a student learn a specific skill by breaking down the assignment or activity into sequential steps. The student learns each step of the task as he moves toward the preferred level of skill achievement.

Content Enhancements

This approach allows teachers to use various techniques that enhance more complex information in the curriculum so students may remember and utilize it more efficiently. Types of content enhancements include guided notes, graphic organizers, and mnemonic strategies.

Graphic Organizers

Graphic organizers are effective instructional tools that help organize information in a more concrete manner. They provide a visual, holistic representation of facts and concepts, depict the relationship of facts within an organized framework, and relate new information to prior knowledge. Graphic organizers may be used before instructional activities to activate prior knowledge and to encourage student prediction. They can be used during instruction to help students process and reorganize information. And, after instruction, graphic organizers help summarize learning, support the organization of ideas, provide a structure for review, and assess the degree of student understanding. Types of graphic organizers include the concept map, sequence chain, story map, main idea table, flowchart, matrix, and Venn diagram.

Wait Time

Wait time (adequate processing time) is the amount of time between the moment a task is presented or a question is asked and when the learner is asked to respond. Research shows that when teachers provide a pause period between a question and student response, students tend to reply with more thoughtful answers as they have time to process the request. Often, students are given only a few seconds to answer a question posed by the teacher, and it results in brief responses or no answers at all.

The amount of response (wait) time will vary based on students' ages and cognitive levels, as well as the complexity of the task, topic, or question. If a task or topic is considerably new, the amount of time allocated to think and formulate a response should be greater than that provided for a task that is more familiar. Some studies showed that at the elementary level, a decrease in achievement was attributed to waiting too long for responses to low-level questions.

Peer Tutoring

Peer tutoring is an effective strategy when used appropriately under the guidance of a teacher. The teacher selects a student with demonstrated mastery and competencies in a particular subject or topic and groups him with a student who needs assistance to gain mastery or access content knowledge. The students work together periodically so the student needing assistance can learn from modeling and practice the observed skills.

Student Responses

Students who are actively engaged in learning achieve greater success. Interactive learning activities keep students involved and provide them with adequate practice. Educators should elicit student responses several times per minute, whether through question/answer periods, student writings, or an activity.

Instructional Pacing

Pacing is the rate at which the instruction is delivered through presentations and in response solicitations. Pacing may be influenced by variables such as the complexity of a task, the newness of a task, and the range of student differences. Research suggests that instruction should be presented at a brisk and consistent pace as the benefits include

- More information may be provided.
- Learners are more engaged in the activity.
- Behavior problems are limited.

Feedback for Correct and Incorrect Responses

Immediate feedback should be provided in the classroom for both correct and incorrect responses. Corrective feedback should be instructional, not accommodating, and the feedback delivered to reinforce correct responses should be consistent and specific. Feedback should be subtle and part of the learning process, while not interfering with the timing of the next question, content, or interaction, or learners may suffer from learning disruptions and have problems with memory and recall.

Important terms regarding instruction include the following:

- **ability grouping**—Placing students together according to performance and academic achievement levels
- **adaptation**—A change made to the environment or curriculum
- **accommodation**—An adjustment that does not change the curriculum, but enables a student to participate in educational activities he might not otherwise be able to do
- **active student response**—The measure of the engagement of a student in tasks and activities
- **chained response**—Breaking down a task into smaller component parts so a person may complete the task, starting with the first step in the sequence and performing each component progressively until the task is final
- **chaining**—A technique in which student performance is reinforced so the student will continue to perform more complex tasks in the sequence
- **choral responding**—Oral response of students (in unison) to a question or problem presented by the teacher
- **chunking**—A strategy that helps a student learn, remember, and organize large amounts of information
- **cloze procedure**—The use of semantic and syntactic clues that aid in completing a sentence
- **cooperative learning**—Students are divided into groups to work together to complete a task, participate in an activity, or create a project
- **concept generalization**—The ability of a student to demonstrate content knowledge by applying the information to other settings without prompts from teacher
- **contingent teaching**—A strategy for helping a student and eventually fading out the support as he gains mastery of the skill or task
- **corrective feedback**—Aids students in understanding correct and incorrect responses while informing them of their progress
- **cues and prompts**—Provides assistance to ensure adequate support of instruction
- **demonstration**—Student observes the teacher or another student completing a task and then makes the attempt at task completion
- **drill and practice**—Use of consistent repetition and rehearsal

- **facilitated groups**—Students engage in active learning with lessons designed and overseen by the teacher but managed by the students
- **fluency building**—A measure that encourages practice of skills to improve the accuracy and rate of use
- **generalization**—The ability to use skills learned across various settings
- **guided practice**—Providing opportunities to gain knowledge by offering cues, prompts, or added sequential information
- **learning centers**—Specific areas or activities that enhance the curricular content and allow independent or small group instruction
- **mnemonics**—Enhances memory through key words, acronyms, or acrostics
- **modeling**—Helps make connections between the material to be learned and the process to learn it by acting out sequences so students may imitate the task
- **naturalistic teaching**—Procedures that involve activities interesting to students with naturally occurring consequences
- **prompting**—A technique in which a visual, auditory, or tactile cue is presented to facilitate the completion of a task or to perform a behavior
- **reinforcement**—The provision of a positive contact or object in order to strengthen the possibility that the student will make a similar response to a similar situation in the future
- **remediation**—A program technique to teach students to reach competency through training and education
- **repetition**—Continual work on a specific skill or content concept to help build rote memory skills
- **response cards**—A method that allows all students to answer simultaneously by using signs, cards, or items held up to demonstrate responses
- **skill drill**—Repetition and practice of new skills until the learner performs without cues and prompts
- **strategic instruction**—A planned, sequential instruction to show similarities and differences between acquired and new knowledge
- **systematic feedback**—Providing positive reinforcement and confirmation to improve learning
- **time trial**—A procedure that improves the fluency of new skills through time limits
- **universal design**—The concept that everything in the environment, in learning and in products, should be accessible to everyone

Motivation

Motivation is the reason students engage in certain behaviors, which may be to satisfy their basic needs, complete projects, or participate in activities. Motivation is a critical component in the academic success of students as it allows them to attain goals and reach accomplishments. Students need to feel motivated to learn and achieve. Educators should naturally want to motivate students and include methods of motivation in their daily and unit plans, which include interesting lessons, various materials, and unique activities.

To assist students in becoming motivated, teachers should develop healthy, trusting relationships and positive rapport with students. Students who are motivated become actively involved in the educational process and responsible for their individual achievements, gain self-confidence and pride in their work which instills enthusiasm for academics. Various rewards and strategies, both extrinsic and intrinsic, may be used to improve motivation in classrooms of diverse learners.

Extrinsic Motivators

Extrinsic motivators are those that come from outside the individual; these may be small tangible items (money, prizes, stickers), grades, special privileges, or verbal or written praise. The motivating factor is an external reward that can provide satisfaction that the completion of the task or activity itself may not provide to the student. Some students need to have something for their efforts, and some students need an extrinsic motivator only for a short period of time, until they feel capable and satisfied with their own efforts. Educators determine which students need this support.

Intrinsic Motivators

Intrinsic motivators are those that come from within the individual; students do not need to receive anything for their efforts as they have their own drive or internal need to be successful. Intrinsic motivators may include the feelings of satisfaction, accomplishment, or enjoyment. Many students are intrinsically motivated to learn for the pure joy of it, and they complete work and projects or activities because they want to succeed and master a subject. Teachers may capitalize on this form of motivation in students by including a sense of curiosity and excitement in the lessons they deliver.

Classroom Management

Effective classroom organization and structure are essential to maximizing student academic success. This management determines the learning environment, the teacher's attitude and behaviors, and the impact on students, their achievement, and behaviors. The basic classroom management components include an appropriate curriculum and motivating instruction, responsible and engaged students, and a teacher who models a positive attitude toward education. Positive classroom management creates an environment that allows students to flourish.

To create an appropriate educational environment for students, teachers must plan and implement the proper design and structure for the classroom, create efficient procedures, plan appropriate lessons, maintain order, use effective communication strategies, manage varying situations, consider proper behavior management strategies, and meet the diverse needs of all learners. A positive environment with effective management, in which students understand the expectations, will result in increased instructional time, reinforce the learning process, promote desired behaviors, and improve student-teacher relationships.

Teachers should use proactive strategies that model and teach students to effectively self-manage their behaviors and encourage them to be actively engaged in their own learning process. Students should be involved in creating the instructional environment, which will stimulate their interest in education, promoting life-long learning. Effective classroom management includes some of these strategies and procedures:

- Use appropriate lessons and materials.
- Vary tasks, assignments, and activities.
- Remove visual and auditory distractions.
- Give directions in concise, repetitive manners.
- Use modeling and demonstration for new tasks.
- Supply appropriate materials with easy access.
- Provide feedback/rewards for desired behavior.
- Reflect positive attitude for learning.
- Be clear about expectations.
- Minimize interruptions and transitions.
- Utilize positive and effective communication.
- Allow adequate time for learning.
- Help students organize work and work area.
- Implement effective transition periods.
- Establish special areas for enrichment.
- Support students when they make mistakes.
- Monitor progress and maintain accountability.
- Listen to the learners.

There are three recognized styles of classroom management:

- **Authoritarian**—restrictive and punitive with the main focus on maintaining order instead of emphasizing instruction and educational activities
- **Authoritative**—encourages students to become independent under an effective management program, with guidelines, expectations, and verbal support appropriate for the learners
- **Permissive**—promotes independence of learners, but offers them limited support for academic skills or managing their behaviors

Interventions

Interventions are the steps teachers take to address student needs when situations arise that imply the student is having difficulty either managing his own behavior or completing academic tasks. Deciding when and how to intervene is an essential classroom management skill.

Teachers should attempt to address issues with students prior to seeking assistance from others, yet knowing the resources available is also important. If students are having behavior issues, the teacher should attempt various interventions suitable to the student, the grade level, and the situation for a reasonable amount of time. If the problems are not resolved, then seeking the assistance of the school social worker, the psychologist, a peer teacher, or the student assistance team should be considered. For students who have problems with academic tasks, setting up structured study times, accessing additional help (such as a tutor), finding more one-to-one time with the student, or contacting the student's family for help should be typical interventions. However, if these are not successful, it may be necessary for the teacher to work with the school assistance team to begin the process of evaluation to determine academic needs.

Behavior Management

Classroom management and response to behaviors are a reflection of the teacher's attitudes about teaching and about students. In order to maintain effective classroom management, student behaviors must be adequate, whether controlled by the teacher or self-regulated by the student. The classroom environment influences behaviors, and behaviors have a significant impact on learning.

Behavior management requires knowledge about human development and the availability of a designed program that integrates the needs of individuals into the environment. Setting standard guidelines and establishing expectations for students' behaviors in a classroom helps to establish a foundation for learning. A system of rewards and consequences helps manage the typical behaviors demonstrated in elementary classrooms.

General strategies of behavior management techniques include the following:

- Create a comfortable and safe environment.
- Involve students in creating rules and procedures.
- Develop expectations and model appropriate behaviors.
- Use immediate feedback and provide consistent reinforcements.

Behavior and Classroom Management Models

Many models of behavior intervention may be used with elementary aged students, and maintaining behaviors is primary to creating an effective learning environment. Establishing rapport, getting to know the learners, and being respectful and trusting helps both the learners and the teacher. Some educators combine models and individualize their approach to address behaviors.

Theorist	Approach	Definition	Concepts
Glasser	Glasser Model	When an individual makes good choices, good behavior results.	Implement consequences for good and bad behavior. Establish class-wide discipline.
Kounin	With-It-Ness	Teacher is able to manage the learners, as he is "with it" and alert to the group.	Address off-task behaviors. Use effective instructional pace. Instill motivation.
Kyle, Kagan, and Scott	Kyle, Kagan, and Scott Approach	Utilizes Win-Win discipline and three pillars: a. no adversaries b. shared responsibility c. long-term learned behavior	Identify disruptive behaviors and create structures. Incorporate Win-Win solutions for preventive results.
Canter	Canter Model	Educator is in charge of the class and manages learners.	Expectations are stated clearly and concisely. Desired behaviors are insisted upon. Educator is calm, but firm.

Theorist	Approach	Definition	Concepts
Jones	Fred Jones Model	Learner motivation and desired behaviors are stressed.	Non-verbal actions are used to prevent undesirable behaviors. Classroom structure and rules are identified early.
Skinner	Neo-Skinnerian Model	The desired behaviors can be obtained by shaping and modeling.	Behavior is shaped by implementing consequences and rewards. Consistency is the key.

Behavior management terms include the following:

- **antecedent**—Stimulus used in behavior management and behavior modification that occurs prior to the behavior and establishes the reason for the behavior
- **behavior intervention**—Strategies or actions used to extinguish, change, or redirect an inappropriate behavior
- **consequences**—Stimulus that follows a behavior action used in behavior management or behavior modification to increase or decrease the behavior
- **contingency contract**—Written agreement between the student and the teacher that outlines the expected performance and the reinforcers to be used
- **modeling**—Use of imitation to set in place the desired behaviors
- **negative reinforcement**—Used in behavior modification in which the student is motivated to use a desired behavior in order to avoid a negative consequence
- **positive reinforcement**—Used in behavior modification in which the student is motivated to use a desired behavior because of the reward to be obtained
- **response generalization**—Application of a learned behavior or skill to another setting
- **target behavior**—The behavior most often to be extinguished or changed, although may be a positive behavior that should be used in other school situations

Cultural and Linguistic Diversity

Since the 1960s, there has been a shift in immigration patterns from non-European countries. The number of English language learners entering public schools has increased in the past 25 years. Hispanic enrollment increased 48 percent and Asian-American enrollment increased 85 percent in the years between 1980 and 1990. More than 3.5 million students whose primary language was not English attended school in the United States in the year 2000.

Language and culture are two factors that influence how children learn. A growing number of students' first languages are not English. Different labels have identified these students, but the current term used is **English Language Learner** (ELL). To aid ELL students in their learning, teachers should remember to

- Use spoken and written language patterns and structure above the learner's abilities.
- Repeat key words, phrases, and concepts.
- Slow the speech rate and clearly articulate sounds.
- Avoid using difficult words and unnecessary vocabulary.
- Simplify instructional materials.

In addition to the numerous languages represented in elementary populations, classes also appear to be culturally diverse. Research on the various cultural groups resulted in generalizations about how these groups interact and communicate. Another form of diversity represented in elementary classrooms is students who present with learning differences, such as those with disabilities.

Due to the range of diversity in schools educators must exercise cultural sensitivity and cultural awareness toward their students. A way to promote this is to create an attitude or environment of cultural appreciation. Children's literature can provide valuable classroom resources that support multicultural education.

Enrichment

Enrichment is a method for extending a lesson or unit for those students who are capable of participating in more instruction or gaining additional information. This list offers suggestions to aid elementary education teachers in planning instruction that addresses enrichment. These strategies are often used with students who are considered gifted or talented.

- Self-paced instruction
- Mentoring programs
- Summer programs
- Ability grouping
- Extracurricular programs
- Compacting or telescoping curriculum
- Tiered lessons
- Additional special focus courses
- Advanced placement courses
- Skipping grade levels

Assessment

A major factor in identifying student success in any academic area is the evaluation of learning. Assessment is part of the educational process in which a teacher may gather, examine, and share information about the skills, abilities, and achievements of individual students. The teacher may use this information to set new goals for learning, create expectations, and determine future outcomes.

The primary purpose of assessment is to evaluate student achievement, make decisions pertaining to instruction, and review the program. An assessment helps to gather data that will allow students to understand their own learning process and aid the teacher in designing activities and selecting strategies appropriate for the students. Whether using daily informal assessment techniques or standardized testing, the results provide valuable information.

Effective instruction can be evaluated through formative and summative assessments, both of which provide educators with valuable information.

Formative assessment is the collection of data through on-going daily lessons or units of study in order to analyze student achievement and assist students in the learning process.

Summative assessment is the collection of data at a specific completion point in order to identify needs and make decisions to support student learning. This type of evaluation is most often used at the end of a unit of study to analyze a particular concept or skill.

Formal Assessment

Formal assessments are systematic with strict procedures for administration and scoring. These are often used to comply with issues of accountability, report card or progress reports, and curriculum effectiveness. Formal, standardized tests

- Provide information on student progress.
- Deliver information on the placement of students.
- Help in planning educational activities for all students.
- Improve instruction.
- Evaluate programs and classrooms.
- Meet the accountability requirements.

Standardized testing has a set of uniform procedures for the administration and scoring, and these must be followed to ensure standard, valid conditions. Standardized testing includes a set of norms, compares students to others at the same age, and evaluates for reliability and validity. At the elementary level, testing includes the very basic skills. Standardized assessments include achievement tests, aptitude tests, competency tests, and performance exams.

High-stakes testing is used to comply with the accountability requirement under education reform and the No Child Left Behind mandate. It is used to measure how schools are educating youth by assessing student achievement levels. Since this is such a new process with very little research on the effect of the tests or the procedures for administration, professionals are unsure of the type of information best gathered through high-stakes testing or how to use the information.

Pros	Cons
Instills higher expectations	Promotes rote memory instead of more complex cognitive skills
Focuses on instruction in specific subject/content area	Focuses the instruction on the content that is on the test
Improves student performance in testing	Lacks funds and guidelines for remediation of learners
Identifies under-performing schools and educators	Discriminates against culturally and linguistically diverse groups

Informal Assessment

Informal assessments are periodic checks that help professionals gather pertinent information about a student in the natural environment. These informal measures may be used to support a more formal assessment or for continued and on-going progress evaluations. Informal assessments may include anecdotal records, running records, portfolio assessments, and dynamic assessments.

Interpretation of Data

Instructional decisions are made based on the information gathered through an assessment. Assessment data helps to identify student achievement during instructional periods and should not only be gathered at the end of an instructional unit but throughout the studies. The data may be collected informally on a daily basis and periodically when using more formal testing. The use of this information helps the teacher adjust instruction for the students and supports the learning process for all individuals. Knowledge of test terms, procedures, and statistics/scoring will help educators understand outcomes related to student tests and learn how to deliver information to other professionals or parents at conferences.

Procedures

Appropriate assessment procedures are necessary to obtain valid and accurate data about students and instruction. The assessment must have a clearly stated purpose and be closely related to the outcomes it seeks. It is best when the assessment is on-going so the information may be used to change the content or alter the situation for the learner to better meet needs. The assessment tools must be appropriate for the student in order to gather relevant academic information.

Education reform has focused on accountability through assessment and how this occurs continues to be a debated issue. Teachers must be knowledgeable about the assessment process and the various techniques, as well as the options that are available for use in their classrooms. Standardized tests, district tests, and high-stakes state tests are best administered in a child's primary language, free from racial or cultural bias.

Types of Assessment Strategies

Assessment in the classroom should not always be separated from the instruction. Creating an environment in which daily instruction and assessment are integrated provides regular and effective information to the teacher. Many different strategies may be implemented to meet the assessment needs of particular situations, and these can be described according to two different categories: authentic and traditional assessment. Traditional assessments are reflected by "paper and pencil" tasks and authentic assessments are those that are alternatives to traditional exams.

Examples of authentic assessments include the following:

- **performance tasks**—Require that students complete a problem or project, which includes an explanation for the answer and addresses a particular skill.

- **observation**—A simple method of assessment to identify the performance of students completing various activities and tasks, using anecdotal records, and checklists for recording documentation.

- **journal writing**—Written reflections allow teachers to informally gauge student learning through their thinking processes, formation of ideas, and development of skills in creative and factual writing.

- **portfolios**—A collection of completed student work selected by the student and the teacher to demonstrate strengths, progress, and skills.

Terms

There are several types of measurement tools that may be utilized in elementary education:

- **achievement test**—Formal tool used to measure student proficiency of a subject area already learned

- **alternative assessment**—Provides more options to students to apply knowledge and use learned skills by solving realistic problems and completing projects using close to real-life situations

- **anecdotal record**—Informal measurement based on observation of student work or performance

- **aptitude test**—Formal measure of standardized or norm-referenced tests to evaluate student ability to acquire skills or gain knowledge

- **authentic assessment**—Method that is less concrete, more subjective to determine a student's understanding and performance of specific criteria (write a story, create a project, give a presentation)

- **criterion-referenced test**—Formal measure that evaluates a student on certain subject area information by answering specific questions, while not comparing one student to another

- **curriculum-based measure**—Helps determine student progress and performance based on the lessons presented in the curriculum, so a teacher may better assist student

- **dynamic assessment**—Determines a student's ability to learn in a certain situation rather than documenting what the student has actually learned

- **diagnostic assessment**—A way to collect information about a student to use in assessment throughout the period of instruction

- **direct daily measurement**—Classroom form of daily assessment of a student's performance on the skills that are taught each day and may be used to modify instruction for particular students

- **ecological-based assessment**—Informal observation of a student interacting with the environment during a regular schedule

- **intelligence test (IQ test)**—Norm-referenced test used to measure cognitive behaviors in order to assess student learning abilities or intellectual capacity

- **norm-referenced test**—Formal standardized evaluation used to compare a student to other peers in the same age group and aids in developing curriculum options

- **observation**—Teacher or other professional watch a student in different settings to obtain information regarding performance and behaviors

- **performance based assessment**—Informal measure used to assess a student's ability to complete a task that is specific to a topic or subject area

- **portfolio assessment**—Informal method of gathering information and samples of completed student work over a period of time (art, projects, reports) and useful to track progress

- **rubric**—A set standard rating scale used to determine performance abilities on a single task

- **standards-based assessment**—Formal evaluation such as a criterion-referenced or norm-referenced test that measures student progress toward meeting goals or standards previously established

General Topics

Teaching involves more than just providing new concepts and content to students. Teaching requires that educators be actively involved in their careers through membership in organizations, seeking training opportunities, working with parents, and collaborating with peers. Teachers should be reflective practitioners who continue to improve professionally, by assessing their knowledge, evaluating their instructional abilities, and using creative new ideas and techniques to address learners' needs.

Professional Development

Education reform over the past several years has focused more on the training of teachers to enhance student academic success. Teacher preparation is an on-going process as standards are refined, high-stakes test are promoted, technology changes, and students evolve. Educators must be realistic in their abilities to utilize state standards, manage accountability factors, and deliver consistent curriculum activities.

Teachers play a key role in the development of students, and in order to be effective, teachers must also develop their own professional repertoire. Teachers need time to work with colleagues both for training and planning. Educators should avoid isolation and support a shared vision and team efforts.

Teaching Styles

Educators often develop a style of teaching early in their career, which is based on their beliefs about teaching, their personal preferences, and their abilities. Some educators believe they should use a style that is teacher-centered, as the information authority, while others prefer a student-centered approach, as a facilitator of learning. Individual teachers cultivate a preferred teaching style, but they may mix elements of various other styles to create something quite unique and effective.

Teaching styles can be described in five ways according to Grasha (1994, 1996):

Teaching Style	Description
Expert	Possesses knowledge of subject and challenges students' competence and skill development in the content
Formal authority	Prefers standard and acceptable procedures, clear expectations and structure; often rigid and nonflexible
Personal model (demonstrator)	Leads by example, models, guides, and directs students; considers various learning styles
Facilitator	Promotes independence, initiative, and responsibility; consults, supports, and encourages students
Delegator	Encourages autonomy in learners and is available as a consultative resource

Collaboration

Working with other teachers and professionals enhances your career as an educator, but these relationships are built on trust and respect, which must be earned and reciprocated. Involving the community in the classroom is another way to collaborate with other adults who have interests in promoting education. Include community mentors and experts and use the community as a resource for culturally and linguistically diverse students. The collaboration of education, recreation, and health services all enhance the well-being of students.

Technology

Technology has impacted education and classroom activities in multiple ways, as it changes students' experiences and the educational environment. Technology provides increased access and refined practices in such areas as communication, research, and record keeping. It offers visual and auditory input, such as access to historical archives and artifacts, research on collections from other libraries or scientists, photographs and visual images, and virtual tours of museums. Elementary educators can offer students a supplemental resource through the use of such technology as television, computers, DVD, video or CDs, Internet, and smart boards.

Parents

Educators should acknowledge the role that parents play in a child's life. Professionals are encouraged to include parents and families as partners in the education process and to involve them in the classroom and school activities. Gain parent support through positive actions and responses. Create an alliance and work together to guide and enhance the student's education.

This partnership is a meaningful component to the education programs. Research shows that actively involved parents can have a positive influence on their child's performance at school resulting in a higher, more successful academic level. Parents may provide continued support to their child and offer resources to the class, which adds opportunities for learning situations.

Communication with parents is necessary for developing a positive partnership and may include class newsletters or websites, parent-teacher conferences, handwritten or emailed messages, telephone calls, home visits, and specific homework activities.

Working With and Supporting Parents		
Approach	**Theorist**	**Description**
Active parenting	Popkin	Parents must establish leadership roles in the family, so they can effectively train, support, and encourage their children, teaching them to make proper choices and use appropriate behaviors.
Step approach	Dinkmeyer/McCay	Parents should implement a system of goals, giving choices, setting limits, and using logical consequences. The use of I-messages, reflective listening, and teaching values are critical to child development.
	Baker	Improving parent involvement programs and providing training and support will enhance learning.
	McCormack-Larkin	Ongoing communication with parents is a critical element in successful school achievement.

Content Area Exercises (0012)

The Praxis II exam for Content Area Exercises (0012) is comprised of questions that cover the topics of curriculum, instruction, and assessment at the elementary school level. The responses to these essays are written by the examinee based on personal knowledge and experience in the content areas of reading/language arts, mathematics, science, social studies, and integrated subjects; however, physical education and fine arts are not included on this exam.

This test was designed to evaluate and measure how well an examinee can respond to specific situations, which require a thoughtful, well-written response. The essays encompass all four subject areas as well as interdisciplinary instruction. The scenarios are meant to be viewed as an event or situation that occurs in an elementary classroom setting. An examinee may be required to discuss instructional approaches, develop instructional goals, solve instructional problems, or outline procedures necessary to achieve a desired academic outcome.

Many different situations arise within an elementary classroom, and the examinee must be prepared to handle each in a competent and thorough manner. Part of the fun of teaching is being consistently challenged and having new experiences surface each day. Some possible scenarios and situations are included in the individual sections of this study guide. Examinees should become familiar with these and practice writing lengthy and complete exercises to prepare for this examination.

Examination Information

Time restriction: 2 hours

Format: 4 essay questions

Scoring: Since this test is in an essay format, a rubric has been created as a standard scoring guide used by examination readers to determine the competence of the examinee's knowledge as evidenced in the answers. A sample has been included here.

Rubric: This scoring format is used consistently across the states and based on levels from 0 to 6, with 6 being the highest, or representative of a well-constructed narrative answer. A brief summary of the expectations at each level in the scoring guide are outlined here.

> **6**—Essay is answered clearly and concisely, with all portions of the questions addressed. Examinee demonstrates **superior** knowledge of the topic, writing an answer that includes well-organized key ideas and supportive details.

> **5**—Examinee provides answers to the important parts of the essay showing a **strong** understanding of the topic. The answer is well organized, and key ideas are explained clearly with examples to support the ideas.

> **4**—The question is answered accurately, suggesting the examinee has **adequate** knowledge. The essay provides a clear description of the main ideas and relevant supportive materials, although the answer is limited in content and in illustrating key points.

> **3**—Examinees demonstrate **some** knowledge and understanding of the topic providing basic explanations of the key ideas. The answer lacks clarity and only a few relevant details are given to support the answers.

> **2**—The answer is written giving unclear or underdeveloped explanations that include inaccuracies and lack details or support examples. The essay shows **limited** content knowledge and deficiencies in the understanding of the topic.

> **1**—The question is inadequately addressed, demonstrating a **serious lack** of understanding. The essay is poorly written, providing no appropriate examples or details, and may be considered incoherent and unorganized.

> **0**—The essay is unwritten, illegible, or completely **inappropriate** to the topic given.

It is recommended that examinees carefully study the examples of situations provided in the individual content sections of this study guide and practice writing answers to them. These questions may be answered in many different ways, but the primary factor in being successful on this exam is to write answers that are clear, concise, and demonstrate a superior or strong knowledge base. As a study tool, examinees are encouraged to ask an experienced teacher or mentor to review their written answers using this scoring guide and share feedback prior to taking the actual examination.

PART I

INDIVIDUAL SUBJECT AREAS

Language Arts

Mathematics

Social Studies

Science

Integrated Subjects

Reading/Language Arts Content Knowledge (0014)

Reading and language arts are essential to the success of all learners. Students must be familiar with the English language, its uses, and its functions. Understanding the structures and functions of the language allow learners to comprehend text, read and write coherently, as well as produces critical thinkers.

Understanding Literature

Literature is based upon ideologies and values of a certain era. Authors, throughout periods of time, assert their own beliefs and values through their work, and the work is often influenced by these biases. For this reason, literature is very deeply linked to the time period in which it was written. Literature is unique as a form of writing as it does not provide a direct message for the reader but rather is discreet and often conceals its message. It is up to the reader to uncover, analyze, and interpret the meaning.

There are four processes/stages essential to readers in the interpretation of literature:

1. **Initial:** ("construction stage") The reader has initial contact with content, structure, genre, and language of the text. The reader uses prior knowledge to begin to build understanding of the literature.
2. **Developing:** ("extending stage") The reader dives into the text world and uses text and background knowledge to build understanding of the literature. New information is taken in and immediately used to ask questions about the literature.
3. **Reflection/Response:** ("extension of reading stage") The reader uses text knowledge to reflect upon personal knowledge. What is read impacts and is reflected upon the reader's own life, the lives of others, and the human condition in general.
4. **Critical Analysis:** ("examining stage") The reader reflects and reacts to the content of the literature. She judges, evaluates, and relates to the literature.

Types of Literature

There are many types of literature, each possessing unique characteristics. Knowing the type of literature one is reading can help the reader better understand the text as well as better extract meaning from what is being read. Following is a brief list of the most common forms of literature.

Allegory—A narrative in which the characters and events represent an idea or truth about life in general.

Autobiography—A narrative in which the author writes about his/her own life.

Biography—A narrative in which an author writes about another person's life.

Comedy—A genre of literature in which life is dealt with in a humorous manner, often poking fun at people's mistakes.

Drama (play)—Uses dialogue to present its message to the audience and is meant to be performed.

Essay—A nonfiction piece that is often short and used to express the writer's opinion about a topic or to share information on a subject.

Fable—A short story, often with animals as the main characters, that teaches a moral or lesson to the reader.

Fantasy—A genre of literature in which the story is set in an imaginary world, involving magic or adventure, in which the characters often have supernatural powers.

Folktale—A story that has been passed down orally from one generation to another; the characters usually follow the extreme (all good or all bad) and in the end are rewarded or punished as they deserve.

Myth—A story that was created to explain some natural force of nature, religious belief, or social phenomenon. The gods and goddesses have supernatural powers but the human characters often do not.

Novel—A fictional narrative of book length in which characters and plot are developed in a somewhat realistic manner.

Parable—A simple, short story that is used to explain a belief, a moral, or spiritual lesson.

Poetry—Literary work which uses colorful, concise, rhythmic language and focuses on the expression of ideas or emotions.

Prose—Literary work that is in ordinary form and uses the familiar structure of spoken language, sentence after sentence.

Realism—Writing in which the reality of life is shown.

Science Fiction—A genre of literature in which real or imaginary scientific developments and concepts are prevalent and is often set in the future.

Short Story—A narrative that can be read in one sitting. Has a few characters and often one conflict or problem. The characters often go through some sort of change by the end of the story.

Tall Tale—A humorous and exaggerated story often based upon the life of a real person. The exaggerations increase and build until the character can achieve impossible tasks.

Tragedy—A genre of literature in which there is a downfall of the hero due to a tragic flaw or personal characteristic; often ends with an unhappy ending.

Narratives

A narrative is a story. Sequence or time is found within a narrative along with description. Characters are an important ingredient within the sequence of events of the narrative. Every narrative has a beginning, middle, and end.

Certain components must be present in order to make a piece of writing a story. These essential components are the elements of a narrative.

- **Pace**—How the details are placed and how transitions are made within the story. Pacing of a narrative consists of episodes or scenes that function to "move" the story along.

- **Tone**—The attitude or feeling that a piece of literature conveys through the characters, word choice, and writing style. For example, humorous, sad, serious, satiric, and so on.

- **Point of View (POV)**—Who is telling the story or what angle the story is being told from. The POV impacts reader response to the story and the characters. There are a five basic POVs:

  - **Objective**—The story is told through actions and dialogue; the reader must infer what the characters think and feel. The narrator is a detached observer.

  - **Third person**—The story is told through an outside voice (the narrator is not one of the characters) but informs the reader about how the characters feel.

  - **First person**—The story is told through an inside voice (the narrator is participating in the story as a character). The reader receives information from a narrator who is directly involved in the action, and the narrator may or may not be reliable or trustworthy; the narrator is biased.

  - **Omniscient**—The story is told by a narrator who is all knowing and knows everything about all characters (inner thoughts included).

  - **Limited omniscient**—The story is told by a narrator whose knowledge is limited to knowing all inner thoughts and feelings of one character (major or minor).

- **Characters**—People, animals, or objects that participate in the sequence of events within a story. Characters are presented in a myriad of ways to the reader. They can be major or minor and either static (unchanging) or dynamic (changing). Readers learn about characters through physical traits, dialogue, actions, responses to situations, opinions, beliefs, and POV. There are two divisions that pertain to the most important characters in a story:

  - **Antagonist**—The person or force that works against the hero (protagonist) in the story.

  - **Protagonist**—The main character in the story who is often good or possesses heroic qualities.

- **Setting**—The location of the events and the time that the narrative takes place. The setting is created through vivid and descriptive language, which details sights, sounds, colors, and moods of the environment.
- **Theme**—A view on life and of how people conduct themselves. In a narrative, the theme is not directly presented but rather left up to the reader to extract from the characters, events, and setting.
- **Plot**—The sequence of events within a story. The plot is the reason that the events occur within the story. A plot pulls the reader into the lives of the characters and allows the reader to understand the decisions and choices made by the characters. Eight elements make up the plot.
  1. **Exposition**—The introduction of the story in which the reader is introduced to the setting, the tone, the characters, and initial understanding of the story.
  2. **Inciting force**—The character or event that triggers (incites) the central conflict.
  3. **Conflict**—The event(s) from which the plot is derived. There are five types of conflicts:
     - **Man versus Man**—Conflict in which one person is pitted against another.
     - **Man versus Nature**—Conflict in which a person (or people) have a run-in with the forces of nature.
     - **Man versus Society**—Conflict in which societal values and customs are challenged by a person or people.
     - **Man versus Self**—Conflict that centers around internal struggles of a character; a test of the values and inner strength of a character.
     - **Man versus Fate**—Conflict in which the problem or struggle appears to be far beyond the person's control.
  4. **Rising action**—The series of events that builds up from the conflict ending with the climax.
  5. **Crisis**—When the conflict reaches a turning point and the two opposing forces in the story meet. The crisis is when the conflict is most intense and occurs either right before or at the same time as the climax.
  6. **Climax**—The point at which the outcome of the conflict can be predicted. It is the highest point of the story and often the one with the greatest emotion.
  7. **Falling action**—The series of events that occur after the climax which wrap up the story.
  8. **Resolution**—The conclusion of the story and the rounding out of action.

Nonfiction

Nonfiction is writing in which the information is presented as fact or as a truth. This does not necessarily mean that the information is accurate or valid. Some examples of nonfiction writing include, but are not limited to, the following:

essays	user manuals	book reports
journals	historic papers	memoirs
scientific papers	encyclopedias	literary critiques
biographies	dictionaries	menus
textbooks	almanacs	letters

Poetry

Poetry is a creative form of writing and employs many ingredients. Poems are meant to be read aloud, and therefore, must utilize many devices to ensure aesthetically pleasing reads. Poetry is written in groups of lines called stanzas. Following the techniques or devices used in poetry.

Technique	Definition	Example
Rhyme	A scheme of how words are organized into patterns. **Internal Rhyme**—The rhyming of words within the line (<u>Peter</u>, <u>Peter</u> pumpkin <u>eater</u>). **End Rhyme**—The rhyming of words at the end of a line (What <u>now</u>/Brown <u>cow</u>)	aa bb cc ab ab ab aaba bbcb ccdc

(continued)

Technique	Definition	Example
Meter	The rhythm of the poem; the accented and unaccented syllables	I love my little hat / My little hat loves me / and when I wear my hat / I'm as happy as can be
Alliteration	A repetition of the beginning consonant sound	The green grass grows slowly
Assonance	A repetition of vowel sounds	What's the story morning glory
Consonance	A repetition of consonant sounds anywhere within words	Bobo boxed Baby's blue baboon
Onomatopoeia	When a word sound relates to its meaning	buzz hiss woof zip swish
Repetition	The stating of a word or phrase more than once which adds rhythm or focus	"I do not like green eggs and ham . . . I do not like them in a box . . . I do not like them with a fox . . . I do not like green eggs and ham."

Poems are written in a unique structure. There can be formal poems and informal poems, free-formed or formed. Structure can lend to the tone and flow of the poem as well as the overall aesthetic effect. The following is a list of poetic structures.

Structure	Definition	Example
Foot	One unit of meter. There are five basic feet in poetry: 1) **Iambic**—An unaccented syllable followed by an accented syllable (da-dum, da-dum) 2) **Trochaic**—An accented syllable followed by an unaccented syllable (dum-da, dum-da) 3) **Spondaic**—Two accented syllables (dum-dum, dum-dum) 4) **Anapestic**—Two unaccented syllables followed by an accented syllable (da-da-dum, da-da-dum) 5) **Dactylic**—An accented syllable followed by two unaccented syllables (dum-da-da, dum-da-da)	1) Whose **woods** / these **are** / I **think** / I **know** 2) **Pet**er, **Pet**er, **pump**kin-**eat**er 3) **Well-loved** of **me** / dis**cern**ing to ful**fill** 4) 'Twas the **night** before **Christ**mas and **all** through the **house** 5) **Wo**man much **miss**ed / how **you** call to **me**
Verse	A line of poetry written in meter and named for the number of feet per line. There are eight common types of verse.	monometer—one foot dimeter—two feet trimeter—three feet tertameter—four feet pentameter—five feet hexameter—six feet heptameter—seven feet octometer—eight feet
Stanza	The sections or lines of a poem. There are six common stanzas.	couplet—two lines triplet—three lines quatrain—four lines sestet—six lines septet—seven lines octane—eight lines

There are many forms in which a poem may be written. The form of a poem aids in the overall effect that the poem creates: it can set the tone, alter the flow and meter, and impact the way the poem is read. Following is a list of some common poetic forms.

Forms of Poetry	
Form	**Description**
Ballad	A poem that tells a story usually written in quatrains. The pattern is first and third lines are four accented syllables and the second and fourth lines are three accented syllables.
Blank Verse	A poem that is unrhymed but has meter. Each line is usually 10 syllables and in iambic meter.
Cinquain	Poems that are five lines in length. There can be both syllable and word cinquains.
Couplet	Two lines of verse that often rhyme and convey one complete idea.
Elegy	A poem about death or the sadness related to the death of an important person (important to the author).
Epic	A poem of lengthy proportions that is a story or tells the adventures of a hero; it must have a hero and villain.
Free Verse	A poem without meter or rhyme scheme.
Haiku	A form of Japanese poetry often about nature. It contains stanzas of three lines with 5, 7, 5 syllables.
Limerick	A humorous poem of five lines. Lines 1, 2, and 5 rhyme and lines 3 and 4 rhyme. The syllables are 9, 9, 5, 5, 9.
Lyric	A short poem with personal feeling; most often put to music.
Ode	Long lyric with much imagery and full of poetic devices.
Sonnet	A 14-line poem that states the poet's personal feelings. There are different types of Sonnets: **Shakespearean (English)**—has three quatrains (four lines), a rhymed couplet with a rhyme scheme of abab cdcd efef gg **Petrarchan (Italian)**—has an octave (eight lines) and a sestet (six lines) with a rhyme scheme of abbaabba and cdecde, cdccdc, or cdedce
Acrostic	The letters of a word are used to begin each line in the poem; can be comprised of adjectives or phrases.

Resource and Research Materials

The type of research being done leads to the type of resources needed. Many resources are available in today's world and a myriad of avenues exist to pursue information. When evaluating literature from a research perspective, the reader must keep in mind the validity and reliability of the source. There are two general categories for source information: primary and secondary.

Primary sources are original sources that give the reader first-hand knowledge (knowledge that was experienced by observing or participating in the activity). Primary sources offer first-hand ideas and details and will often allow the reader to get closer to the truth about a subject. A primary source can be traced back no further than its author.

There are five major types of primary sources:

1. **Interviews**—An interview allows one to talk directly with a person who has expert knowledge about a subject or topic.
2. **Presentations**—Lectures, displays, and exhibits provide first-hand information.
3. **Surveys**—Questionnaires help gather opinions and preferences directly.
4. **Diaries, journals, and letters**—Personal writings supply an excellent way to gather information first hand.
5. **Observation and participation**—Watching an event, people, or activity in person furnishes the observer with a first-hand account. Actively taking part in an event or activity yields the participant with first-hand experience and information.

Secondary sources share information from a primary source. Facts and data have been collected and gathered from a variety of primary sources and then organized, summarized, and presented in a new format. A secondary source can be traced back beyond its author to at least one other person and often times more than one. Some examples of secondary sources are magazines, newspapers, news programs, encyclopedias, and business presentations.

Readers have the responsibility of making an informed assessment on the resources they use to gain facts, opinions, and ideas. Information is everywhere in today's society: television, Internet, newspapers, magazines, libraries, schools, neighbors, coworkers, friends, and so on. It is up to the reader to judge whether or not the information provided is reliable and trustworthy. To evaluate this, the reader must look at the source that provides the information. Key questions readers must ask themselves when analyzing sources are as follows:

What type of source is this? Whether the source is primary or secondary can play a large role in determining the validity and reliability of the information. Did the source actually witness or experience the information or is she simply relating it to the reader second hand?

Who is the source? Anyone can write literature or essays and post it on the Internet, claiming the information is valid. Check to see if the source is an expert or authority on the subject or topic before judging the validity. Explore the background of the individual providing the information.

Is the information accurate? The information provided needs to be clear, concise, and of high quality. Check to see if there are other sources which express similar information.

Is the information up to date? Make sure that the information given is the most current.

Is the source biased? Check to see whether the source is an objective observer/participant or if the source has something to gain by using the facts and providing the information (ex: politicians, TV infomercials, drug company findings, and so on).

Text Structure and Organization for Reading and Writing

Structure is the way writing is organized. Authors must construct what they have to say in a pattern or form in order to convey their message to the reader. Understanding the organization of a piece of writing helps the reader comprehend the text.

Specific patterns can be found within fiction, poetry, and nonfiction. The structure often can be used as a type of formula when reading various forms of literature. If the reader understands the organization of the literature, she may better understand the message that is being portrayed by the author.

Following is a list of the patterns of organization found within each:

Fiction	*Poetry*	*Non-Fiction*
Story and plot	Poetic devices	Description and details
Theme and meaning	Assonance	Main idea and supporting details (introduction of the subject
Conflict and climax	Rhythm	and the support to prove it)
Resolution and epiphany	Alliteration	Compare and contrast
	Metaphor	Chronological order (time pattern)
	Simile	Cause and effect (situations/events and the reasons it occurs)
	Verses	Process (describes how an event happens)
	Stanzas	
	Diction	

Literacy Acquisition and Reading Instruction

Literacy acquisition is acquired through a myriad of practices such as letter knowledge, familiar word reading, and symbol or picture reading. Literacy acquisition is essential for readers as it leads the reader into procedural knowledge (knowing how) and conceptual knowledge (knowing why). When children are able to assess themselves as readers as well as assessing the text then their literacy and comprehension will flourish.

There are three components to the acquisition of language:

- Letter knowledge—Giving sounds for an individual letter and writing letters in response to their individual sounds
- Logographic foundation—Reading familiar and common words (sight words)
- Alphabetic foundation—Reading aloud and having the student write the letter spoken based upon the sound spoken or the letter name uttered

Reading is the foundation upon which all formal education is constructed. Reading skills and proficiency pervade all aspects of education and life. Academic success, employment, and personal autonomy are all dependent upon reading and writing proficiencies.

Foundations of Literacy and Reading Instruction

Development of literacy skills is dependent upon language and listening skills. There are many ways to practice literacy and encourage the construction of literacy foundation:

- Learn to listen—Make eye contact and attend to the speaker, determine background noise from foreground sounds, develop attention span, social listening skills, mental imaging, and auditory memory.
- Time to speak—Practice social speaking skills, be aware of audience, take turns, develop vocabulary, sentence structure, descriptive language, and use predicting, planning, recalling, and analyzing.
- Memory and music—Develop rhythm, voice control, articulation, turn-taking, sense of time and beat, cooperation with others, auditory memory, language patterns, and prediction skills.
- Learning about print—Understand the function of print, recognizing the alphabet and letters, reading and writing concepts, and sight word and high frequency words.
- In harmony with sound—Use listening skills, learning the awareness of language, the recognition of rhyme and rhythm, the use and impact of poetic devices within language, and the influences of basic skills such as phonemic awareness, blending and segmenting, and phonics.
- Development of writing—Development and honing in of motor skills, hand-eye coordination, letter shapes and formations, development of hand and finger muscles, and control of pencil or pen.

Foundations

Reading encompasses the acquisition of a wide array of skills. If students gain these skills early and have basic foundations set at an early age, they will continue to be successful and achieve greater overall achievement in school and in life. The process of reading is complicated and detailed, but instruction in this area should cover general principles. There are specific foundations, which remain basic throughout elementary education.

The core of reading instruction should include the following four areas:

1. Understanding of psychology and development
2. Understanding of language structure
3. Application of best practices in all aspects of instruction
4. Using reliable, efficient, and validated assessments

Specifically when reading, good readers process the letters of each word in detail unconsciously and very quickly, which can appear as skimming text. Because word recognition is accurate and fast, the reader's mind is able to expend energy mulling over the meaning of the text rather than focusing energy on decoding words. Sound symbol mapping allows the reader to develop word recognition, which leads to comprehension. Good readers are familiar with and possess linguistic structure, recognize patterns, and connect letter patterns with sounds, syllables, and meaningful word parts. The detailed foundations are included here.

Foundation	Definition	How to obtain the foundation
Print concepts	Letters have sounds, and they form words.	Structure of a book Learning through repeated reading and exposure to text/print
Phonemic awareness	Speech is broken into individual sounds; in the English language, there 44 found within the 26 letters of the alphabet.	Exposure to nursery rhymes or common jingles Use of oral language and sound patterns
Alphabetic principle	Letters represent sound and speech.	Exposure to text and print
Word identification	Various strategies are used to recognize vocabulary.	Decoding by sound Decoding by comparison to known words Sight words
Fluency	Reading is done with expression, is automatic and flowing (does not require comprehension).	Practice reading
Comprehension	Critical thinking and processing of content read.	Practice of reading and writing qualities. Reading qualities may include: use of background knowledge, summarizing, visualizing, forming inferences, making connections, asking questions, synthesizing, and determining the main idea. Writing qualities refers to: ideas, organization, voice, word, choice, sentence fluency and mechanics.

Children's Literature

A literary genre designed especially for children. It is defined as literature that is read and selected by children. There are six basic categories found within children's literature.

1. Early childhood—Picture books, concept books (counting and alphabet), pattern books, and non-print books
2. Traditional—Myths, fables, folk songs, legends, tales (fairy and folk), traditional rhymes
3. Fiction—Fantasy, historical, science, contemporary materials
4. Biography and autobiography
5. Nonfiction and reference—Encyclopedia, dictionary, almanac, historical, scientific resources
6. Poetry and verse—Anthologies

Strategies for Word Recognition

Readers use certain techniques to identify printed text and words. These techniques are crucial to text comprehension and reading foundation.

Instant recognition—Being able to fluently identify words leads to text comprehension. There are 100 words that make up 50 percent of the words read by adults and children. The high-frequency words (slight words) should be learned so they may be recognized instantly to assist in reading fluency and comprehension.

For example: the, to, from, in, said, he, it, she, read, you, me, and

Context clues—The ability to use words, meanings, and context to extract the meanings of unknown words. Context clues alone are not enough to predict word meaning and, therefore, must be accompanied by other clues such as phonics or comparison or word structure. There are three types of context clues that readers may use:

- Semantic clues (meaning)—Based upon the subject read, the reader can determine what type of language will be used. For example, when reading a story about dogs, the reader will expect to see words such as teeth, woof, bark, tail, ball, play, ears. Within sentences (*My dog likes to _____*) the reader can use context to determine reasonable vocabulary: run, bark, play, jump.

- Syntactic clues (word order)—Looking at the order and structure of words the reader can determine meaning based upon the part of speech. (*My dog likes to _____*. Since the missing word is at the end the reader can reason that the word needed is a verb to make a real sentence.)

- Symbolic clues (pictures)—Illustrations and graphics can provide assistance in the identification of words. (If a dog is chasing a ball in the picture, the word "play" seems a reasonable choice for the sentence *My dog likes to _____*.)

Word structure clues—Recognizing frequent letter groups. Included in this category are prefixes, suffixes, and inflectional endings. This helps readers become more rapid and efficient word identifiers.

Analogy clues—Readers are able to draw connections between patterns, simple words, and syllables. Being able to compare known words to unknown words helps readers determine sounds and make-up of new words.

Strategies for Comprehension

Reading comprehension is the level of understanding of a specific passage of text. Many reading strategies are available for students to use.

- **Think and read**—Before reading, the reader asks self what is already known about the subject, skims the text, pauses throughout the text to take notes or write questions, and reads difficult parts aloud; after reading, reader writes or tells what was learned, and summarizes.

- **Inferential reading**—Draws upon prior knowledge; the reader draws conclusions and makes inferences, and the reader recognizes the effects that personal biases and point's of view may have in analyzing text. For example, context clues, pronoun recognition, POV, gives details of setting, evaluates author's message, draws connections between text and own life, draws conclusions from information.

- **Annotating text**—Develops questions in response to text, analyzes and interprets elements of poetry, draws conclusions based on literal and figurative meaning, labeling and interpreting literacy devices, determines and labels main idea and supportive details.

- **KWL**—K represents "what do I know," W represents "what do I want to know," and L represents "what I learned or want to learn."

- **Metacognition**—Thinking about thinking, monitoring understanding, clarifying purpose, identifying difficulty and planning to solve, looking through text to review key concepts, and adjusting reading speed depending upon the difficulty of text.

- **Graphic organizers**—Help readers focus on text structure, show relationships within a text, organize ideas for better summarizing, and illustrate concepts. Some examples include Venn diagrams, storyboards, chain of events, story maps, story webs, graphs, charts, and cause and effect.

- **QAR** (Question-Answer Relationship)—Readers learn how to answer questions, delineate between explicit information and implicit information, and draw on background knowledge. There are four types of questions:
  - "Right there" questions within the text that ask the reader to find the answer that is located in one place as a word or simple phrase.
  - "Think and search" questions that force the reader to recall information directly from the text. The answer is found in more than one place, requiring the reader to search the text.
  - "Author and You" questions that require the reader to use what they already know coupled with what they just learned from the text.
  - "On Your Own" questions based upon the reader's prior knowledge and background knowledge in which the text may not be helpful in answering.
- **Summarizing**—Identifying and/or generating main ideas, connecting main ideas, eliminating unneeded information, and recalling what was read.
- **Story Structure Recognition**—Being able to recognize patterns within literature aids in the readers' comprehension, identifying categories of content, recognizing the type of literature based upon elements, and organization of text.

Language in Writing

Language is the foundation upon which writing is based. Having a firm grasp upon language allows the writer to express meaning in a clear and concise manner. There are many facets to writing, which must be studied and understood in order to develop the ability to communicate effectively.

Grammar and Usage

Grammar can be defined as the rules and guidelines that are followed to write and speak in an acceptable manner. In the English language, parts of speech assist an individual in the understanding of words and how to use words.

Parts of speech

There are eight parts of speech in the English language. Every word is a part of speech.

A **noun** is a word that names a person, place, thing, concept, idea, act, or characteristic. Nouns give names to everything that exists, has existed, or will exist in the world.

Common nouns refer to general ideas, objects, places, and concepts and are NOT capitalized. For example, girl, man, house, bridge, class.

Proper nouns refer to specific ideas, people, concepts, places, and objects and ARE always capitalized. For example, Haley, Chip, White House, Golden Gate Bridge, English.

Concrete nouns name things that are physical and able to be touched. For example, desk, bottle, phone, space shuttle.

Abstract nouns name something that cannot be seen or touched but can be thought or felt. For example, love, hate, Buddhism, happiness, sickness.

Collective nouns name a group or collection of people, things, places, concepts, or characteristics. For example, tribe, family, team, flock, gaggle, litter, bunch, dozen.

Compound nouns are made up of two or more words. For example, basketball, middle school, mother-in-law.

Singular nouns refer to only one thing, person, place, idea/concept, or characteristic. For example, dog, teacher, dress, test, giraffe.

Plural nouns refer to more than one thing, person, place, idea/concept, or characteristic. The following rules apply when making nouns plural:

- Most words, simply add "s." For example, teachers, stethoscopes.
- If a word ends in ch, s, ss, x, or z add "es." For example, boxes, witches, dresses.
- If a word ends in a "y" preceded by a consonant, change the "y" to "i" and add "es." For example, butterflies.
- If a word ends in "o" with a vowel right before the "o", add "s." For example, radios.
- If a word ends in "o" with a consonant right before the "o", add "es." For example, echoes.
- If a word ends in "f" or "fe" in which the final sound is a v sound, change the "f" or "fe" to "ve" and add "s." For example, lives, loaves.
- If a word ends in "f" and the final sound remains the f sound, add "s." For example, roofs.

Nouns can be used in a variety of ways within a sentence.

Noun Type	Definition	Example
Subject noun	When the noun does something or is being talked about within a sentence	The dog ran quickly around the fence to catch the red ball.
Predicate noun	When the noun repeats or renames the subject	A classroom is a great place to learn new things.
Possessive noun	When the noun shows ownership	My mother's face beamed with pride at my book's success.
Object noun	When the noun is used as the direct object, the indirect object, or the object of the preposition	You will love the sandwich on wheat bread.

A **verb** is a word that shows **action**(s) or a state of being. Verbs can also be known as **linking verbs** that link the subject to the words that describe it. Such as is, has been, and was.

Action Verbs	Linking Verbs
Mabel chases squirrels.	Mabel is happy.
Mabel barked in the yard.	Mabel's face was dirty.
The squirrel shrieks at Mabel.	The dog treats were on sale.
The squirrel fell.	The sun has been bright today.

Helping verbs are words that aid in the formation of tense. For example, shall, will, should, would, could, must, can, may, have, had, has, do, did, is, are, was, were, am, being, been.

Verbs have three principle tenses: past, present, and future. Verbs must be conjugated into these different tenses depending upon the time that the action is taking place.

- **Present tense**—Shows the action is happening now
- **Past tense**—Shows the action happened in the past or before (uses "ed")
- **Future tense**—Shows that the action will happen (uses "will")

Present	Past	Future
Chip enjoys his vacation.	Chip enjoyed his vacation.	Chip will enjoy his vacation.
I jump over the rock.	I jumped over the rock.	I will jump over the rock.

Verbs in a sentence should **agree** with one another and should coincide or match time sequences. If an action happened at the same time as another action, then the verbs must have the same tense. This holds true within sentences and also within paragraphs and narratives. For example,

Justin *sleeps* while his dog *runs* up and down the stairs. (*both present*) CORRECT

Justin *slept* while his dog *runs* up and down the stairs. (*past and present*) INCORRECT

Justin *slept* while his dog *ran* up and down the stairs. (*both past*) CORRECT

Present perfect tense is when the action begins in the past but concludes in the present. (Add "has" or "have" to the past participle.) For example, It *has taken* a very long time to write this book.

Past perfect tense is when the action begins in the past and is completed in the past. (Add "had" to the past participle.) For example, I *had hoped* to be finished by November.

Future perfect tense is when the action will begin in the future and will be completed by a specific time in the future. (Add "will have" to the past participle.) For example, By the end of the year, we *will have completed* the manuscript.

Verbs can also be **regular** and **irregular.** Regular verbs follow a distinct pattern and are predictable (past = ed, future = will). Irregular verbs have their own, individual form for each tense that does not follow a pattern.

Irregular Verbs to Know		
Present	*Past*	*Future (are preceded by the word "has," "had," or "have")*
am, is, are	was, were	been
begin	began	begun
break	broke	broken
bring	brought	brought
catch	caught	caught
choose	chose	chosen
do	did	done
eat	ate	eaten
give	gave	given
go	went	gone
grow	grew	grown
know	knew	known
lay	laid	laid
lie	lay	lain

The **voice** of a verb tells whether the subject is doing the action or receiving the action:

- **Active voice**—The subject is doing the action in the sentence. For example, I found the treasure chest in the sand.
- **Passive voice**—The subject is receiving the action in the sentence. For example, The treasure was found in the sand.

Verbs can be used in a myriad of ways. The verb type allows the reader to better comprehend the meaning of what is being read. If the reader recognizes the use of the verb it may help in the understanding of the sentence content.

Verb Uses		
Verb Type	*Definition*	*Example*
Transitive verb	When the verb transfers its action to an object; the noun must receive the action of the verb for the verb meaning to be complete.	The girl **threw** the ball. (Threw transfers its action to the ball. Without the ball, the meaning of the verb threw is incomplete.)
Intransitive verb	When the verb completes its action without an object.	His shoulder **felt** sore. (Sore is a predicate adjective, not a direct object.)
Transitive and intransitive verbs	When the verb can be either transitive or intransitive depending upon the sentence.	He **read** the paper. (transitive) He **read** aloud. (intransitive)

Verbals are words that are made from verbs, have the power of a verb, but act like another part of speech.

- **Participle**—When a verb ends in "ing" or "ed," and it is used like an adjective. For example, The *shaking* windows broke in the aftermath of the tornado. (*Shaking* modifies *windows*.)
- **Infinite**—When a verb is preceded by "to" and it is used as an adjective, noun, or adverb. For example, *To climb* Mount Everest is one of my goals. (*To climb* is used as a noun and is the subject of the sentence.)
- **Gerund**—When a verb ends in "ing" and it is used as a noun. For example, *Screaming* is pointless. (The noun *screaming* is the subject.)

An **adjective** is a word used to describe a noun or pronoun. For example, purple, loud, minuscule, gigantic, colorful, sweet.

The *purple* shirt is *pretty*.

The child was *loud*.

A *miniscule* fish rides on the back of a *gigantic* whale in the ocean.

A **proper adjective** is formed by a proper noun and is always capitalized. For example, The *San Francisco* bridge stretches a long way.

A **common adjective** is any adjective that is not proper and is not capitalized. For example, The *long, elegant* bridge stretches for miles across the *angry* sea.

Types of Adjectives

Type	Description	Example
Demonstrative adjective	An adjective that singles out a specific noun: this, that, these, those (a noun must immediately follow).	This lake is huge but that ocean is larger.
Compound adjective	An adjective that is made up of two or more words and is hyphenated.	The self-centered boy refused to share his snack with the starving children.
Indefinite adjective	An adjective that gives the reader approximate information and does not tell exactly how much or how many.	Some rivers flow quickly.
Predicate adjective	An adjective that follows a linking verb and describes the subject.	The Colorado river was once humongous, but now is small.

Adjective Forms

Form	Definition	Example
Positive	When an adjective describes a noun or pronoun without comparing it to anyone or anything else.	Mountain biking is an exciting sport that requires skill and balance.
Comparative	When an adjective compares two or more people, places, things, ideas, concepts, or characteristics. The adjective usually ends in –er.	Mountain biking is better than road biking.
Superlative	When an adjective compares three or more people, places, things, ideas, concepts, or characteristics. The adjective usually ends in –est.	Mountain biking is the most exciting sport in the Olympics. or Mountain biking is the hardest type of biking.

(continued)

Adjective Forms *(continued)*		
Form	*Definition*	*Example*
Two-syllable	When the adjective shows comparison by the suffixes (er/est) or modifiers (more/most).	spicy, spicier, spiciest or boring, more boring, most boring
Three- (or more) syllable	When the adjective is three or more syllables long, it requires the words more/most or less/least to express comparison.	more terrifying, most terrifying, less terrifying, least terrifying
Irregular	When the adjective uses a completely different word to express the comparison.	good, better, best bad, worse, worst

An **article** is a word placed before a noun, which introduces the noun as specific (the) or nonspecific (a, an). "The" delineates a specific person, place, thing, concept, idea, characteristic, or a plural noun. For example,

> Please get *the* pencil from *the* desk.

"A" or "an" delineates a nonspecific person, place, thing, concept, idea, or characteristic. "An" is used for nouns that begin with a vowel. For example,

> *A* car can travel faster than *an* elephant.

A **pronoun** is a word used to replace or in the place of a noun. Pronouns include the following:

> I, me, myself
>
> you, yours, yourself
>
> we, us, ours
>
> he, she, his, her, hers
>
> they, their, theirs
>
> it, its

For example, As the ball sailed over the net, *it* spun to the left. (*It* replaces *ball*.) Poppy kicked *her* soccer ball after *it* was passed to her. (*Her* refers to *Poppy,* and *it* refers to the *soccer ball.*)

The **antecedent** is the noun that the pronoun replaces or to which it is referring. Every pronoun has an antecedent. The antecedent can be in the same sentence as the pronoun or in the previous sentences. All pronouns must coincide and agree with their antecedent in person, number, and gender. For example,

> The dog chased the Frisbee in the park. When *she* brought *it* to *her* owner *she* was praised. (*Dog* is the antecedent for *she* and *her,* and *Frisbee* is the antecedent for *it.*)

Personal pronouns replace nouns in a sentence. There are three types of personal pronouns:

- Simple—I, you, we, it, he, she, they
- Compound—myself, herself, himself, itself, ourselves, themselves, yourself
- Phrasal—one another, each other

Singular pronouns express one person, place, thing, concept, idea, or characteristic. For example, I, you, he, she, it.

Plural pronouns express more than one person, place, thing, concept, idea, or characteristic. For example, we, you, they, us, you all, them.

The **person of the pronoun** tells the reader whether the pronoun is doing the action or speaking, experiencing the action or receiving the speaking, or is being spoken about:

- First person (I, me, we)—Used to show the pronoun is doing the action or is speaking; replaces the name of the noun. For example, *I* am writing.

- Second person (you, you all)—Used to show the pronoun is experiencing the action or is being spoken to. For example, Eric, will *you* please go kayaking?

- Third person (he, she, it, they)—Used to show the pronoun is being spoken about. For example, Basta needs to cook dinner if *she* wants to eat.

Pronouns can be used in many ways within a sentence. A pronoun can represent a subject, an object, or to show possession.

The pronoun can be used as the sentence's **subject** (*I, you, he, she, it, we, they*). For example, *I* like to eat peanut butter and jelly sandwiches. (*I* is the subject).

The pronoun can be used as the **object** of a verb or prepositional phrase (*me, you, him, her, it, us, them*). For example, "You hit *me*!" screamed Elizabeth. (*Me* is the object pronoun because it receives the action *hit*.)

The pronoun can show ownership or **possession** (*my, mine, our, ours, his, hers, their, theirs, its, your, yours*). For example, The red jacket was *hers*. (*Hers* shows ownership of the *jacket*.)

Pronoun Uses			
Type	**Definition**	**Example**	**Pronoun**
Relative	A pronoun that connects a subordinate clause to the main clause and uses a connecting word.	The girl who has curly hair is in fourth grade. (Who relates to girl.)	that who
Intensive	A pronoun that emphasizes the noun it refers to; most sentences are complete without the intensive pronoun.	The rattlesnake curls before it strikes and the snake itself can strike up to three times its body length. (Itself intensifies snake.)	itself myself himself herself yourself
Demonstrative	A pronoun that identifies the noun without naming it specifically.	This was a fabulous party. or Those drinks were delicious.	this that these those
Interrogative	A pronoun that asks a question.	Who wants ice cream? Whom would you take to dinner? Which ice cream is your favorite? Whose car will you take?	who whom which whose
Indefinite	A pronoun that does not specifically name the antecedent.	Will somebody make me dinner?	somebody anybody anyone someone
Reflexive	A pronoun that places the action back upon the noun.	A rattlesnake protects itself by rattling and then striking.	itself herself himself

An **adverb** is a word that modifies a verb, an adjective, or another adverb. Adverbs tell how, when, where, why, how much, and how often. (Many adverbs end in -*ly* but not all.) For example,

> The scorpion scurries *quickly* across the floor. (*Quickly* modifies the verb *scurries*.)
>
> Bark scorpions are *very* deadly. (*Very* modifies the adverb *deadly*.)
>
> Bark scorpions are *extremely* dangerous. (*Extremely* modifies the adjective *dangerous*.)

There are three types of adverbs.

Positive adverbs describe a verb, adjective, or adverb. For example, She performed *poorly* on her presentation.

Comparative adverbs compare two things. For example, He plays the drums *more loudly* than his brother.

Superlative adverbs compare three or more things. For example, Blue whales are the *largest* animals in the world.

Adverb Uses		
Type	***Definition***	***Example***
Time adverbs	When the adverb tells how often, when, or how long	She will kayak tomorrow. She always goes kayaking.
Place adverbs	When the adverb tells where, to where, or from where	The music blared outside. The boy walked backward out the door.
Manner adverbs	When the adverb tells how something is done (often ends in –ly)	The rock climber meticulously chose holds to use. The rock fell slowly down the mountain.
Degree adverbs	When the adverb tells how much or how little	I rarely eat sushi.

A **preposition** is a word or group of words that tells position, direction, or how two ideas are related to one another. For example,

> The phone slid *off* the wall.
>
> The mustache grew *above* Chuck's lip.
>
> He walked *across* the grass.
>
> *During* the game, Andrea scored four goals.

A **prepositional phrase** contains the preposition, the object of the preposition, and the modifiers of the object. The phrase can function either as an adjective or adverb. For example,

Shirley skied *down the large, hairy cliff*. (Within the prepositional phrase, down = preposition; long, hairy = modifiers; cliff = object.)

Common Prepositions (not a comprehensive list)				
above	below	except	off	since
across	beneath	for	on	through
after	beside	from	on top of	to
against	between	in	onto	together with
along	beyond	inside	opposite	under/underneath
among	but	into	out	until
apart of	by	like	outside	up/upon

Common Prepositions (not a comprehensive list)				
around	down	near	over	with/within
at	during	of	regarding	without

A **conjunction** is a word that joins together words or groups of words. Some examples include *when, and, but, so, or, because*. There are three types of conjunctions:

A **coordinating conjunction** joins a word to a word, a phrase to a phrase, or a clause to a clause; the words, phrases or clauses joined must be equal or of the same type. They include *and, or, but, for, nor, yet, so*. For example, if you want to hang out with me, we can go see a movie *or* get coffee.

A **correlative conjunction** is used in pairs. For example, *Either* you sit quietly *or* you leave the room.

A **subordinating conjunction** connects two clauses that are not equal or the same type; it connects a dependent to an independent clause. They include *if, although, as, when, because, since, though, when, whenever, after, unless, while, whereas, even though*. For example, Running a marathon is hard work *because* of the taxation on your body.

An **interjection** is a word or phrase used to show strong emotion or surprise. Interjections are usually delineated by an exclamation point or commas. For example,

> *Whoa!* Slow down.
> *Ah,* a shark!
> *Look,* a falling star!
> *Yippee!* I won a bike.
> *Look out,* there's a moose in the road!
> *Yea,* it's time for recess!

Syntax and Sentence Types

The manner in which words are organized and put together in a sentence (syntax) shows the reader what type of sentence is being read and how to read the information presented. A sentence must have a **subject** and a **predicate.** The **subject** is the part of the sentence that is doing the action or is being talked about. There are three types of subjects:

- **Simple subject**—The subject without all the words that describe or modify it. For example, The team *sports* at school encourage cooperation and teamwork.
- **Complete subject**—The simple subject and all the words that modify or describe it. For example, *The team sports at school* encourage cooperation and teamwork.
- **Compound subject**—Has two or more simple subjects. Ex: *Basketball*, *volleyball*, and *football* are all team sports at school.

The **predicate** is the part of a sentence that discusses or adds information to the subject. There are three types of predicates:

- **Simple predicate**—The predicate without all the words that modify or describe it (only the verb). For example, The snow *falls* heavily every night in the month of December.
- **Complete predicate**—The simple predicate with all the words that modify or describe it. For example, The snow *falls heavily every night in the month of December.*
- **Compound predicate**—The compound predicate has two or more simple predicates. For example, The snow *falls* and *sticks* to the ground.

Direct objects include nouns and pronouns that directly receive the action of the predicate (answers the question "what?" or "whom?"). For example, Young, preschool *children* need to be read to on a daily basis.

Indirect objects include nouns and pronouns that indirectly receive the action of the predicate (answers the question "to whom?" or "from whom?"). For example, I read the *class* a book. If an indirect object follows a preposition, it is the object of the preposition, NOT an indirect object.

Independent clauses can stand alone as a sentence because they express a complete idea or thought. For example, If the vegetables are picked, *they could be used to make a delicious, organic salad.*

Dependent clauses cannot stand alone as a sentence because they do not express a complete idea or thought. For example, *If the vegetables are picked*, they could be used to make a delicious, organic salad.

Phrases are groups of words that are related but lack a subject or a predicate or both and are, therefore, not complete sentences. For example, two girls (lacks a predicate); has dirt on it (lacks a subject). There are five types of phrases. Each type is named for the function it serves within a sentence:

1. noun phrase
2. verb phrase
3. adverb phrase
4. verbal phrase
5. prepositional phrase

Sentences are made up of one or more words and express a complete thought. Sentences begin with a capital letter and end with a punctuation mark (period, question mark, or exclamation point). There are four sentence forms that may be used.

Form	*Definition*	*Example*
Simple sentence	A sentence with one complete thought (independent clause)	My hand hurts. Her shoulders and arms are sore.
Compound sentence	A sentence with two or more simple sentences, which are joined by a conjunction and/or punctuation	I usually stretch my arms in the morning, but I forgot to this morning.
Complex sentence	A sentence with one independent clause and one or more dependent clauses	Since my arms are sore, I think I will not lift weights today.
Compound-complex sentence	A sentence with two or more independent clauses and one or more dependent clauses	My friend Hal wants to go running, but I want to go biking when we get together on Saturday.

There are four major categories in which sentences can be divided. The type of sentence helps the reader recognize voice and mood of the text as well as determine meaning and lends to the overall comprehension of text.

A **declarative (.) sentence** makes a statement or tells something and ends with a period. For example, Charles Darwin wrote *The Origin of Species.*

An **interrogative (?) sentence** asks a question and ends with a question mark. For example, Who wrote the book, *The Origin of Species?*

An **imperative (.) sentence** gives a command, often with you as the understood subject and ends with a period. For example, read this book.

An **exclamatory (!) sentence** expresses strong feeling or shows surprise and ends with an exclamation point. For example, I love this book!

Orthography and Morphology

Orthography is the study of the spelling systems of language. It examines how letters are combined to represent sound and form words. In language, morphology is the study of the forms of words and examines how words develop.

Semantics

Semantics is the study of meaning within linguistics. It includes sense, reference, implication, logical form, word meaning, word relations, and structure of meaning. Readers use semantics to help fluency, comprehension, and language acquisition.

An **affix** is an attachment to a base or root word. There are two types:

- **Prefix**—Word or letters placed at the beginning of a root or base word to create a new word or alter the meaning of the root. For example, un-, pre-, non-, a-, tri-, bi-, dis-.
- **Suffix**—Morpheme added to the end of a root or base word to form a new word or to alter the meaning of the root. For example, -ing, -er, -tion, -fy, -ly, -it, -is.

A **derivational affixation** occurs when affixes are added to root or base words, which modify meaning and function. For example, sing (verb) add *–er* to create singer (noun); slow (adjective) add *–ly* to create slowly (adverb).

A **digraph** is a combination of two letters possessing a single sound. For example,

head = *ea*

chance = *ch*

swing = *ng*

graph = *ph*

A **dipthong** is two vowels in which the sound begins at the first vowel and moves toward the sound of the second vowel. For example,

snout = *ou*

boy = *oy*

A **grapheme** is a letter or letters that represent one phoneme (includes every letter in the alphabet); the smallest meaningful unit within a writing system. For example, cat = c, a, t = three graphemes

A **homonym** occurs when two words that have the same pronunciation and spelling but different meanings. For example,

left (direction, opposite of right) and left (past tense of leave)

bear (animal) and bear (to carry)

mouse (animal) and mouse (computer component)

mean (rude) and mean (average) and mean (to define)

A **homophone** occurs when two words are spelled differently, pronounced identically, but have different meanings.

two, to, too	hour, our
aero, arrow	air, heir, err
isle, aisle	ball, bawl
sweet, suite	holy, wholly
hear, here	pair, pear
pain, pane	rain, reign
rheum, room	sighs, size

A **homograph** occurs when words have the same spelling but different meanings and may or may not be pronounced differently. For example,

> read (past tense), read (present tense)
>
> dove (bird), dove (past tense of dive)
>
> close (shut), close (near)
>
> wind (to turn), wind (blowing air)

A **morpheme** is the smallest meaningful unit of speech that can no longer be divided. For example, in, come, on.

A **phoneme** is a distinct unit of sound found within language that helps distinguish utterances from one another. For example,

> bat: b = "buh" + at
>
> pat: p = "puh" + at

Vocabulary in Context

Context helps readers decode words, extract meaning, and comprehend text. There are five major clues readers can use to assist them while reading.

Clue	Definition	Key Vocabulary	Example
Antonym clue	Words or phrases that indicate the opposite of an unknown word or concept	but, however, unlike, yet, in contrast, instead of	Instead of singing in a mellifluous voice, she sang with a harsh and grating voice.
Synonym clue	Words or phrases that have a similar or have the same meaning as the unknown word or concept	that is, in other words, sometimes called, or, known as	The ursine, commonly known as the bear, tore through the camp garbage.
Definition clue	Words or phrases that explain or define the unknown word or concept	means, the term, is defined as, can be delineated as a phrase by commas, italics or bold-face	Raucous sounds, loud and harsh noises, can be heard in the jungle.
General knowledge	Meaning is acquired from background knowledge or prior experience of the reader	the information is either familiar or common	The plethora of balloons floated in the sky. There were a myriad of colors in the atmosphere.
Word analysis	Breaking down words into roots, prefixes, and suffixes to determine meaning	the meanings of individual roots, prefixes, suffixes (un- = not, -able = having a quality of)	The home team was undefeatable in their tournament play. un – defeat – able not having the quality of being beaten

Figurative Language

Writing that compares one person, place, thing, idea, concept, or characteristic to another in order to improve, magnify, strengthen, refine, and clarify meaning. Figurative language is any language that goes beyond the literal meaning of the words used.

Alliteration is when language repeats the consonant sounds, which occur at the beginning of words or within words, creates mood and melody, brings attention to important words, and points out similarities and differences. For example, The coffee cup was carefully cradled in her convulsing arms.

Hyperbole is an exaggeration or overstatement that may or may not be realistic and is not meant to be taken literally. For example,

> It was such a cold winter that even the penguins were wearing jackets.
>
> I was so tired I spoke in snores rather than words.

Imagery is language that appeals to the readers' senses; describes people or objects by using the five senses. For example,

> I walked calmly to the dark side of the moon where the winds of time blew softly through my hair.

Idiom is when words are used in a special way that is different than their literal meaning. For example, steal one's thunder (to take the credit away from someone else) or cut corners (to rush through a project or job just to finish quickly).

A **metaphor** is a comparison of two unrelated objects, concepts, or ideas without using the words *like* or *as*. For example, the cloud was a soft pillow of down.

Onomatopoeia are words that mimic sounds. For example, buzz, hiss, crackle.

An **oxymoron** occurs when combining two words with opposite meanings. For example, jumbo shrimp, military intelligence, small fortune.

Personification is giving a nonhuman thing (object, idea, animal) human characteristics. For example, the tree fell with a silent, crackling cry of relief.

A **simile** is a comparison of two unrelated objects, concepts, or ideas using the words *like* or *as*. For example,

> The dog ran like a pinwheel in the wind.
>
> Her glance was as cold as ice.

Social, Cultural, and Historical Influences

Language, both written and spoken, plays a vital role in building societies, cultures, cities, and countries. Socially, humans gather together according to understandings and beliefs about the things and events around them. People have the capacity to respond to these situations and events and social bonding is generated through discussion and understanding. Communication is strong before, during, immediately after, and long after an event occurs. The ability to talk, discuss and respond to such events develops social, cultural, and community cohesion. There are four ways in which a society or culture communicates.

Means of Communication

Mean	Definition
Symbolic names	Names identify people and places with groups, differentiate communities, and declare known and recognizable groups.
Specific vocabulary Jargon Lingo	Cultures and communities develop characteristic vocabulary. Being able to use this specific vocabulary demonstrates membership within the culture and society.
Heroes and villains	People in groups tend to single out certain people to talk about. Some are praised and their actions endorsed (hero). Others are condemned and their actions reprimanded. Both reflect a society's values and beliefs.

(continued)

Mean	Definition
Proverbs	A set of values or sayings that impart wisdom within a culture and guide the society in their actions. ("A penny saved is a penny earned.")
Stories Myths Histories	Every culture, society, and community has symbolic narratives. Knowing the stories identifies a person as a member of the group. Most tell tales of success in crisis or the growth of a hero or the defeat of a villain.

Types of Communication

Communication occurs in a variety of forms within a culture and society. There are written and spoken, direct and indirect, explicit and implied forms.

Encounters—Day-to-day communications occur as people interact within their environment. Encounters take place at school, home, work, the grocery store, gas station, library, mall, TV, over the phone, and on the Internet.

Rituals—Can be meetings or other established times to gather as a group to hold discussions. They are used to demonstrate unity (holidays) and response to situations (rally or protest). Rituals can be determined by the clock or calendar (Martin Luther King Jr. Day) or by the events of life (wedding).

Crisis—These are times that demand communication and attention. Society is forced to deal with a pressing issue/situation. The society must cooperate and respond properly to ensure success and cohesion.

Deviants—Encountering misfits or people who deviate from the accepted societal norms also cause society and cultures to communicate. Communities must identify deviant behavior and also delineate the norms of society (laws).

Communication Skills

Communication is the ability to impart and share knowledge, opinions, ideas, feelings, and beliefs. Communication can be spoken or written, explicit or implied, simple or complex, positive or negative, and passionate or reasonable.

Stages of Writing Development

There are eight stages in the development of writing. Writers must progress through each stage in order to fully comprehend language and evolve writing.

- **Scribbling**—Appears as a random collection of marks on a paper. The marks may be large, circular, and resemble drawings. The marks do not resemble letters or print but are highly significant as the young writer uses the marks to express ideas.
- **Letter-like symbols**—Letter forms begin to emerge at times although still randomly placed and numbers may be strewn throughout. The writer is able to explain and tell about the "writing."
- **String of letters**—Some letters are legible and are usually written as a capital letter. The writer is developing an awareness of sound-symbol relationships but does not necessarily match the letter to the sound.
- **Beginning sound emergence**—The message within the writing begins to make sense and matches the picture drawn with it. The writer is beginning to see the differences between a letter and a word, although spacing may not be apparent.
- **Consonants represent words**—Spaces are becoming more frequent between words and lowercase letters begin to appear with upper case letters. The writer begins to write sentences that express ideas.
- **Initial, middle, and final sounds**—Sight words, familiar names, and environmental print are spelled correctly and are frequently used. Most other words are spelled phonetically. The writer is writing legibly and the writing is readable.

- **Transitional phases**—The writing is readable and is beginning to advance toward conventional spelling. The writer begins to use standard form and standard letter patterns.
- **Standard spelling**—Most words are spelled correctly in this stage. Understanding of root words, compound words, and contractions are developing. The writer is able to decode words and spell using analogies of known words.

Stages of the Writing Process		
Stage	*Description*	*Techniques Used*
Prewriting	generate ideas for writing gathering details	brainstorm read literature create life maps webs story charts word banks determine form, audience, voice
Rough draft	write ideas on paper ignore conventions	notes outlines webs
Reread	proof the work fit purpose order details	read aloud to self peer edit
Revise	improve how information is presented improve details	remove unneeded words add details and adjectives accept peer suggestions add imagery
Edit	review writing for mechanics and grammar usage	spell check grammar check
Final draft	prepare final copy	review, rewrite, and type final copy

Spelling Development

Children navigate through various stages of spelling. Each stage is crucial to the development of language acquisition as well as good spelling habits.

Invented spelling is when a young child attempts to spell words using his best judgment. The child can identify letters and relate letter sounds to words.

Stages of Spelling Development		
Stage	*Description*	*Example*
Precommunicative	When symbols are used to represent the alphabet; letter-sound does not correspond, no deciphering of upper and lowercase letters, and no concept of left-to-right direction	scribbles (elephant)
Semiphonic	When letter-sound correspondence begins to arise; single letters are used to represent words or sounds or syllables; initial sounds are used first to spell words, then final sounds, and lastly, medial sounds	single letters (U = you) (elephant)

(continued)

Stages of Spelling Development *(continued)*		
Stage	*Description*	*Example*
Phonetic	When every sound heard is represented by a letter or group of letters; vowels appear at this stage	"-ed" endings are often written with a "t" or "d" "dr" and "jr" sound the same and are interchanged "ch" is written as "tr" and vice versa LFENT (elephant)
Transitional	When the child stops relying only on sounds and mapping alone to spell words; vowels appear in every syllable; all letters are present in a word but may not be in the correct order; conventions and rules of spelling are learned (long vowels, doubling of consonants, and social conventions)	gril = girl elefent = elephant Jhon = John

Following are some basic spelling guidelines:

- *i* before *e* except after *c* or when the sound produced sounds like *a* (n*ei*ghbor); (exceptions to this rule: counterfeit, either, financier, foreign, height, heir, leisure, neither, seize, sheik, species, their, weird)
- Silent *e* at the end of a word means to drop the *e* before adding the suffix that begins with a vowel. (state = stating = statement; like = liking = likable; use = usable = useful)
- If *y* is the last letter in the word preceded by a consonant, change the *y* to *i* when adding a suffix. (hurry = hurried; happy = happiness; beauty = beautiful)
- One-syllable words ending in a consonant preceded by one vowel, double the final consonant before adding a suffix that begins with a vowel. (pat = patting; god = goddess; hum = humming)

Aspects of Speaking and Listening

Listening is an active process that requires the listener to hear, understand, and judge. Speaking requires the speaker to be knowledgeable, confident, clear, and concise. Being a good listener and a well articulated speaker is dependent upon an individual's grasp of language.

There are three components to listening, which are essential to comprehension:

- **hearing**—Being able to repeat a fact or concept that was stated
- **understanding**—Being able to process information heard, asking pertinent questions, forming responses to the information presented
- **judging**—Being able to form opinions and analyze information stated

When presenting information the speaker must consider four points:

1. Subject—What information is being presented and how (direct or indirect)?
   a. informative
   b. persuasive
   c. entertaining
2. Audience—What is the background, needs, and wants of the people in the crowd?
3. Themselves as a speaker—What preparations need to be made?
4. Occasion—The time and place of the speech or presentation; does the subject fit the occasion?

Reading/Language Arts Curriculum, Instruction, and Assessment (0011)

Reading and language arts are two critical components in a student's education. The acquisition of language begins even before birth. Educators must build upon a child's experiences and knowledge of the language in order for the student to achieve success in school. However, learning to read and understanding how to use the components of language is a difficult area to master.

The subject of language arts is comprised of the areas that include reading, spelling, and composition that aim at developing reading and writing skills. This includes comprehension and written and oral language skills most often taught at the elementary level and continuing through high school.

Reading achievement is the single most essential skill for success in school, as all subjects require that students be able to read to gain information. Three factors that will predict reading achievement are

- The ability to recognize and name letters of the alphabet
- Basic general knowledge about print
- The awareness of phonemes

The National Institute for Literacy and the Center for Education Statistics suggests that more than 40 million adults are functionally illiterate and that students at the elementary school level still lack the basic skills. Gaining these skills requires strong oral language ability and an understanding of the use of language. Learning reading skills is not a natural process supported by literacy rich environments and the acquisition of certain skills through practice. It is much more.

Reading is the act of finding meaning from print. It is a multifaceted process that requires motivation and skills in word recognition, comprehension, and fluency. Children learn to read when their teacher is knowledgeable about language development and skilled in the reading process, as well as focused on the appropriate instruction and strategies. Research shows that the most important variable in a reading program is the teacher's knowledge and possession of skills to execute a comprehensive program. For children to succeed, educators must be careful diagnosticians and focus on individual skills as they approach instruction.

Reading and the use of language arts skills is a basic necessity in our society. Students need these skills to function on a daily basis as children and later as adults. A program of rigor and teaching reading and language arts with fidelity will ensure that students gain proper skills. Implementing an integrated curriculum based on national and state standards for reading and language arts that includes developmentally appropriate activities, as well as motivational and meaningful tasks will help all students gain skills to the best of their abilities.

Standards Overview

Together, more than ten years ago, the International Reading Association (IRA) and the National Council of Teachers of English (NCTE) published 12 Standards for English Language Arts. The purpose of the standards is to provide an outline that ensures that all students are proficient language users in school, in the community, and in their work. These standards, developed through work by educators, parents, researchers, and others, delineate the language skills necessary for students to become productive citizens, who appreciate and contribute to the culture and society, who pursue a life full of personal goals directed at their own interests, and who continue to communicate and learn in the world around them.

Students need appropriate opportunities and adequate resources to acquire language skills, which are developed based on the experiences they have and the materials they are presented. These standards should help educators in the development of curriculum and instruction to encourage students to use emerging literacy abilities. These are general statements so teachers may continue to be innovative in their teaching and use a variety of instructional strategies for their diverse students.

Following is a summary list of the standards, and examinees should notice that the concepts are interrelated. For further information about standards, individuals may want to visit the web. Students will:

1. Read a variety of print and nonprint texts to develop an understanding of texts and the world; to gain new information; to respond to personal and societal needs.

2. Read a wide range of literature in several genres, from different periods, to expand their understanding of the various dimensions of the human experience.

3. Apply strategies to comprehend, interpret, and evaluate texts in the process of learning to appreciate various uses and pleasures gained from text. (This will draw from prior experience, knowledge of word skills, and text features.)

4. Modify the use of spoken, written, and visual language in utilizing more effective communications applied to various audiences and purposes.

5. Implement strategies for writing and use a variety of writing process elements to learn how to deliver a message for a purpose to different audiences.

6. Use and apply knowledge of language structure, grammar, techniques, and genre to compose print and nonprint texts.

7. Perform research and evaluate and synthesize data to communicate findings that align with the purpose and suit the audience.

8. Use technology-related and other resources to collect and interpret information and to create and communicate knowledge.

9. Develop an understanding of and respect for diversity in language across cultures, ethnic groups, geographic regions, and social roles.

10. Use their first language to develop competency in the English language arts and to gain access of the curriculum.

11. Participate as knowledgeable members of a variety of literacy communities.

12. Use spoken, written, and visual language to accomplish personal purposes.

The reading and language arts portion of the Praxis II 0011 exam assesses an examinee's overall knowledge and application of information regarding curriculum, instruction and assessment, specifically in reading, grammar, writing, and speaking. In this section of the study guide, examinees will find content specific to these topics and the more general elementary practices will be found in the "Overview" of 0011 at the front of the study guide. Use both of these sections to study for this particular topic that will be included on the exam.

The 0011 exam measures how well an examinee knows how to develop and deliver instruction based on reading and language arts content knowledge. This exam utilizes examples of elementary school situations in a multiple choice question format. This section of the study guide includes the information necessary for the examinee to clearly utilize the content of 0014 in the implementation of curriculum and instruction and the use of assessments in reading and language arts instruction.

Curriculum

Language arts integrates the areas and skills of reading, spelling, writing, and grammar. In elementary school, students learn the basic components and structures of these individual areas and practice the skills in order to apply them across the curriculum to other academic subjects.

Language Acquisition

Language acquisition is a phenomenal undertaking and depends on the background, experiences, and exposure a child has at a very young age. Linguistic awareness, which is the ability to understand the sound structure of language, is an oral language skill and listening skill that is essential to learning how to read and write. Young children need to hear how language is separated into different parts. They must learn to recognize rhyme, match words by sound and begin to understand syllables. Some of the following activities will aid children in gaining language knowledge:

- Play games with sounds.
- Use clapping to emphasize syllable breaks.
- Sing songs with rhymes and rhythms.
- Recite poems with alliteration passages.

- Read stories with predictable sound patterns.
- Utilize jokes and silly riddles for verbal play.
- Use pictures in books and encourage oral language.

Print Knowledge

Encouraging interest in reading is a primary factor in developing future reading skills. Children must gain knowledge about the printed word, understanding that letters become words, words become sentences, and sentences have meaning. Reading aloud and having children talk about the story, providing a special area for children to look at reading materials independently, using environmental print in the classroom, and playing alphabet and word games all contribute to print knowledge.

Reading

Children learn to read and write from the many opportunities available in the home and at school on a daily and regular basis. When parents read aloud and use reading and writing in the home, children become aware of the importance and gain skills indirectly. When teachers promote vocabulary and allow children to interact with books and writing materials, children become interested in learning more. Children need experiences with reading and writing, so they may draw upon this previous knowledge to apply it to word meanings, cues, and language structures in their academic work.

The purpose of teaching reading is to help students

- Gain information from text
- Improve communications
- Increase pleasure

Creating a curriculum that focuses on reading and integrates other subject areas can be a challenge for educators. Educators must be cognizant of the scope and sequence established for the school curriculum as well as the standards set at the state level and requirements at the district level. A reading program requires that teachers use a variety of strategies and methods and base their instruction on conducting individual diagnostics on all students. Curriculum development for reading and language arts should include instruction in phonemic awareness, phonics, spelling, reading fluency, grammar, writing, and reading comprehension strategies. A curriculum is a guide and not a substitute for a well-trained and effective teacher.

Developing **decoding skills** is the process of understanding that letters in text represent the sounds (phonemes) in speech. In order to learn how to decode words, a student must understand that letters in text represent the phonemes in speech. Some students have difficulty developing decoding skills as they lack phonological processing skills, while others may not have received adequate instruction in the domains that are essential for acquiring decoding skills (print concepts, letter knowledge, understanding of the alphabetic principle).

Literature

Students gain insight into cultures, historical periods, ideas, and values from reading literature and these readings may be influential on student's writings later. Reading various types of literary works allows students to learn to analyze and interpret the message delivered by the author. Students should be taught the components and types of literature available, as investigating literature will continue throughout their school career and hopefully throughout their lifetimes. They need to know the genre, the content, the structure, and the language of the text and use their prior knowledge in gleaning the appropriate information from the context of the passage or story. Merging new information with prior knowledge will help build upon their skills.

A **narrative** is a piece of literature that tells a story and incorporates the elements of sequential events, time, characters, and plot to deliver a description to the reader. It may be fictional or nonfictional and in the format of a poem, a song, a story and so on. Using narratives in the classroom, not only improves a student's reading skills, but it moves them toward developing writing skills. Narratives include new vocabulary, descriptive words and phrases, and realistic views of people and the environment. Incorporate reading narratives with writing in journals, creating personal stories, improving oral and written vocabulary, and comparing format to other types of literature.

The instruction of **poetry** should focus on an understanding of literal and figurative meanings of words, and the instruction of metaphors, similes, and patterns of language. Studying the structural elements such as assonance, alliteration, rhyme, and rhythm will also guide students to improve word knowledge and the use of language.

Writing

Writing goes hand in hand with reading. These are often taught simultaneously with increased skill development as children mature. Both are necessary for all content areas. Learning to write involves a complex cognitive process and can be very difficult for the many diverse learners in a classroom. Teachers often use the opportunity of a writing workshop to teach the stages of writing and help children master the skills.

Spelling

Research has shown that spelling is a developmental process with five complex stages. More than one stage may be present in a sample writing by one student. Instruction in spelling is essential to the developmental process. These include

- **Precommunicative**—Uses symbols from the alphabet but no knowledge of letter-sound correspondence
- **Semiphonetic**—Begins to understand letter-sound correspondence
- **Phonetic**—Uses a letter or group of letters for every speech sound heard and may not conform to the more conventional spelling
- **Transitional**—Understands conventional alternative for sounds and structure of words
- **Correct**—Knows the orthographic system and the basic rules, making generalizations

Invented spelling is students' attempts to use their personal judgment or guesses about how a word is spelled. It may be a step for some students in the process of learning to spell and reaching the final stage of **correct spelling,** where they apply spelling principles appropriately. Even students who are receiving standard spelling instruction may continue to use invented spelling for a couple of years.

Grammar

All languages follow grammatical principles and patterns. It is an essential component to a reading and language arts program, as students need an understanding of grammar in order to grow in their reading level and improve their writing. It involves the type of words and word groups in a language, and how to contrive sentences and paragraphs that deliver a message that is understandable to the reader.

Instruction

Researchers believe there are certain types of knowledge and specific skills necessary for students to become successful in learning how to read and how to write. Educators should be familiar with the developmental stages of language acquisition, as well as promote the use of oral language and vocabulary. Children must have speaking and listening skills prior to gaining reading and writing skills. Three skills that are critical to learning to read and write include:

- Print knowledge—understanding of print letters, words, and books
- Emergent writing—using print in meaningful ways
- Linguistic awareness—comprehending language use

Reading and writing foundations are built upon a student's previous knowledge as well as increasing and improving their language with experiences that include listening, thinking, and speaking opportunities. Creating letter-sound relationships is a part of the stories that children may read and the content they write. This should be tied to meaning. The use of big books, trade books, class books, and other sources rich in rhyme, rhythm, and repetition engage young children and should be used daily in the classroom.

Reading

The National Research Council recommends that instead of simply developing a program that focuses on phonics instruction and whole language instruction, educators should include alphabetic principle (understanding that word sounds are linked to certain letters and patterns), phonemic awareness, vocabulary, fluency, and comprehension in a comprehensive approach to reading instruction. Educators should integrate their approach and utilize appropriate activities and materials.

Reading Levels

Research studies indicate that grouping students according to their reading abilities can be instrumental in improving their skills. Screening tools and diagnostic instruments aid in grouping students based on abilities. Students may be grouped in a three tier system of below level learners, on-level learners and independent learners. If time is scheduled each day for the teacher to provide direct instruction students will be better able to grasp skills that are lacking. Ongoing diagnostics aid the teacher in regrouping students as skills are mastered, although research suggests leaving students in their groups for extended periods in order to ensure attainment and build confidence in their reading.

Print Awareness

To learn how to read, students must first learn that print has meaning. This occurs at different ages and stages depending on a student's previous experiences with print. After students are taught the process of print awareness, they are able to become successful readers and these skills of reading emerge.

- Be aware that sounds are represented in printed words, which is **phonemic awareness.**
- Identify words in print, which is vocabulary development or **word recognition**.
- Decode the sounds of familiar and unfamiliar words, which is the use of **phonics.**
- Construct understanding from the words, which is **comprehension**.
- Coordinate the words and meaning so reading becomes automatic, which is called **fluency**.

Reading Approaches

There are several leading perspectives about the instruction of reading at the elementary level. These approaches have proven to be effective for different types of learners, yet each may suggest that there needs to be more variety for the learner if only one approach is used. Combining approaches, or selecting core principles of several approaches are recommended, since classes vary year to year and needs are diverse.

Whole language is an approach based in both research and practice. These studies include the psycholinguistic and social nature of the process of reading, how individuals may learn concepts and express ideas, how reading and writing are interrelated with the structures of language, and the basics of literacy. This approach coincides with the constructivist theory of learning. It promotes the use of a student's language knowledge and their experiences to increase and improve their reading ability. Key concepts include:

- **Meaningful context**—Reading materials are based on content and information that has meaning for the student and the age group.
- **Acceptance of all learners**—Teachers work with students to create the environment and the instructional activities.
- **Flexible structure**—Allow ample time to engage students in meaningful projects and lessons where they are responsible for their learning.

- **Supportive classroom**—Teachers expect students to cooperate and interact to enhance learning.
- **Integrated approach**—Other subject areas in thematic units and lessons are included.
- **Focused expectations**—Teachers provide whole texts and encourage reading and writing at a higher level.
- **Context skill development**—As students read and write, teachers interject skills in spelling, grammar, reading, and writing.
- **Collaboration and scaffolding**—Teachers provide ongoing support to students and work together to meet learner needs.
- **Authentic assessments**—Regular diagnostics, based on student work, are integrated across the curriculum.

Phonics instruction is an approach that evolved around the same time period as the whole language approach. One method of reading instruction, it promotes the relationships between the sounds in spoken language (phonemes) with the letters that represent the sounds when written (graphemes) for word recognition. Systematic, explicit phonics is considered an effective method as the instruction includes sets of letter-sound relationships that are organized into sequences and the directions for the instruction are precise and clear. This method of instruction may be used either separately or in combination with other methods. Key points of phonics include the following:

- Explicit instruction in phonemic awareness and functional phonics is necessary.
- Phonics instruction may be best suited to use in context.
- Children learn phonics when they address reading and writing activities.

Terms related to phonics instruction include the following:

- **Analogy-based phonics**—A strategy taught that helps students use parts of words they have learned to attack words that are unfamiliar
- **Analytic phonics**—A method taught so students will be able to analyze letter sound relationships from learned words to those not familiar while not pronouncing sounds in isolation
- **Embedded phonics**—Use of explicit instruction for using letter-sound relationships during the reading of connected text as a way to sight read new words
- **Intrinsic phonics**—Taught gradually in the context of meaningful reading
- **Onset-rime phonics**—Instruction of separating onsets and rimes in words so students may read them and then blend the parts into the word
- **Phonics and spelling**—A method of teaching children to segment words into phonemes and creating words by writing the letters for the phonemes
- **Synthetic phonics**—The method of teaching students to convert letters or combinations of letters into sound sequences and then blend the sounds to form words

In the **basal reading approach (whole word)** students are often taught through a series or program that includes readers, manuals, workbooks, flash cards, and tests. There have been some programs with adjustments to this approach as publishers are considering the stages of reading as they design their series. Due to the emphasis on emergent literacy, programs have been moved down to the kindergarten and even the preschool level and include a preprimer, a primer and first reader. Basal programs can be either **meaning-emphasis** or **code-emphasis** programs and developers often recommend that teachers use a directed approach to reading.

In the **literature-based reading approach** children's literature and trade books are utilized in a leveled format. The readers are selected through a specific criteria based on reading stages or grade level. Using this approach helps students to become interested and motivated to read and to select various types of literature. Components include the following:

- Teacher reads aloud to the class
- Student oral reading periods
- Shared reading activities
- Sustained silent reading blocks

The **linguistic approach** focuses on the mastery of words rather than using isolated sounds. The materials that teachers use in this approach generally lack pictures so students will not be distracted from the reading; however, this limits oral language development.

The **language experience approach** integrates the development of reading skills with listening, speaking, and writing. Students dictate stories to the teacher and they become the basis for students' first reading experiences. In the language experience approach, it is assumed that writing is a secondary system derived from oral language, while whole language looks at writing and reading as structurally related.

The **individualized reading approach** is a less structured approach to reading in which students are allowed to choose the reading selections and work at their own rate on improving reading skills and comprehension. The educator facilitates the program by completing diagnostics, meeting with students individually to listen to their oral reading, and evaluating their comprehension. This approach may be complicated for some learners who lack motivation and basic reading skills.

Comprehension Skills

Reading comprehension skills enable students to become "active" readers. Active readers not only read text but interact with the text read. Readers who are active can do the following:

- predict outcomes or actions using clues from the text
- create questions about the plot or message of the text
- monitor understanding of characters, plot sequence, or context
- clarify confusing text
- connect events to prior experience or knowledge

Students make personal connections to text they read by using background knowledge and prior experience. It is imperative that teachers help students engage background knowledge before, during, and after reading a text. There are 3 essential types of connections students may utilize:

- text to self (T-S) is when a reader draws upon personal experiences to relate to a text. For example, "This story reminds me of my summer job at a camp."
- text to text (T-T) is when a reader is reminded of something she has read before. For example, "This character reminds me of the main character from a book I read last year."
- text to world (T-W) is when a reader compares something from the real world to the text he is reading. For example, "I saw a documentary about wolves and it showed some of the things discussed in this book."

Teachers must model these connections in order to ensure students are making meaningful connections and are actively reading.

Comprehension Strategy Instruction

Teaching explicit techniques helps instill effective comprehension skills. Using explicit instruction includes the following:

- **Direct instruction/explanation**—Teacher describes why a strategy helps and how and when to apply it.
- **Modeling**—Teacher demonstrates how to use and apply the strategy.
- **Guided practice**—Teacher assists students in how to learn the strategy and when to apply it.
- **Application**—Teachers support the students in practicing the strategy until they are independent in its use.

Writing

In process-based writing instruction, teachers may scaffold instruction as they

- Model the trait or strategy.
- Use guided practice with the trait or strategy.

- Allow individual practice of the trait or strategy.
- Promote application of the trait or strategy.

In the **six traits approach,** the key components aid learners of all abilities to access and use good writing. It breaks the difficult process of writing into six smaller processes.

- **Ideas**—The message that presents the purpose, includes the theme, the main idea, and the details to engage the reader and deliver understanding
- **Organization**—Constructing the piece into the proper format, using a beginning, a middle and an end to pursue the purpose
- **Voice**—The personal and unique style of the writer that provides the reader a connection and an interest in the piece
- **Word choice**—The use of words, phrases, and language selected by the writer to create the appropriate meaning
- **Sentence fluency**—The manner in which the writer composes the sentences and paragraphs to give a flow to the piece that is rhythmic, and easy to read
- **Conventions**—The grammar, spelling, punctuation, and word use that is considered when the piece is edited to support its meaning and purpose

Emergent Writing

Young children are playful with writing when given the opportunity to use the proper materials (paper, pencils, and so on). Setting up centers in the classroom will help to instill a desire to write for purpose. When writing activities are attached to meaningful purpose, children become more interested, and develop skills that lead to success with writing. Younger children should begin using writing instruments to draw and scribble. They must develop their fine motor skills in order to have proper control for more formal written assignments. Materials and activities should be age appropriate and easily accessible.

Once a child has mastered the stage of scribbling, he will move to one-letter spelling and then writing a few words. This leads a child into talking as he works and experimenting with the sounds of language. He may write his name or the name of a pet, use simple phrases, and move toward constructing invented spelling of words.

Spelling

When teachers are knowledgeable about the developmental stages in the spelling process, they are more apt to create an appropriate plan for instruction. It is recommended that students learn phonetic relationships, sound-spelling correspondences, and be able to adjust the principles and rules of spelling as they move through the stages. At each stage, teachers will instruct students in different strategies on how to approach spelling. They should learn alphabet knowledge, letter-sound correspondences, left-to-right directionality, word families, spelling patterns, phonics, word structures, irregular spellings, and manipulating or building words.

There are several ways to promote spelling in the classroom, aside from the formal standard spelling instruction. Some professionals believe that providing students with meaningful and frequent writing assignments will help them improve their spelling skills, as they may apply what they have learned through the stages. During these writings, teachers should beware of their focus on correctness, as it may inhibit growth in this area. Teachers may also use games, puzzles, and alphabetizing words to promote spelling skills. Teachers may use words from various sources to enhance spelling practice, such as those words from student writing assignments or from a list of high frequency words.

- **Regular spelling**—Words in which the pronunciation can be predicted based on the spelling as the spelling reflects one or more patterns. These are useful in reading selections when there are unfamiliar words.
- **Irregular spelling**—Does not follow the regularly established patterns of spelling and these words must be memorized.

Grammar

Grammar instruction is best provided as an element of literature instruction. Students may explore the details of sentence structures and design in poetry and other narratives which is a more authentic and meaningful way to teach grammar. Research suggests that learning grammar may best be accomplished in the context of reading, writing, and speaking.

Strategies

There are numerous strategies used for the instruction of reading and language arts; some are commercially designed and some are teacher constructed. Most include components of the critical core skills that students need to improve their skills and experience success in school. Some of the strategies come from instructional programs that are philosophically formatted and educators must identify the programs and strategies best suited to their personal style and individual students.

Reading Aloud

Research stresses that opportunities for reading aloud have a profound effect on children and their success in reading as well as their overall academic achievement in school. Reading aloud helps promote language acquisition, improves oral vocabulary and usage, and increases reading comprehension skills. There appears to be a direct correlation to the amount of time **reading aloud** occurs in homes with the education of the mother, which is a significant contributing factor to a child's interest in reading. Reading aloud to young children is one of the most critically important activities for parents and caregivers to involve themselves in order to better prepare children to be successful readers.

Building Vocabulary

Educators continually work on increasing students' oral vocabulary which improves their reading and writing abilities. Using strategies that help students determine the meanings of unfamiliar words, and instilling a curiosity for exploring word meanings and use of these words adds to reading comprehension and writing ability.

Phonemic Awareness

A strong correlation exists between phonemic (phonological) awareness and future reading success. Research indicates that successful independent readers have an excellent grasp of phonemic awareness which results in proficient decoding skills and the skill development may come at an earlier rate than for those who are not aware of phonemes. Poor readers generally exhibit a lack of phonemic awareness.

It is recommended that phonemic awareness instruction be accomplished in a natural and authentic manner. Teachers should use playful, fun ways to teach young children to be aware of the sounds (phonemes) in spoken words. They may use music and songs, poetry and rhymes, games and puzzles to instill a desire to learn and use words.

Five levels of phonological awareness from simple to complex:

1. rhyming and alliteration
2. sentence segmentation
3. syllable blending and segmentation
4. onset rime, blending, and segmentation
5. phoneme blending and segmenting words into phonemes

Phoneme Instruction

All words have phonemes and most words have more than one. Helping students understand phonemes assists them in becoming successful readers. Several different strategies promote an understanding of phonemes so they may apply this knowledge to developing reading skills.

- **Phoneme addition**—Making new words by adding a phoneme to a word. (For example, add /t/ to the word rain, which is train.)
- **Phoneme blending**—Provide a sequence of spoken phonemes and then form a word. (For example, /s/ /i/ /t/ is sit.)
- **Phoneme categorization**—Identifying words that do not belong in a set. (For example, ton, tea, sit, tug; the word sit does not belong as it does not start with a /t/.)
- **Phoneme deletion**—Identifying the word that remains when a phoneme is removed from an existing word. (For example, remove /c/ from crock and it leaves rock.)
- **Phoneme identity**—Recognizing the same sounds in a variety of words. (For example, the same sound in these words [sit, sat, sin, son] is /s/.)

- **Phoneme isolation**—Recognizing separate sounds in words. (For example, the first and last sounds in the word top are /t/ and /p/.)
- **Phoneme segmentation**—Breaking a word into separate sounds and counting them. (For example, three sounds in the word pig /p/ /i/ /g/.)
- **Phoneme substitution**—Changing one phoneme for another to make a new word. (For example, in the word bed, change the phoneme /d/ to /t/ and the new word is 'bet'.)

Phonics Instruction

There are various ways to promote phonics in the classroom. Using student names, reciting nursery rhymes, playing sounds games, reading poems and singing songs, while also reading alphabet books, discussing words and sounds, making word banks, and pointing out consonants and vowels are just a few examples of ways to instill phonics.

Instructional Approaches

The following strategies are used across the curriculum at the elementary level. These may be more fully described in the "Overview" of 0011 earlier in this study guide along with others that are helpful to reading and language arts instruction.

Direct Instruction

This approach teaches children complex skills and strategies through the introduction of specific principles. Concepts may be separated into smaller components that are taught in steps until the students fully understand the skills. Students are allowed to practice the skills to mastery and then exhibit their ability to generalize or apply the skill to other venues and subject areas. This approach is most useful in teaching reading and language arts skills that require students to proceed with a series of steps before completely understanding and using the process.

Inquiry Based Instruction

Inquiry-based instruction is useful in advancing reading skills, language development, and writing abilities. Inquiry-based instruction presents situations for students to solve, often used in science and math instruction. This method may be used to integrate subject areas of the curriculum. The students can then link their previous experiences and knowledge to the activity and ask questions as they investigate it. Students may communicate their findings through journal writing, oral presentations, and written reports.

Cooperative Learning

Cooperative learning is used with small teams of students who are generally grouped by the teacher either in a homogeneous or heterogeneous manner. A successful teaching strategy, it incorporates a variety of learning activities across the curriculum. Its pertinence to reading and language arts comes in the rich oral language, writing, and reading that occurs as students proceed through the process. Team members aid one another in advancing in the subject area and mastering skills. Particularly helpful to reading and writing is to group students of varying levels of abilities, so peer mentoring and tutoring is included in the activity.

Assessment

Proficiency in reading demonstrates the ability to read text in an automatic and fluent manner. There are many children who do not read well and have difficulties decoding words, recognizing words, and gaining meaning from the words in context. Analyzing student progress is essential in helping them to become more skilled in reading and language arts.

Steps in monitoring student achievement in reading and language arts may be identified in three stages:

1. **Pre-reading**—Prior to instruction of new skills, check for independence, use of vocabulary, and application of background information to discover the areas that may need further attention; often completed through a screening tool.
2. **Reading**—As students are involved in the learning process and are working on gaining and practicing skills, teachers can monitor skill development through on-going classroom assessments; often completed through the use of authentic and informal evaluation measures.

3. **Post-reading**—After a certain set of skills have been taught and students have been exposed to practice and application opportunities, teachers will want to identify the level of mastery of the skills and focus on addressing problematic areas that appear through the use of modified instruction and future planning.

Following are some types of assessment tools used in elementary education, not only for checking reading and language arts skills, but may also be utilized for other subject areas. These types are commonly used in the area of reading and language arts.

- **Standardized reading test**—Often conducted by classroom teachers, with imposed time limits, standard reading tests evaluate word recognition, vocabulary, and comprehension, but do not have direct relevance to improving instruction. Generally computer scored, these norm referenced tests can offer an overview of student achievement in reading and language arts.

- **Portfolios**—A collection of samples of student work in one or more areas to demonstrate student achievement. Portfolios are useful in monitoring student writing progress.

- **Profile**—A profile differs from a portfolio as it does not include samples of work, but rather is a collection of ratings or descriptions about the student. It provides information about what a student knows and what the student can do in various areas.

- **Performance task**—Using a performance task delivers beneficial information to the teacher, particularly for writing tasks and checking language arts skills (grammar, spelling, and so on). A task, a problem, or question that requires students to construct responses using strategies, organize data, formulate and generalize, and justify answers through writings.

- **Anecdotal records**—Descriptions of meaningful events observed by the teacher are collected as notes so the teacher may interpret the information in order to modify and adjust instruction for individual students. These are particularly useful to educators in observing reading and writing skills for future academic planning.

Terminology

The topic of reading and language arts is extensive, as there is a broad span of philosophies about how to teach students in this area, and there are multiple programs that may be used in classrooms. How an educator proceeds in this area with students reflects a composite of their background, personal teaching beliefs, state standards, district requirements, and the diverse students awaiting instruction. The examinee should be familiar with the following:

- **Alphabetic principle**—The concept that written language is comprised of letters that represent sounds in spoken words

- **Blend**—A sequence of consonants before or after a vowel in a given syllable (tr, sh)

- **Comprehension strategy**—Specific techniques that promote reading comprehension such as predicting and gaining word meanings from context

- **Decoding**—An ability to sound out new words or to interpret a word from print to speech through the skill of sound-symbol correspondence

- **Morpheme**—The smallest unit of language that has meaning and may be a part of a word (syllable, prefix, or suffix) or an entire word

- **Onset and rime**—Parts of words in the spoken language smaller than syllables; an onset is the initial consonant sound of a syllable such as in track (tr-); a rime is the portion of the syllable with the vowel and the remainder of the word such as in track (-ack)

- **Oral language**—Development of spoken language system (vocabulary, listening skills, and grammar ability)

- **Orthographic knowledge**—Comprehending that sounds in language are represented by printed or written symbols

- **Peer response and edit**—A process for students to share feedback with one another on their writing

- **Phoneme**—The smallest unit of sound that may change the meaning of spoken words; there are about 41-44 phonemes in the English language

- **Phonemic awareness**—Blending sounds in a word to say the word, a critical component of reading

- **Phonics**—Promotes understanding of alphabetic principles and the relationship between phonemes and graphemes

- **Phonological awareness**—Understanding that sounds are related to written words

- **Print awareness**—Knowing the basic concepts about written words, such as print organization, reading left to right, and separating words by spaces
- **Shared writing**—A cooperative effort between students and the teacher to compose a written piece by providing thoughts, ideas, and content
- **Word attack**—Reading strategies that help a learner read written words
- **Word roots**—Words from other languages that are the origin of English words
- **Writing aloud**—A strategy where a teacher shares her thoughts as she composes a written piece with students; modeled writing

Reading/Language Arts Content Area Exercises (0012)

This Praxis II exam (0012) assesses an examinee's ability to apply the knowledge gained in the content knowledge section (0014) as well as that found in the curriculum, instruction, and assessment information (0011). Examinees will have 2 hours to answer four essay questions; one question will be focused on reading/language arts. Review the information from the Praxis II 0014 and 0011 reading/language arts study guide, as well as the "Overview" of 0011 in this book.

There are endless possibilities on what questions may be presented on the exam, so examinees should prepare for this exam by considering how to use the reading/language arts information they already know. Read through the following list of questions that relate to the topic of reading and language arts education at the elementary level and try to answer these questions using a separate sheet of paper. You will notice that answers are not provided, as there are many different ways to answer these open ended questions. A rubric is used in the scoring of the actual exam (explained in the "Overview" of 0012).

The exercises posed on this exam will test the examinee's ability to prepare an extended, in-depth response to one question in the reading/language arts area. When preparing to answer questions on this exam, remember that some of the questions presented may have multiple components and therefore require multidimensional answers.

1. Discuss how to integrate language arts into a unit of study on explorers at the fifth grade level. List the learner objectives for language arts, describe three activities, explain how to assess students on those activities, and outline how parents might be involved in this unit specifically related to language arts.

2. Identify the five stages of the writing process, and with a third grade class in mind, write a developmentally appropriate activity to implement with these students that will reinforce their knowledge of the stage and the generalization of the skills.

3. Compare and contrast the following terms: read-alouds, shared reading, sustained reading, guided reading, choral reading, and reader's theatre. Identify how these different methods would be used in an elementary classroom and state the benefit of each.

4. This question requires knowledge of Bloom's taxonomy and its application to writing and implementing lesson plans. Use this structure to design a lesson plan for a fourth grade class who is studying the various types of figurative language (select one type, such as expressions, slang, or idioms).

5. Explain what role the home environment plays in a child's literacy development. Cite specific examples of components that play a vital factor in this development (for example, adult attitude toward literacy).

6. Informal assessments can provide invaluable information to teachers about their students and their needs. Read the following list of informal assessments for reading, describe how each type of assessment is used, what type of information it will provide, and how this information may be used to help structure the learning. Informal assessments: running record, miscue analysis, and informal reading inventory.

7. Invented spelling has its place in the stages of spelling development. Define invented spelling and identify its importance in the overall process of learning to spell. Then explain four ways that teachers may nurture spelling in the classroom for elementary students.

8. Children enter classrooms with diverse skills in reading and this requires teachers to utilize differentiated instruction to meet each learner's needs. Given that some children will be below grade level and some will be above grade level in reading, create two activities (at the second grade level) related to vocabulary development; one focused on remediation and one that emphasizes enrichment for these two groups of learners.

9. The use of journals is an effective strategy in the area of language arts at all elementary grade levels. For grades K–6, describe how journals could be implemented and identify the differences for use and objectives at each grade.

10. Graphic awareness plays a key role in establishing early literacy. Define graphic awareness and explain how it is an important prerequisite to invented spelling, decoding, and independent reading.

Mathematics Content Knowledge (0014)

Mathematics is the academic discipline centered around concepts such as quantity, structure, space, and change. Math draws systematic conclusions and explains relationships between numbers, patterns, solutions, and problems. It is used in many fields ranging from medical to educational to science to business to engineering to economics. Math is apparent in daily living situations such as balancing a checkbook, calculating sales percentages, grocery shopping, and paying bills.

Critical Thinking

Critical thinking is the process of conceptualizing, applying, analyzing, synthesizing, and evaluating information. The information being processed is gained through observation, reflection, reasoning, experience, and communication. Critical thinking is not a general or universal skill found among humans. All individuals experience and observe in unique and personal manners. Critical thinking is an ability that must be continually practiced and encouraged throughout life. In mathematics there are three types of reasoning associated with critical thinking:

- Deductive reasoning
- Inductive reasoning
- Adaptive reasoning

Deductive Reasoning

This is the process in which conclusions are made based upon prior knowledge, facts, and truths. It is a step-by-step process of drawing conclusions. Deductive reasoning is only valid and reliable when all the premises are true and each step follows the previous step logically.

For example, imagine you have lived in California your whole life and experienced many earthquakes. One day you are at the store when the shelves begin to shake and the ground buckles. You reason that there is an earthquake occurring.

Inductive Reasoning

This process of reasoning is based not upon proofs but upon observation. Inductive reasoning is drawing conclusions based upon a set of observations. It does not provide valid or reliable conclusions, but is used instead to develop hypotheses or ideas. After the ideas are formed, systematic methods are used to confirm or deny the ideas.

For example, you observe an ice cream shop one summer day. You notice that bubble gum flavored ice cream is ordered by children. You reason that children exclusively order bubble gum ice cream.

Adaptive Reasoning

This process is defined as the ability to justify strategies and to analyze the strengths and weaknesses of solutions proposed by others.

Problem Analysis

Problem analysis is the ability to apply and adapt a variety of mathematical strategies to solve problems.

Number Sense and Numeration

Number sense is the ability to understand numbers and their relationships. This skill develops gradually through experiencing numbers in a variety of contexts, exploring numbers, and relating numbers. Number sense should encompass all kinds of numbers (whole, fraction, decimal, percent, integer, rational, and so on). It is also the capability to progress beyond basic numeration concepts and the reading and writing of numerals. Number sense should include:

- **Relative magnitude**—The size relationship between numbers; is the number smaller, larger, close or the same?
- **Real world connections**—How do numbers affect our lives; where do we use numbers; what do you do with numbers?
- **Approximations and rounding**—Estimation skills are important for mental computations and verification of solutions.

Types of Numbers

In the subject of mathematics, numbers obviously play an important role. Numbers can be used in a variety of ways to construct mathematical problems and equations. There are several different types of numbers which are categorized according to the following.

- **Natural numbers**—The counting numbers: 1, 2, 3, 4, 5, 6, 7, ...
- **Whole numbers**—All the natural numbers and zero: 0, 1, 2, 3, 4, 5, 6, ...
- **Integer**—The natural and whole numbers and the negatives of the natural numbers: ... –4, –3, –2, –1, 0, 1, 2, 3, 4, ...
- **Rational numbers**—All integers are rational numbers. They are also fractional numbers or fractions, any integer over any integer: 1/2, 1/4, 4/1, 7/8, ...
- **Prime numbers**—An integer other than zero and one that has only two factors, itself and 1; a number that can be divisible only by itself: 3, 5, 7, 11, 13, 17...
- **Even numbers**—An integer divisible by two: $2n$
- **Odd numbers**—An integer that is not divisible by two: $2n-1$
- **Complex numbers**—The numbers with 'i' in them: $6 - 2i$

Meaning and Use of Numbers

Number is a broad and expansive concept that requires continual study and practice. Students must develop a strong foundation of numbers in early grades in order to support the extension of operations, large numbers, facts, and computations. Key concepts in using numbers include:

- Counting tells how many items or objects are in a set or group.
- Numbers are related to one another through a multitude of number relationships.
- Number concepts are intertwined and essential to the world around as they help make sense of the world.

Number development in early grades relates to the following:

- Relationship of more, less and the same
- Counting
- Number writing and recognition
- Counting forward and back

General number relationships important to elementary children include the following:

- **Spatial**—Learn to recognize sets of items in patterns and without counting to tell how many items are present.
- **More and less**—Begin with the one and two more or the one and two less.

- **Five and ten anchors**—Useful relationships to know as 10 plays a large role in the numeration system.
- **Part-part-whole**—Learn to recognize that a number is made up of two or more parts, as this will help students construct and deconstruct process numbers.

The Standard Algorithms for Four Basic Operations

An algorithm is a routine process used to obtain a result to a problem without using extreme concentration, thus freeing the mind to focus on more difficult and important tasks.

Addition

Carrying (regrouping) is the basic algorithm used in addition. Count by ones in the right hand column, tens in the next column to the left, hundreds in the next column to the left and so forth. Once the sum of two numbers in any column exceeds nine (reaches ten) the amount over ten is kept and the rest carried into the next column on the left.

24 added to 67

Adding the first column 7 plus 4 yields 11 or one 10 and one 1. The 10 is carried to the left and the 1 remains in the column. Then add the tens column, 2 and 6 and 1 which yields the sum of 9 tens. Therefore, the sum of 24 and 67 is 91.

Subtraction

Borrowing (regrouping) is the algorithm for subtraction. Subtract the ones column first and if the subtrahend (number subtracted from another) is larger that the minuend (number to be subtracted from), one must be borrowed from the next column to the left. Then subtract the tens column, then the hundreds and so on, borrowing as needed.

42 subtract 17

First subtract the units column 2 minus 7. The subtrahend is larger than the minuend, so we must borrow from the tens column. 40 now becomes 30 and the ten borrowed is moved to the 2 to make 12. Now the units column becomes 12 minus 7 which yields 5. Then move on to the tens column, 40 minus 30 equals 10, so the difference of 42 and 17 is 25.

Multiplication

The algorithm for multiplication is labeled long multiplication or grade school multiplication. When faced with a multiplication problem, multiply the multiplicand by each digit in the multiplier. Once this has occurred, add up the results. This algorithm is based upon three concepts:

- Place value system
- Memorization of multiplication table
- Distributive property of multiplication over addition

27 multiplied by 5

27 is 2 tens and 7 units. 7 units taken five times is 35 and 2 tens taken five times is 10 tens (100); therefore, 100 and 35 added together gives the final product of 135.

Division

The division algorithm involves the quotient, remainder, divisor, and dividend. The algorithm here is long division. The divisor (how many times to divide) is placed into the dividend (the number being divided) to yield a quotient (answer). When dividing the operation is conducted from largest place value to the smallest place value (left to right). Division requires a firm grasp on basic multiplication facts, subtraction, and place value.

5412 divided by 4

The 4 can be put into 5 (in the thousands place) one time, leaving a remainder of 1. The 4 (in the hundreds place) is then dropped down to make 14. 4 goes into 14 three times yielding 12 with a remainder of 2. The 1 (in the tens place) is dropped down to make 21. 4 can be put into 21 five times for a product of 20 and a remainder of 1. Finally the 2 (in the units place) is dropped down to yield 12. The 4 can be divided evenly into the 12 three times with no remainder. Therefore the quotient is 1353.

Appropriate Computations, Strategies, and Reasonableness of Results

There is no one best strategy for every student and every problem. Computation strategies used are based upon the numbers in a problem, the background knowledge of the individual person, and the number of the relationships known. Strategies assist students in being able to clearly and concisely write down work and solutions, keep track of steps, check work, and allow others to understand the process that was used.

Mental computation is placing emphasis on the mental processes used to reach an answer. Being able to explain how one arrived at an answer and then compare that strategy to others is essential to building mental computation acuteness.

As students build up their mental computations, they begin to understand the reasonableness of results. Checking solutions to see if it seems possible is a higher order process as students must analyze and evaluate their solutions. Encouraging students to walk through their computations enables them to self-check (analyze) and justify (evaluate) their answers. A keen grasp of number sense is essential to the ability to determine reasonableness of results.

$$27 + 69 =$$

When looking at this problem, students need to use their number sense and critical thinking skills to estimate or approximate a reasonable answer.

It is not reasonable for students to say $27 + 69 = 120$.

It is reasonable for students to say $27 + 69 = 95$ (Estimated answer)

Methods of Mathematical Investigation

Mathematical investigations allow students to examine math situations using various techniques. This process of discovery helps the students develop skills that can be applied to other problems. When approaching a mathematical investigation, students must use mathematical processes to understand and comprehend the problem.

Processes developed by mathematical investigations include the following:

classifying	justifying	proving
following patterns	conjecturing	hypothesizing
extending patterns	generalizing	predicting
symbolizing	data collecting	abstracting
communicating	evaluating	analyzing

After students have developed the processes through mathematical investigations, they are better able to relay and transmit the knowledge to new problems and situations.

Number Patterns

Number patterns are a string of numbers that follow some logical rule for the continuation of the string. Generally speaking, number patterns involve a progression of some form. The challenge of number patterns is to find and extend the pattern, but also to recognize a general rule that will produce the *n*th number in the pattern.

Common Number Patterns

Pattern	Name	Explanation
2, 4, 6, 8, 10, 12, ...	Even numbers	$2n$
1, 3, 5, 7, 9, 11, ...	Odd numbers	$2n - 1$
1, 4, 7, 10, 13, 16, 19, ...	Arithmetic sequence	Add the same value each time; add 3 each time
1, 4, 9, 16, 25, 36, ...	Squares	Square each number; $1^2, 2^2, 3^2$
2, 4, 8, 16, 32, 63, 128, ...	Geometric sequence	Multiply by the same value each time; the previous number is multiplied by 2
1, 8, 27, 64, 125, 216, ...	Cube	Cube each number in the pattern $1^3, 2,^3 3^3$
0, 1, 1, 2, 3, 5, 8, 13, 21, 34, ...	Fibonacchi numbers	The next number is found by adding the two numbers before it together; 2+3 = 5, 3+5 = 8

Place Value

Place value is a concept based upon groupings of 10. It is an imperative concept for students to grasp, as it is the basic foundation for all mathematical operations.

Whole Numbers

Millions	Hundred thousands	Ten thousands	Thousands	Hundreds	Tens	Units
1000000	100000	10000	1000	100	10	1
10 hundred thousands	10 ten thousands	10 thousands	10 hundreds	10 tens	10 units	one

Therefore, 78 is 7 tens and 8 units.

243 is 2 hundreds, 4 tens and 3 units.

Place value is also used for decimal concepts.

Units	Decimal point	Tenths	Hundredths	Thousandths	Ten thousandths	Hundred thousandths	Millionths
1	.	.1	.01	.001	.0001	.00001	.000001

Equivalence

Equivalence is being equal in value or amount. Equivalences are used to demonstrate information in a variety forms.

Common Equivalences

Simplified Fraction	Fraction	Decimal	Percentage
$^1/_5$	$^2/_{10}, ^3/_{15}, ^4/_{20}$	0.2	20%
$^1/_4$	$^2/_8, ^3/_{12}, ^4/_{16}$	0.25	25%

Simplified Fraction	Fraction	Decimal	Percentage
⅓	²/₆, ³/₉, ⁴/₁₂	$0.3\overset{\infty}{3}$	33%
½	²/₄, ³/₆, ⁴/₈	0.5	50%
⅔	⁴/₆, ⁶/₉, ⁸/₁₂	$0.6\overset{\infty}{6}$	66%
¾	⁶/₈, ⁹/₁₂, ¹²/₁₆	0.75	75%

Factors and Multiples

Factors and multiples are used when comparing numbers and analyzing numerical value.

A **factor** is a prime or composite number that is multiplied to obtain a product. Factoring is the process of taking a number apart and expressing it as the product of its factors. A factor is a breakdown of a larger number.

Factors of 18 = 1, 2, 3, 6, 9, 18.
Factors of 24 = 1, 2, 3, 4, 6, 8, 12, 24.
Factors of 45 = 1, 3, 5, 9, 15, 45.

Factor Rules

1. 2 is a factor of ALL even numbers.
2. 10 is a factor of ALL numbers ending in 0.
3. 5 is a factor of ALL numbers ending in 0 or 5.
4. 3 is a factor of a number if it is also a factor of the sum of the individual digits found within the number.
   65,331   6 + 5 + 3 + 1 = 18
   27   2 + 7 = 9
5. 9 is a factor of a number if it is also a factor of the sum of the individual digits found within the number.
   36   3 + 6 = 9
   89,172   8 + 9 + 1 + 7 + 2 = 27
6. 11 is a factor of a three digit number if the middle digit is the sum of the two outside digits.
   682   6 + 2 = 8
   594   5 + 4 = 9

Multiples

Multiples of a number are gathered by multiplying that number by a whole number.

Multiples of 3 are 3, 6, 9, 12, 15, 18, and so on.
Multiples of 25 are 25, 50, 75, 100, 125, 150, and so on.

Lowest Common Multiples (LCM)

This is used when comparing two numbers. The LCM is a number that is a multiple of each of the two numbers being compared and is lower than all other multiples.

6 and 4
The LCM is 12.

Multiples of 6 = 6, 12, 18, 24, 30, 36, 42, 48, and so on.

Multiples of 4 = 4, 8, 12, 16, 20, 24, 28, 32, 36, 40, 44, 48, and so on.

12 is the lowest common multiple because it is the smallest value multiple that both 6 and 4 have in common.

Ratio, Proportion, Percent

These three terms are imperative in not only mathematics, but in business and science as well. Each represents mathematical information in a similar manner yet each is very distinct in its own way.

Ratio

A **ratio** is a comparison between a pair of numbers. For example, if there are five dogs and three cats in a house, the ratio of dogs to cats is 5:3 or 5/3 or 5 dogs to 3 cats.

Proportion

A **proportion** is two ratios written with an equal sign between them; two ratios that are equal to one another (For example, 5/3 = 10/6 or 2:3 = 4:6).

> The ratio of apples to oranges in a grocery store is 6:7, and there are 246 apples. How many oranges are there?

Set up a proportion.	$6:7 = 246:x$
Write the proportion in fraction form.	$6/7 = 246/x$
Solve for x using cross multiplication.	$(a/b = c/d \rightarrow a*d = b*c)$
	$6*x = 246*7$
	$6x = 1722$
Isolate the variable using division.	$x = 1722/6$
	$x = 287$

Therefore, there are 287 oranges in the store.

Percent

Percent broken down means "per one hundred." A percent is represented by the % symbol. Percentages can be written in three mathematical expressions; all are equivalent to one another:

fifty percent   50%   .50   50/100

There are many ways to use percentages in calculations.

> **1.** What is 35% of 105?

1. 35% of "something" requires a set up for cross multiplication. Simply stated this means the percentage multiplied by "the something." (.35 * 105 = 36.75).

> **2.** What percentage of 105 is 36.75?

2. Set up the cross-multiplication fractions.

$x/100 = 36.75/105$ (cross multiply)

$105x = 3675$ (divide by 105 to isolate the variable)

$x = 35\%$

3. 18 is what percent of 20?

Divide the number you have by the number possible and multiply by 100 to obtain the percentage.

$18 \div 20 = .9$

$.9 * 100 = 90\%$

4. A pair of shoes is on a 20% off sale rack. They have a sale price of $60. What is the original price? The regular price is denoted by x, and the discount is 20% less than x. There is enough information to solve. The equation is written as follows:

$x - (0.20)x = 60$ Remember there is an invisible 1 in front of the first x, so it really states $1x - 0.2x = 0.8x$

$0.8x = 60$

$x = 60 \div 0.8$

$x = \$75$

Representations

There are many types of mathematical representations. A few types are mental representation, mathematical representation, models, physical representation, and representation of integers. Students should be able to do the following:

- Develop and utilize representations to organize, record, and communicate ideas.
- Choose, apply, and translate mathematical representations to solve a variety of problems.
- Use representations to model and interpret physical, social, and mathematical ongoings.

Three things that mathematical representations help students do:

1. Identify the object.
2. Deduce some properties of the object.
3. Calculate something about the object mathematically.

Calculator Strategies

The calculator allows students to solve problems that are both challenging and intriguing. The calculator is helpful in mathematics for all children as intellectual development is usually at a higher level than the mathematical skill. Using calculators to support learning will help students build up a strong number sense.

Calculators provide the following educational supports:

- Support counting (skip counting—using the repeat function).
- Promote basic fact memorization (visual representation).
- Aid learning of place value (can see the number on the screen in its column).
- Assist in computation (improves speed and accuracy and encourages self-reliance and autonomy).
- Show reasonableness of answers (allows students to validate work).

Number Lines

A number line is a one dimensional illustration of a horizontal line that has integers shown/placed at specifically indicated points, evenly spaced on the line. It is used as a tool for teaching addition, subtraction, and negative numbers. There are many variations on a number line, but normally each end depicts an arrow where the line goes on forever in each direction. "0" is usually represented at the origin and placed in the middle of the line. Negative numbers are to the left of the 0 and positive numbers are to the right of the 0.

Number lines help students grasp the relationship between numbers and their relative magnitude.

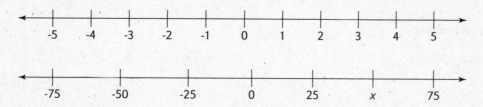

A child with number sense knows that x is larger than 25 but smaller than 75.

Algebraic Concepts

Algebraic concepts include expressions with numbers, variables, and arithmetic operations. It is a branch of math that studies structures, relationships, and quantities. Algebraic concepts at the elementary level introduce children to the fundamental ideas of adding and multiplying numbers, variables, definitions of polynomials, factorization, and determining number roots.

Algebraic Methods and Representations

Methods to solving algebraic equations and problems rely upon the ability to represent unknown and missing quantities. Vocabulary is critical to understanding algebraic representations. Common phrases or key words alert students to the operations and skills needed to solve problems.

Addition	Subtraction	Multiplication	Division	Equals
more than	less than/fewer than	product	quotient	is
in addition to	decreased by	times	divided	are
exceeds	diminished	twice	separated	was
increased by	take away	of	distribute	were
altogether	difference	multiplied by	per	will be
sum	deduct	increased by	out of	gives
and			percent	yields
extra			ratio of	
combined				
total of				

Examples:

3 more than a number	=	$3 + x$
10 less than 5 times a number	=	$5x - 10$
2 times a number increased by 8	=	$2x + 8$
4 less than a number divided by 3	=	$(x - 4)/3$

Properties

There are four basic properties of numbers. All mathematic systems/branches follow and obey these properties. Students must be familiar with these properties in order to solve algebraic problems.

Associative Property

States that numbers can be grouped or regrouped in an operation in any manner without changing the answer; does not matter the order or how the numbers are combined, the answer will always be the same. Addition and multiplication are both associative.

General addition formula:

$a + (b + c) = (a + b) + c$

$$3 + (4 + 6) = (3 + 4) + 6 \qquad (-5 + 25) + 10 = -5 + (25 + 10)$$
$$3 + (10) = (7) + 6 \qquad (20) + 10 = -5 + (35)$$
$$13 = 13 \qquad 30 = 30$$

General multiplication formula:

$a * (b * c) = (a * b) * c$

$$4 * (2 * 6) = (4 * 2) * 6 \qquad (1/2 * 2) * 4 = 1/2 * (2 * 4)$$
$$4 * (12) = (8) * 6 \qquad (1) * 4 = 1/2 * (8)$$
$$48 = 48 \qquad 4 = 4$$

Commutative Property

States that numbers in an operation can change order without altering the end result; changing the order does not change the answer. Addition and multiplication are both commutative.

General addition formula:

$a + b = b + a$

$$60 + 15 = 15 + 60 \qquad 10 + 8 + 2 + 15 = 2 + 15 + 8 + 10$$
$$75 = 75 \qquad 35 = 35$$

General multiplication formula:

$a * b = b * a$

$$10 * 5 = 5 * 10 \qquad 1/2 * 1/2 * 4 = 1/2 * 4 * 1/2$$
$$50 = 50 \qquad 4 = 4$$

Distributive Property

Distribute means to share something or to deal out something (from the Latin *distribut*, meaning divided up). It states that one operation may change to another. In math, this property is used to make equations simpler by breaking them apart. An easy way to remember this property is that it can be used when multiplying with parentheses.

General formula:

$a (b + c) = ab + ac$

$$4(3 + 2) = 4(3) + 4(2) \qquad 8(a + 12) = 8(a) + 8(12)$$
$$4(5) = 12 + 8 \qquad 8a + 96 = 8a + 96$$
$$20 = 20$$

Transitive Property

States when an operation is applicable between successive numbers in a sequence then it also applies to any two numbers taken in order; if x is related to y and y is related to z then x is related to z.

General formulas:

Whenever $a > b$ and $b > c$ then $a > c$.

Whenever $a < b$ and $b < c$ then $a < c$.

Whenever $a = b$ and $b = c$ then $a = c$.

For example,

If $5 > 4$ and $4 > 3$, then $5 > 3$.

If $3x + 2 = y$ and $y = 8$, then $3x + 2 = 8$.

Additive and Multiplicative Inverses

The **additive inverse** of a number (n) is the opposite number or the number that when added to (n) results in a sum of zero. For example,

The additive inverse of x; is $-x$.

The additive inverse of 4 is -4 (because $4 + (-4) = 0$).

The additive inverse of 0.13 is -0.13 (because $0.13 + (-0.13) = 0$).

To calculate the additive inverse of a number, multiply the number by -1. $n * -1 = -n$.

Have additive inverses	Do not have additive inverses
integers	natural numbers
rational numbers	cardinal numbers
real numbers	ordinal numbers
complex numbers	

The **multiplicative inverse** for a number (n) is the reciprocal or a number that when multiplied by n results in the product of 1. For example,

The multiplicative inverse of x is $1/x$ or x^{-1}.

The multiplicative inverse of 6 is $1/6$ or 6^{-1} (because $6 * 1/6 = 1$).

The multiplicative inverse of 0.25 is 4 (because $.25 * 4 = 1$).

Function Machines

Functions are expressed using words, graphs, equations, and tables. They describe relationships between sets of numbers and are often thought of in terms of input and output (algorithms). When a number is plugged in (input) to an algorithm, and steps are followed, then a solution (output) is obtained. A function has two requirements:

Consistency—Every time the same input is plugged in, the same output is received.

One output—Each input will produce only one possible output.

Function machines allow students to picture algorithms/functions as little machines.

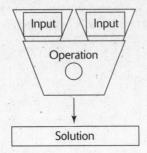

If you place a 6 and a 4 into your machine along with the addition operation, what is the outcome?

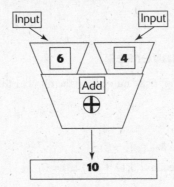

Not only can you work from input to obtain output, but you can also work inversely from the output to gain the input.

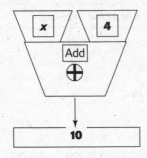

$x = 6$ because $10 - 4 = 6$.

Properties of Zero and One

Zero and one are unique numerals. They possess special properties that no other numbers have. Here is a list of their important properties (x = any number).

- **Addition property of zero**—Adding a 0 to a number does not change its value.

  $x + 0 = x$ or $0 + x = x$

- **Multiplication property of zero**—Multiplying a number by 0 always results in the product of 0.

  $x * 0 = 0$ or $0 * x = 0$

- **Multiplication property of one**—Multiplying a number by 1 does not change its value.

  $x * 1 = x$ or $1 * x = x$

- **Powers of one**—The number one raised to any power always yields the value of 1.

  $1^x = 1$ ($1^5 = 1 \times 1 \times 1 \times 1 \times 1 = 1$)

- **Powers of zero**—The number 0 raised to any power always yields the value of 0.

  $0^x = 0$

- **Zero as a numerator**—0 divided by any number is 0.

  $0/x = 0$

- **Division by zero**—Any division problem with 0 as the denominator or divisor is undefined.

- **Quotient of one**—Any number other than 0 divided by itself equals 1.

  $x \div x = 1$

- **Additive inverse yields zero**—Any number added to its opposite equals 0.

  $x + (-x) = 0$

- **Multiplicative inverse yields one**—Any number multiplied by its inverse yields a product of 1

  $x * 1/x = 1$

Equalities and Inequalities

Equalities are equations that are the same on both sides without having to solve either side. There are six properties of equalities to remember (x, y, z = any number).

- **Reflexive property**—Any number is equal to itself.

  $x = x$.

- **Symmetric property**—If one number is equal to another number, then vice versa.

  If $x = y$ then $y = x$.

- **Transitive property**—If one number is equal to another number and that number is equal to a third number, then the first and third numbers are also equal.

  If $x = y$ and $y = z$, then $x = z$.

- **Substitution property**—If two numbers are equal, then they are interchangeable in any situation.

  $x = y$ so x may be replaced by y or $x = y + z$ so x may be replaced by $y + z$.

- **Addition and subtraction property**—If two numbers are equal, then they will remain equal if the same value is added to or subtracted from them.

  If $x = y$, then $x + z = y + z$ or $x - z = y - z$.

- **Multiplication and division property**—If two numbers are equal, then they will remain equal if they are multiplied or divided by the same number.

  If $x = y$, then $xz = yz$ or $x/z = y/z$.

Any mathematical problem containing $<$, $\leq$, $>$, $\geq$ is called an inequality. Solutions to inequalities are any numbers that make the inequalities true. For example, $5 > 3$ or $6 > 3$ or $9 > 3$.

Addition principle for inequalities: When the same quantity is added or subtracted to both sides of an inequality, the truth of the inequality does not change.

  If $a > b$, then $a + c$ is $> b + c$.

Multiplication principle for inequalities:

  If $a > b$ and c is positive, then $ac > bc$.

  If a > b, and c is negative, then ac < bc. (Note the sign reversal.)

Patterns and Algebraic Formulas

Patterns litter the world around. We use patterns to organize information that we see and hear, analyze data that we receive, and evaluate situations that we encounter. Recognizing patterns is an important problem solving skill to help generalize specific concepts into broader solutions. Being able to find, describe, explain, and utilize patterns to make educated predictions is a vital skill in mathematics. Pattern recognition is dependent upon each individual person and individual perceptions. Being able to communicate patterns effectively is an important concept to master. Algebra is a tool used to describe patterns in a universal manner.

Pattern recognition skills are as follows:

- **Finding**—Looking for repetition or regular features
- **Describing**—Communicating clearly and concisely
- **Explaining**—Determining why and how the pattern occurs
- **Predicting**—Foreseeing the next steps or future situation

For example, 15, 13, x, 9, 7, 5. . .

1. **Find** the missing number—Look at the regular feature of odds.
2. **Describe** the pattern—The numbers are decreasing in a descending order by 2.
3. **Explain** the pattern—The difference between each number is 2, and every number is an odd number.
4. **Predict** the numbers—After recognizing a pattern, the missing numbers can be solved ($x = 11$).

Algebraic Formulas

Algebraic formulas follow specific rules. Formulas are used in equation format which help state a fact/rule and use one or more variables. A formula can be solved for any of its variables by using equation solving rules. Here are a few of the fundamental formulas needed to be able to solve problems.

- **Absolute value**—The value of a number is never negative. If x is greater than or equal to 0, then the absolute value of x will be the same as its usual value. If x is less than 0, then it will be opposite its usual value.

  The absolute value of 3 is 3.

  The absolute value of -6 is 6

- **Difference of squares**—$a^2 - b^2 = (a - b)(a + b)$
- **Distance formula**—The coordinate points on a plane are (x_1, y_1), (x_2, y_2).

  $d = \sqrt{\left(x_2 - x_1\right)^2 + \left(y_2 - y_1\right)^2}$

- **Fundamental theorem of algebra**—Every polynomial equation that exists must have at least one solution.
- **Laws of exponents**:

  $(a^m)(a^n) = a^{m+n}$

  $(ab)^m = a^m \cdot b^m$

  $a^{-m} = 1/a^m$

  $(a^m)^n = a^{mn}$

  $a^0 = 1$

  $a^m/a^n = a^{m-n}$

- **Mid-point formula**—Used to find the mid-point coordinates on a plane with two points.

  $([(x_2 + x_1) \div 2], [(y_2 + y_1) \div 2])$

- **Negative exponents**—Any number taken to a negative exponent is the same as one over that number with a positive exponent.

  $x^{-y} = 1/x^y$ Example: $6^{-2} = 1/6^2$

- **Parallel lines**—Non-vertical lines in a plane with the same slope. The symbol for parallel lines is //.
- **Perpendicular lines**—Two lines in a plane with the product of the slopes equaling –1. The symbol for perpendicular is ⊥.
- **Pythagorean Theorem**—Used to explain the lengths of the sides of a right triangle. The two legs (a and b) squared yield the length of the hypotenuse (c) given any two values of the three, the third value can always be found.

  $a^2 + b^2 = c^2$

- **Quadratic formula**—The standard form of a quadratic equation is $ax^2 + bx + c = 0$. The quadratic formula is a tool used to solve the equation. The roots of the equation will yield where the graph touches the x-axis.

$$x = \frac{-b \pm \sqrt{b^2 - 4ac}}{2a}$$

- **Remainder theorem**—When a number is divided, the dividend = quotient * divisor + remainder. This is used to check division solutions.

- **Slope**—Given two points, (x_1, y_1), (x_2, y_2), to find the slope (m), use

$$m = \frac{y_2 - y_1}{x_2 - x_1} \quad (x_1 \neq x_2)$$

- **Slope intercept formula**—$y = mx + b$ (m = slope, b = y-intercept, and x = x-intercept) The graph of this formula is a straight line.

- **Standard form of an equation**—A, B, C are variables, and x and y are unknowns.

$Ax + By = C$.

Informal Geometry and Measurement

Geometry and measurement pervade the world around us. These math topics help students develop critical thinking skills, basic reasoning abilities, and knowledge of spatial relationship concepts.

Real World Properties and Relationships in Figures and Shapes in Dimensions

The field of geometry encompasses a wide array of topics. It is the study of properties and the relationships of points, lines, angles, surfaces, and solids.

Figures and Shapes in Two Dimensions

A two-dimensional figure is also called a plane figure. It is defined as a set of lined segments (sides) and/or curved segments (arcs) lying within a single plane.

Parts of a Two-Dimensional Figure		
Part	*Description*	*Illustration*
Edges	sides or arcs of the figure that are one-dimensional	
Vertices	the end points or corners of the figure which are zero dimensional	
Angles	when two sides meet at a vertex measured in degrees	

Two-dimensional figures include the following:

equilateral triangle	trapezoid	ellipse
rhombus	right triangle	circle
square	kite	parallelogram
isosceles triangle	chevron	
rectangle	scalene triangle	

Polygons are two-dimensional figures in which

- All edges are segments.
- Every vertex is the end point of two or more edges.
- No two sides cross each other.

Polygons are named and classified according to the number of sides they possess (which also equals the number of vertices). Polygons can be both regular (all sides and angles are equal) or irregular (unequal sides and angles).

Common Polygons	
Number of Sides	*Name*
3	triangle
4	quadrilateral
5	pentagon
6	hexagon
7	heptagon
8	octagon
9	nonagon
10	decagon
11	undecagon
12	dodecagon
n	n-gon

Figures and Shapes of Three Dimensions

A three-dimensional figure is also called a **solid figure.** It is defined as a set of surface regions (faces that are two-dimensional) and a set of plane regions all lying within a three-dimensional space.

Parts of a Three-Dimensional Figure	
Part	*Description*
Edges	the arcs or sides of the faces
Face	the surface region that is two-dimensional
Vertices	the end points of the edges that are zero-dimensional

Three-dimensional figures include the following:

sphere	ovoid	cylinder	pyramid
ellipsoid	cone	prism	

Polyhedrons are three-dimensional figures/shapes in which

- All faces are plane regions.
- Every edge is the edge of two faces.
- Every vertex is the vertex of three or more faces.
- No two faces cross each other.

Polyhedra are classified and named by the number of faces it possesses.

Common Polyhedrons	
Number of Faces	*Name*
4	tetrahedron
6	cube
8	octahedron
12	dodecahedron
18	icosahedron

Pythagorean Theorem

The **Pythagorean Theorem** was discovered by the Greek mathematician, Pythagoras. This equation presents a simple relationship among three sides of a right triangle so that if any of the lengths of any of the two sides is known, the length of the third side can be found.

The square of the hypotenuse of a right triangle is equal to the sum of the squares of the other two sides:

$a^2 + b^2 = c^2$

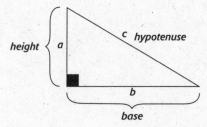

Transformations

A **transformation** (transform equals "to change") changes the position of a shape upon a coordinate plane resulting in the same value and magnitude. The shape moves from one place (coordinate) to another.

There are three basic transformations:

Name	Description
Rotation (turn)	the shape is turned on a 360 degree axis
Reflection (flip)	the shape is a mirror image
Translation (slide)	the shape moves by sliding to another area in the plane

Geometric Models

Geometric models are used to define and describe the shape of an object in geometrical terms and concepts. Geometric models can be built for any object, any dimension, and any space.

Nets

A geometrical net is when a three-dimensional shape is broken down into a two-dimensional or plane diagram. The edges of the net should never intercept. There are five solid shapes which can be broken into a net. They are known as the cosmic figures or Platonic figures.

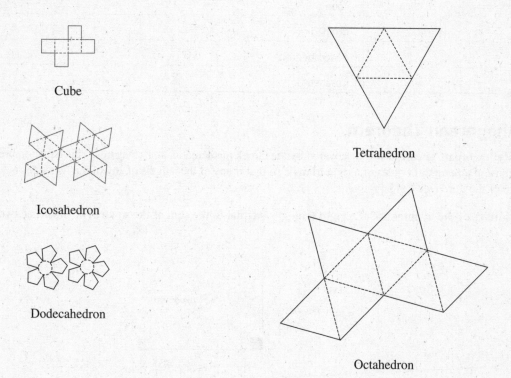

Cube

Tetrahedron

Icosahedron

Dodecahedron

Octahedron

Standard Units of Measurement

Students at the elementary level first learn measurement by using informal units of measure, but they soon advance to learning about the standard units of measurement. These include specific types of measuring tools, devices, containers, and units. They are used for measuring length, areas, volume, capacity, and weight of objects. The key for students is to understand what is being measured and what is needed to complete the task. Both customary U.S. and metric systems include various units that can be used in standard measurement.

Metric Units and Conversions

The most common prefixes you will see within the Praxis and within schools are the following: kilo-, hecto-, deka-, (unit), deci-, centi-, and milli-. It is easy to remember the order by using a simple sentence such as:

King Henry Doesn't Usually Drink Chocolate Milk

The unit refers to the measurement you are using: grams (weight), meters (length), or liters (volume/capacity). Metric measurement is usually written using decimals and whole numbers. When converting between the various sized units you simply move the decimal point as you travel along the chart.

kilo-	hecto-	deka-	unit	deci-	centi-	milli-
0.001	0.01	0.1	1	10	100	1000

For example, convert 1000 mL to L.

Look at your chart and count the number of moves you need to make. You need to move 3 spaces to the left.

1.000 L or 1 L = 1000 mL

Convert 68.94 cm to kilometers.

Look at your chart and count the number of moves you need to make. You need to make 5 moves, which means moving the decimal point 5 spaces to the left and then add 3 zeros for your space holders.

0.0006894 km = 68.94 cm

Customary Units and Conversions

Customary measurement is what we use in the United States. Customary measurements are usually written in fractions and whole numbers. There are four categories for customary measurement: length, weight, volume, and time.

Units of Length

Inches   Feet   Yards   Miles

1 foot (ft. or ') = 12 inches (in. or ")

1 yard (yd.) = 36 inches (in.)

1 yard (yd.) = 3 feet (ft.)

1 mile (mi.) = 5,280 feet (ft.)

1 mile (mi.) = 1,760 yards (yd.)

Units of Weight

Ounces   Pounds   Ton

1 pound (lb.) = 16 ounces (oz.)

1 ton (T.) = 2,000 pounds (lbs.)

Units of Volume/Capacity

Fluid Ounces   Cups   Pints   Quarts   Gallons

1 cup (c.) = 8 fluid ounces (fl. oz.)

1 pint (pt.) = 2 cups (c.)

1 quart (qt.) = 4 cups (c.)

1 quart (qt.) = 2 pints (pt.)

1 gallon (gal.) = 4 quarts (qt.)

Units of Time

Seconds   Minutes   Hours   Days   Weeks   Months   Years

1 minute (min.) = 60 second (sec.)

1 hour (hr.) = 60 minutes (min.)

1 day = 24 hours (hr.)

1 week (wk.) = 7 days

1 year (yr.) = 52 weeks (wk.)

1 year (yr.) = 12 months (mo.)

1 year (yr.) = 365 days

Coordinate Graphing

Coordinate graphing is a visual method for demonstrating relationships between numbers. Coordinate graphing uses a coordinate grid which has two axis (perpendicular lines). The horizontal axis is called the x-axis and the vertical axis is called the y-axis. The origin is where the x- and y- axis intersect. A coordinate grid uses numbers to locate points. Each point is identified by an ordered pair of numbers: an x coordinate and a y coordinate. When writing ordered pairs, the x coordinate always comes first, and the y coordinate is second. The pair is written in parentheses with a comma between the two coordinates. (x, y)

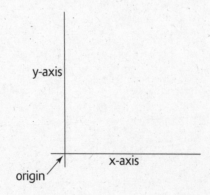

Perimeter, Areas, Volume

Rectangle	Perimeter	$P_{rect} = 2l + 2w$
	Area	$A_{rect} = lw$
Triangle	Perimeter	$P_{tri} = s_1 + s_2 + s_3$ or $a + b + c$
	Area	$A_{tri} = 1/2\, bh$
	Pythagorean Theory (side lengths)	$a^2 + b^2 = c^2$
	Angles	$\angle_1 + \angle_2 + \angle_3 = 180°$
Square	Perimeter	$P_{sqr} = 4s$
	Area	$A_{sqr} = s^2$
Circle	Perimeter	$C_{cir} = 2(\pi)r$ or πd
	Area	$A_{cir} = (\pi)r^2$

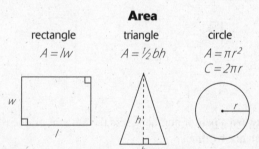

Area

rectangle
$A = lw$

triangle
$A = \frac{1}{2}bh$

circle
$A = \pi r^2$
$C = 2\pi r$

(π, or pi, is the number approximated by 3.14159 or $\frac{22}{7}$.)

Volume

The volume of an object is measured in cubes and is the amount of cubes that is required to fill the object completely.

Common Volume Formulas	
Shape	**Formula**
Cube	a^3
Rectangular prism	$l * w * h$ l = length w = width h = height
Prism	$b * h$ b = base h – height
Pyramid	$1/3\ b * h$ b = base h = height

Shape	Formula
Cylinder	$\pi r^2 h$ r = radius h = height π = 3.14 or 22/7
Cone	$1/3\ \pi r^2 h$ r = radius h = height π = 3.14 or 22/7
Sphere	$4/3\ \pi r^3$ r = radius π = 3.14 or 22/7

Volume

rectangular solid   right circular cylinder

$V = lwh$ $V = \pi r^2 h$

Rates

The rate explains a relationship between a pair of numbers. It is the amount of one thing needed to find the amount of another. To find the **rate**, divide distance by time.

rate = distance / time

Rate is written as a fraction with the distance units as the numerator and the time units as the denominator.

To find **time**, use: time = distance / rate.

To find **distance**, use: distance = rate * time.

Be sure to keep the units organized and consistent. Sometimes, time will need to be converted in order to make the units match.

Angles

An angle consists of two rays that share the same end point (vertex). The two rays are the sides of the angle. Angles are measured in degrees.

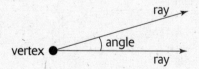

There are many types of angles:

Acute angle—Any angle that is less than 90 degrees but greater than zero degrees.

Obtuse angle—Any angle that is greater than 90 but less than 180 degrees.

Right angle—Any angle measuring exactly 90 degrees. Two lines that meet at a right angle are said to be perpendicular.

Complimentary angle—When two angles are measured, the sum of their degrees is equal to 90 degrees.

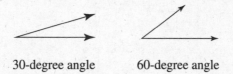

      30-degree angle   60-degree angle

30 degrees + 60 degrees = 90 degrees

Supplementary angle—When two angles are measured, the sum of their degrees is equal to 180 degrees (straight line).

90 degrees + 90 degrees = 180 degrees.

Data Organization and Interpretation

Organizing data into a useable form and interpreting the meaning are critical skills to possess. There are many ways to record, organize, and communicate data. Students must learn how to use charts, tables, and graphs in order to better organize and interpret collected data.

Visual Displays of Quantitative Information

Visual displays of quantitative information simply refer to different types of informational graphics which display measured quantities. These include but are not limited to the following:

illustrations	maps	3-D computer graphics
diagrams	photographs	interactive models
tables	pictograms	charts

Graphics (visual displays) are used to reveal data, often in a more precise and direct manner than conventional computations. The most common visual representation used in math is the graph.

Types of Graphs	Description	Illustration
Line	Uses either vertical or horizontal lines to connect plotted data points. This graph shows change or information over a period of time.	
Bar	Bars can be displayed vertically or horizontally. Each bar represents a specific set of information, and the value is based upon the height or length of the bar.	
Pie	Has the shape of a circle and displays the information in relation to a whole. Data is usually shown in percentages.	
Pictograph	Pictures or symbols are used to represent numbers of specific items. Value of items is obtained by counting the pictorial representation.	

Outcomes

An outcome is the end result or the consequence of a single trial of an experiment. A possible outcome is one of three things:

1. A choice
2. A possibility
3. A result

A **favorable outcome** is what someone wants to happen.

A **total outcome** is all the things that could happen.

For example, at a restaurant, there are the following choices of drinks: coffee, ice tea, soda, and juice. What are the outcomes? The outcomes are the four choices of drinks: coffee, ice tea, soda, and juice. The favorable outcome is the one type of beverage chosen or desired.

For example, what is the probability of rolling an even number on a standard 6-sided die? What are the outcomes?

The favorable outcomes are even numbers (2, 4, 6). Therefore, there are 3 *favorable* outcomes and 6 *total* outcomes.

Simple Probability

Probability is the measure of the likelihood that an event will occur. Probabilities are expressed as fractions, ratios, decimals, or percentages. To calculate the probability of an event, count the number of times the event is true (favorable) and divide that number by the possible (total) number of outcomes.

Event = number of favorable outcomes/number of possible outcomes

Formula: $P_{event} = O_f / O_p$

For example, what is the probability of rolling a 3 on a standard 6-sided die?

> There are 6 possible total outcomes = 1, 2, 3, 4, 5, 6.
>
> There is only 1 favorable outcome = 3.
>
> Therefore, the probability of rolling a 3 is 1:6 or 1/6 or 1 to 6 or .1666 or 16.7%.

For example, if a coin is flipped twice, calculate the probability that it will land on tails both times.

> Favorable outcomes = 1 (TT)
>
> Possible outcomes = 4 (HH, HT, TH, TT)
>
> Solve: P_{tails} = favorable outcome / possible outcome
>
> Therefore, the probability that the coin will land on tails each time is 1/4 or 1:4 or 25%.

For example, a cookie jar contains 5 peanut butter, 3 oatmeal raisin, 8 chocolate chip, and 4 sugar cookies. If a single cookie is chosen at random from the jar, what is the probability of choosing a peanut butter cookie? An oatmeal raisin cookie? A chocolate chip cookie? A sugar cookie?

What do you know?

> Outcomes = peanut butter (5), oatmeal raisin (3), chocolate chip (8), sugar (4)
>
> Total number of cookies = 20
>
> Probabilities: P_{pb} = # of peanut butter cookies to choose from/total # of cookies = 5/20 = 1/4
>
> Probabilities: P_{or} = # of oatmeal raisin cookies to choose from/total # of cookies = 3/20
>
> Probabilities: P_{cc} = # of chocolate chip cookies to choose from/total # of cookies = 8/20 = 4/10= 2/5
>
> Probabilities: P_s = # of sugar cookies to choose from/total # of cookies = 4/20 = 1/5

The outcomes in this example are not equally likely to occur due to the different values. The most likely outcome is chocolate chip and the least likely outcome is oatmeal raisin.

Events

An event is the set of outcomes found with in a probability; it is the occurrence (one or more outcomes) of a probability.

The probability of an event is written: P_{event} = # of ways an event can occur / total # of possible outcomes.

For example, Megan grabs a sock from her drawer at random. The drawer has 6 white, 5 black, 4 blue, and 2 red socks. What is the probability she will grab a black sock?

> One event of this probability is grabbing a black sock.
>
> Another event of this probability is grabbing a white sock.
>
> Another event of this probability is grabbing a blue sock.
>
> Another event of this probability is grabbing a red sock.
>
> Another event is grabbing a primary colored sock (red or blue).

Sample Spaces

Sample space refers to the set of all possible outcomes of an event. The number of different ways something is chosen from the sample space is the total number of possible outcomes.

Since probabilities are fractions (decimals and percentages) of a sample space, the sum of the probabilities of all the possible outcomes is equal to 1. Therefore, the probability of the occurrence of a specific event is always 1 minus the probability that it does not occur. Within the sample space, the probability of any outcome is equal to the product of all possibilities along the path which indicates the outcome on the tree diagram.

For example, a moose has 3 mooselings. How many outcomes in the sample space indicate the combinations of the gender of the mooselings? (Assume that the probability of male (M) and female (F) is each 1/2.)

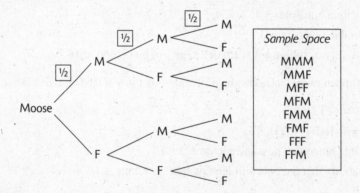

The probability of each outcome is 1/2 * 1/2 * 1/2 = 1/8.
(There are 8 outcomes in the sample space.)

Counting Techniques

The fundamental counting principle states that the total possible number of ways, in a sequence of events, for all events to occur is the product of the possible number of ways that each individual event can occur.

Tree Diagrams

A tree diagram is used in math to decipher the probability of obtaining specific results. Tree diagrams are graphical representations that list all possible outcomes of an event. It helps organize the possible outcomes in an orderly manner beginning with event 1 and branching off into sequential events thereafter. Final outcomes are determined by tracing each branch to its end.

For example, a tree diagram shows the following possible outcomes when flipping two coins:

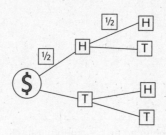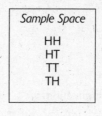

Combinations

A **combination** is a selection of numbers or objects in which order is not important and there is no repetition.

$$C_{(n,\,r)} = \frac{n!}{\left[(n-r)!\,r!\right]}$$

n = objects r = size c = combination

(! = this symbol means a factorial; the number counted down multiplied)

For example, $5! = (5 * 4 * 3 * 2 * 1)$

---

1. How many different groups of 4 dogs can be chosen from a group of 15?

$n = 15$ $r = 4$

$_nC_r = 15!/(15-4)!4!$

$_nC_r = 15*14*13*12*11*10*9*8*7*6*5*4*3*2*1$

$(11)!4*3*2*1$

$_nC_r = \dfrac{1307674368000}{(39916800)24}$

$_nC_r = \dfrac{1307674368000}{958003200}$

$_nC_r = 1,365$

There are 1,365 different groups.

---

2. There are 7 colors of cars. How many different combinations of 3 cars can be chosen?

$n = 7$ $r = 3$

$_nC_r = \dfrac{7!}{(7-3)!3!}$

$_nC_r = \dfrac{5040}{(4)!6}$

$_nC_r = \dfrac{5040}{144}$

$_nC_r = 35$

There will be 35 different combinations.

Permutations

A permutation is an arrangement of numbers (objects) in which order is important and there is no repetition. A factorial is a number that is successively multiplied down to the number 1, denoted by !.

For example, 5! is 5 * 4 * 3 * 2 * 1.

The **Formula of Permutation** is

$$_nP_r = \frac{n!}{(n-r)!}$$

n = objects r = size P = permutation

---

1. How many ways can 5 students from a class of 10 be lined up for a photograph?

$n = 10, r = 5$

$$_nP_r = \frac{10!}{(10-5)!}$$

$$_nP_r = \frac{3628800}{120}$$

$$_nP_r = 30240$$

The students can be arranged in 30,240 ways.

---

2. How many three-letter permutations can you make from the word BEND?

$n = 4, r = 3$

$$_nP_r = \frac{4!}{(4-3)!}$$

$$_nP_r = \frac{24}{1}$$

$$_nP_r = 24$$

Therefore, there are 24 three-letter permutations for the word BEND.

Mean, Median, Mode

Mean, median, and mode are used in math to determine three kinds of averages.

To determine the **mean,** add up all the numbers in the set and divide the sum by the number of numbers. For example, the mean of 3, 6, 9, 12, 15 is found as follows:

3 + 6 + 9 + 12 + 15 = 45

Divide 45 by 5 (there are 5 numbers in the set).

The mean is 9.

To determine the **median,** which is the middle value in a set of numbers, list the numbers in numerical order. For example, the median of 5, 8, 3, 16, 12 is found as follows:

Place in numerical order: 3, 5, 8, 12, 16.

The median is 8.

If the set has an even amount of numbers (3, 5, 8, 12, 16, 20), add the two middle values together and divide by 2 to obtain the median (8 + 12 = 20, 20 / 2 = 10).

The **mode** is the number that occurs most often. If there is no number that is repeated, then there is no mode. For example, in this list of numbers: 1, 1, 2, 3, 5, 6, 10, the mode is 1.

The **range** is the difference between the largest and smallest value. For example, the range of 13, 24, 7, 32, 29 is determined as follows:

32 – 7 = 25

---

1. Find the mean, median, mode, and range of the following list of values.

21, 16, 13, 7, 5, 11, 2

---

1. Mean = (21 + 16 + 13 + 7 + 5 + 11 + 2) ÷ 7

75 ÷ 7 = 10.7 (rounded)

Mean = 10.7 (rounded)

Median = 2, 5, 7, 11, 13, 16, 21

Median is 11.

Mode = There is no mode.

Range = 21 – 2 = 19

Range = 19.

---

2. Chip has been racing slalom snowboarding. He needs to maintain an average race time of 56 seconds to qualify. In his last 5 races, he has gotten 55, 58, 56, 54, and 59 seconds. What time does he need to get on his last race to maintain his qualifying average of 56 seconds?

---

2. Let x represent the unknown value that is needed.

Set up the formula

$$\frac{\left(x+55+58+56+54+59\right)}{6}=56$$

Multiply each side by 6.

$$\frac{\left(x+282\right)}{6}\cdot 6=56\cdot 6$$

Solve for x by subtracting 282 from each side.

$x + 282 - 282 = 336 - 282$

$x = 54$

Chip needs to get a race time of 54 seconds to qualify.

Mathematics—Introduction to Curriculum, Instruction, and Assessment (0011)

Our world is full of mathematical situations. The expectations for individuals in today's society to know, understand, and apply math is beyond that of times past. People face math problems daily when making store purchases, using measurements in cooking, applying time concepts, and using spatial organization to move furniture. They must apply and use math when they create spreadsheets, balance a checkbook, select insurance, and numerous other examples in school and at work.

Students will need to develop math competence in order to function in the world. Since they are exposed to math on a daily basis they must be aware of its importance. Although individuals have different interests and abilities when it comes to the subject of math, educators should be prepared to teach the basic concepts and help students understand how to apply and generalize this knowledge. To help them retain a positive attitude and feel competent in their math knowledge, educators should engage students in successful and meaningful opportunities to study and use mathematics.

Mathematics education begins in preschool and continues through adulthood, even beyond the academic rigor and structure. The world is changing rapidly and math is an essential skill that is necessary for individuals to master. Implementing a well-balanced curriculum that includes the national standards for mathematics and activities that are exciting, developmentally appropriate and realistic will aid students in learning the value of math and pursuing further study of this subject. In addition, multidisciplinary and integrated approaches need to be utilized to further increase mathematics concept knowledge and application.

Students may easily see the connection of math in their current lives beginning as early as elementary school, if educators implement meaningful activities and connect children's lives to the use of mathematics. Later, when students begin to make career choices, they may be interested in jobs related to this subject, such as being a mathematician, a statistician, an engineer, a teacher, a scientist, or an actuary.

There are six principles set forth for school mathematics by the National Council for Teachers of Mathematics (NCTM) that address primary topics of math:

- **Equity**—Focuses on expectations and support for students
- **Curriculum**—Emphasizes appropriate activities and concepts aligned with standards and articulated by grades
- **Teaching**—Educators must be knowledgeable about math concepts and principles so they may engage the learners
- **Learning**—Encourages students to gain math understandings and build upon prior knowledge
- **Assessment**—Evaluations of the learner and the program are instrumental in mathematics education
- **Technology**—This area impacts math in numerous ways and should influence what and how it is taught

The NCTM submit to 10 core beliefs related to mathematics education in school programs. These beliefs emphasize the improvement of these programs, promote competence in math, and suggest how to utilize it in today's world. They are summarized here.

- Students should be challenged in mathematics instruction to meet their needs in the future.
- Qualified teachers, knowledgeable about math and children, should deliver the mathematics instruction.
- Mathematics curriculum should focus on the primary standards and concepts through all grade levels.
- Students in elementary school must be able to utilize and apply number, algebra, geometry, measurement, and statistics concepts.
- The classroom environment and learning activities should be related to mathematics content; teachers should focus on mathematical thinking and reasoning.
- Mathematics understanding is broadened when it is meaningful to students and integrated with other subject area concepts.

- Technology is a critical component to mathematics instruction and should include computers and calculators regularly.
- Students may require alternative approaches to learning math concepts, using math strategies and understanding the different algorithms.
- Assessments should be incorporated with and related to the mathematical content.
- The learning of mathematics and math programs must be channeled by ongoing research.

The NCTM has created a broad band of standards, and these are available for review. These standards provide educators with an overall view of the needs of students in this academic area. An overview and a brief outline of the standards for elementary school-aged students, in grades pre-K to 6, are included.

Standards Overview, Grades Pre-K to 6

The general academic standards for mathematics instruction detail a comprehensive series of goals that students should acquire in pre-K through grade 12, although this guide emphasizes those in grades pre-K to 6th grade. These standards illustrate the mathematic knowledge, skills, concepts, understanding, and application that students should learn. The mathematical content in the first five standards include numbers and operations, algebra, geometry, measurement, and data analysis and probability. The mathematical content in the second set of five standards include the processes of problem solving, reasoning and proof, communication, connections, and representation. These 10 standards represent the basic skills and concepts that are necessary for students to apply as they live and work in the world.

Standards Pre-K to 6

Included here are the 10 general standard strands and the primary objectives related to the strands. More detailed information on the standards is available through national mathematics organizations.

1. **Numbers and Operations**

   Understand numbers, ways of representing numbers, relationships among numbers, and number systems.

   Understand meanings of operations and how they relate to one another.

   Compute fluently and make reasonable estimates.

2. **Algebra**

   Understand patterns, relations, and functions.

   Represent and analyze mathematical situations and structures using algebraic symbols.

   Use mathematical models to represent and understand quantitative relationships.

   Analyze change in various contexts.

3. **Geometry**

   Analyze characteristics and properties to two- and three-dimensional geometric shapes and develop mathematical arguments about geometric relationships.

   Specify locations and describe spatial relationships using coordinate geometry and other representations systems.

   Apply transformations and use symmetry to analyze mathematical situations.

   Use visualization, spatial reasoning, and geometric modeling to solve problems.

   Use visualization.

4. **Measurement**

   Understand measurable attributes of objects and the units, systems, and processes of measurement.

   Apply appropriate techniques, tools, and formulas to determine measurements.

5. **Data Analysis and Probability**

   Formulate questions that can be addressed with data and collect, organize, and display relevant data to answer them.

   Select and use appropriate statistical methods to analyze data.

   Develop and evaluate inferences and predictions that are based on data.

   Understand and apply basic concepts of probability.

6. **Problem Solving**

   Build new mathematical knowledge through problem solving.

   Solve problems that arise in mathematics and other contexts.

   Apply and adapt a variety of appropriate strategies to solve problems.

   Monitor and reflect on the process of mathematical problem solving.

7. **Reasoning and Proof**

   Recognize reasoning and proof as fundamental aspects of mathematics.

   Make and investigate mathematical conjectures.

   Develop and evaluate mathematical arguments.

   Select and use various types of reasoning and methods of proof.

8. **Communications**

   Organize and consolidate their mathematical thinking through communication.

   Communicate their mathematical thinking coherently and clearly to peers, teachers, and others.

   Analyze and evaluate the mathematical thinking and strategies of others.

   Use the language of mathematics to express mathematical ideas precisely.

9. **Connections**

   Recognize and use connections among mathematical ideas.

   Understand how mathematical ideas interconnect and build upon another to produce a coherent whole.

   Recognize and apply mathematics in contexts outside of mathematics.

10. **Representations**

    Create and use representations to organize, record, and communicate mathematical ideas.

    Select, apply, and translate among mathematical representations to solve problems.

    Use representations to model and interpret physical, social, and mathematical phenomena.

The mathematics portion of the Praxis II 0011 exam assesses an examinee's overall knowledge and application of the information regarding curriculum, instruction, and assessment, specifically the number concepts, four mathematical properties, number theories, problem solving, geometric concepts, measurement, probability, and use of technology. In this section of the study guide, examinees will find content specific to these math topics and the more general elementary practices are found in the "Overview" to 0011 at the front of the study guide. Use both of these sections to study for this exam.

The 0011 exam measures how well an examinee knows how to develop and deliver instruction based on mathematics content knowledge. This exam employs examples of elementary situations through multiple choice questions. This section of the study guide includes the information necessary for the examinee to clearly utilize the content of 0014 in the implementation of curriculum and instruction and the use of assessments in mathematics education.

Curriculum

The primary goal in teaching mathematics is for students to understand that math makes sense in their lives. It is used regularly and the concepts are applicable to a variety of situations, so instruction should focus on the meaningful aspects of using mathematics. Learning math is like building with blocks; each one added supports the next and is important to the previous. Without the general foundations (basic math skills), more complex structures (complicated math concepts) could not be attained.

Number Sense

Number sense is an individual's basic understanding of numbers and operations and how to apply this knowledge to solve dilemmas and make decisions about mathematical problems and concepts. This area of math, according to research, develops gradually by experimenting with numbers, visualizing them, using them, and understanding their relationships.

At the elementary level, the curriculum will focus on numeral relationships, writing numbers, and recognizing numbers. Students will move from basic counting techniques and concepts to understanding the size and relationships of numbers. They will be able to learn place values and operations because they have gained number sense.

It is important to provide children with opportunities to "play" with numbers and develop activities that allow them to count numbers, and make adjustments to their groups of numbers. Manipulatives such as blocks, counters, buttons, popsicle sticks, and other small objects that can create a larger group will aid young children in learning to count to 3 place numbers and group similar items in small groups of 10.

When students understand number relationships, they build a foundation of basic concepts or mastery. Basic facts mean the addends and the factors in addition and multiplication problems that are less than 10. In subtraction and division it means that the facts relate to addition and multiplication and both parts equal less than 10.

Basic facts understanding can be categorized by grade levels and means that the knowledge and concepts are mastered and solutions are recalled quickly by the learner.

First grade: Addition and subtraction without manipulatives or using fingers
Second grade: Addition and subtraction usage on worksheets and timed tests
Third grade: Multiplication and beginning division
Fourth and fifth grades: Refined mastery of multiplication and division

Counting Objects

Children learn to count at a very young age, even before they enter school. They must have the vocabulary to count (names of numbers) and the ability to sequence the numbers. In the early grades, educators can play games, sing songs, and read children's literature that includes the numbers, the sequential order, and the counting activities to enhance a child's automatic knowledge of numbers and how to count. After children can count with ease, an educator should begin to challenge them with such strategies as *counting on* and *counting back*. Using mathematics tools such as number lines and counters, students can conceptually and procedurally practice these skills.

Comparing/Classifying Objects/Sets

Once elementary students develop number sense, they gain the idea that numbers have relationships to one another. Concepts in number sense such as *more* or *less* demonstrate a basic relationship of numbers. Since they know these concepts from their basic numbers, it may be applied to learning more about sets.

Children need opportunities to practice using these skills. Manipulatives can be used to construct sets to compare and classify. Activities with manipulatives such as *make sets of more/less/same* or *find sets with the same amount* will provide practice in visualizing the concept of sets, comparing and classifying them.

Exploring Sets

Students should be exposed to various types of sets that exist, not just in math. They should be able to apply their knowledge of sets to daily life, such as groups of animals, or books and how these might be arranged according to specific numbers (a set of 6 hippos live in one cage and a set of 4 in the other; therefore the zoo has 10 hippos). Set models may be used to help students visualize the organization of sets. These may be drawings or objects within a perimeter or border.

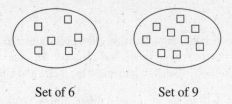

Set of 6   Set of 9

Number Patterns

When students have gained skills in counting, they can move forward in their knowledge of numbers by learning to recognize the patterns and relationships. Patterns exist throughout the world and in our daily lives. Learning to recognize patterns and their purpose through math instills a skill that will be used again and again.

Four types of number relationships exist in the set of 1–10:

1. **Spatial**—Recognizing sets of objects in number patterns and figuring out how many exist without counting
2. **One and two more, one and two less**—Comprehending the relationship of one number position to another number's position (3 is one more than 2).
3. **Anchors**—Discovering how the combinations of numbers are related to each other
4. **Part-part-whole**—Establishes that two parts consist of a whole (2 and 2 make the whole of 4).

Three types of number activities help in the study of number relationships from 10–20:

1. **Pre-place-value**—Connects the ideas of sets (a set of 5 buttons and a set of 3 buttons equal a set of 8).
2. **More and less**—Promotes understanding of numbers 10–20 (use of sets of 10 can help children understand that a set of 10 counters and 2 more are 12).
3. **Doubling or near-doubling**—Learning larger numbers (more than 10) may be easier if students understand that doubles make another larger number (the double of 5 is 10, the double of 8 is 16), while near-doubling is a double and one more (17 is the double of 8 and one more).

Base-Ten Numeration Systems

Students pre-K through grade 2 must develop a solid understanding of the base-ten numeration system. They need to recognize that the word "ten" represents a single entity (1 ten) and/or ten separate units (10 ones). They should learn that these representations are interchangeable, as they have the same value. Use of developmentally appropriate concrete materials and even calculators will support students in learning these concepts.

Place value

Students learn place value over a period of time and as they proceed through the grade levels, which may be outlined as:

- Kindergarten—Counting to 100
- First and second grade—Work with units and tens, learning place value strategies
- Third and fourth grade—Use of place value in hundreds and thousands
- Fifth grade—Begin work with decimals

Students must have the skills of counting and grouping in order to understand and use place values. Using manipulatives is a significant method to process place value understanding in young children, as it provides the students with visual and kinesthetic access to count a group. Not all children will learn place-value concepts at the same time.

Estimation

Estimation skills may be developed once students are experienced with mental computation and number sense, as well as understand and use invented strategies, since those require the ability to manage numbers. In the beginning, the opportunities provided to students to learn estimation should be simple, flexible number activities, instead of rigid algorithms, as these will help students understand computational fluency and develop computational estimation skills. The instructional goal in estimation is for students to learn how to approximate an answer appropriate to the situation they are faced with (planning a trip, purchasing an item, the tip on a restaurant bill).

The instruction of estimation should include different types of manipulatives (such as base-ten models, 100s charts) and various estimation strategies (such as front-end addition and subtraction, front-end multiplication and division, rounding addition and subtraction, and rounding multiplication and division). In addition, estimation instruction should be taught using situations that reflect or pertain to real life situations. Estimation is an important life skill as it is used almost daily by most adults. It is an important skill to use in measurements and figuring quantities of objects. Teach students using such phrases as about, a little less than, a bit more than, close to, between, and so on, as these indicate that an exact number is not necessary.

Reading and Writing Numbers

Children's literature is full of stories and other written passages with examples of number usage, so reading and writing should be an essential component of math education. Incorporating reading and writing skills into an integrated curriculum with math will boost skill development in many specific areas and provide motivation, excitement, and interest in math for the students.

Extending Numbers

After students have an understanding of number relationships, they will begin to use larger numbers. Teachers can help extend the number relationships the students know by helping them count by 10s. The use of a *tens frame* as a tool to count in relationships to 100 is very beneficial. Students can use these frames to represent various numbers and developing this skill of extending numbers supports skills in learning to estimate, compare, and compute.

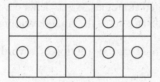

Tens Frame

Mathematical Operations

The four basic mathematical operations—addition, subtraction, multiplication, and division—are the focus of the elementary mathematics education curriculum beginning in about first grade. However, students must have a solid foundation of number recognition, counting, and number relationships up through 20 before instruction begins on these mathematical operations. Story problems and manipulatives are recommended methods for instructing students on the meanings of the operations and the function of the operations.

Addition and Subtraction

Students must use the operations in a variety of ways in order to master the concepts. Using interesting and different strategies to entice students into learning the basic math operations of addition and subtraction will provide the foundation they need to complete other operations and solve problems.

Following are some addition strategies with which students should be familiar:

- **One-More-Than and Two-More-Than Facts**—Requires that the student count from a specified number. For example, 2-more-than 6, count on 7, 8.
- **Zero Facts**—Students must learn not to count on when using zero and that zero does not add another number, but holds a place. In addition a number added to zero is that same number. For example, $5 + 0 = 6$ is incorrect; $5 + 0 = 5$.
- **Doubles**—Ten of the basic facts are doubles. For example, $2 + 2 = 4$, $3 + 3 = 6$.
- **Near-Doubles**—Concept of doubles plus one, in which learners round the smallest addend and then add one more. For example, $3 + 4 = 7$, but thought of as $3 + 3 = 6 + 1 = 7$.
- **Make Ten Facts**—When one of the addends is 8 or 9, then part of the other addend is added to make 10, and the remaining is added for the total. For example, $9 + 4 = 13$. The learner takes 1 from the 4 and adds to the 9 to make 10, which leaves 3 and that is added to 10 to equal 13.

Other addition strategies include adding single digits, adding tens and hundreds, and adding two-digit numbers.

Following are some subtraction strategies with which students should be familiar:

- **Subtraction as Think-Addition**—Focuses and builds upon the part-part-whole relationship. For example, $4 - x = 2$: count 4 manipulatives, cover 2, so how many are left?
- **Subtraction Facts with Sums to 10**—Basic addition facts must first be mastered, as learners must use fact families to learn subtraction facts. For example, $3 + 2 = 5$, $5 - 2 = 3$.
- **Sums Greater than 10**—Builds upon the relationship of addition and subtraction up to 10 and back down to 10 or extension of the think-addition method.

Other subtraction strategies include subtracting single digits, subtracting tens and hundreds, subtracting two-digit numbers, and subtracting by counting up.

Story problems engage students more than simple computation problems, as they are interesting and realistic. Frequent opportunities should be included for solving story problems and a combination of methods that help students through the progression of direct modeling and invented strategies. As students develop various strategies for addition and subtraction, the traditional algorithm should be discussed as the final development in the operation.

Use these sequential steps to teach students to attack the solution of a word problem:

1. Understand the problem.
2. Determine the essential information.
3. Make a plan to solve the problem.
4. Follow the plan.
5. Check the answer to be sure it makes sense.

Whole Number Computation

Whole number computation is based on *place value* concepts and the understanding of operations. Students should be permitted to invent strategies for addition and subtraction problems without having to use specific algorithms. Invented strategies differ from the traditional algorithms because they focus on the number not just a digit within the number. Use of invented strategies seems to provide benefits over using traditional algorithms, such as enhancing *base ten* instruction and ensuring that students can explain their work.

Before inventing strategies, students should use math tools such as counters in direct modeling activities. Students will also benefit from guided activities to share how they solved the problems. Depending on learning styles, some students will then be able to mentally solve the problems and some will be better at expressing it in written form. The teacher should be supportive and allow time to use the strategies so students retain skills in whole number computation.

Multiplication and Division

Multiplication and division are the more complex operations using basic facts. However, in order to learn these principles, an individual must master the concepts of addition and subtraction.

Following are some multiplication strategies with which students should be familiar:

- **Doubles**—Equivalent to doubles in addition problems. For example, 2 * 5 = 10, 5 + 5 = 10.
- **Fives Facts**—Builds on the counting by 5 concept.
- **Zeros and Ones**—Generalizations that when one factor is zero then the answer is 0, and when one factor is 1, the answer is the other number. For example, 0 * 8 = 0 and 4 * 1 = 4.
- **Nifty Nines**—The basic math facts have a factor of 9 and students use the pattern. For example, 4 * 9 = 36 (3 + 6 = 9), 9 * 9 = 81 (8 + 1 = 9).

Other multiplication strategies include complete-number, compensation, multiples of 10 and 100, and two-digit multipliers.

Students can master **division** facts and operations, but it will depend on how well they mastered multiplication facts and operations. Division represents the recall of a multiplication problem. Students should be made aware of this relationship through class discussion and practice using these concepts.

Use of **fact families** can aid in the explanation and concept development for young children. For example,

4 * 5 = 20
5 * 4 = 20
20 ÷ 4 = 5
20 ÷ 5 = 4

Concepts of Number Theory

Number theory is the area of mathematics related to the properties of numbers in general. It includes the properties of integers and the use of both. There are several subcategories of number theory and these are established by the methods used and the types of investigations done. Individuals who work in this field of mathematics are considered number theorists.

The specific fields of number theory have historical value and include

- **Analytic number theory**—Includes solutions of calculus and complex analysis (also squares, cubes, integers, primes)
- **Algebraic number theory**—The study of the concept of numbers expanded to algebraic equations
- **Geometry of numbers**—Pertains to basic geometric concepts
- **Combinatorial number theory**—Defines the use of algebraic and analytic methods
- **Computational number theory**—The study of algorithms pertinent to number theory
- **Greek number theory**—Refers to integer solutions to linear indeterminate equations (beginning in third century)
- **Classical Indian number theory**—Solutions to equations involving fractions, integers, and so on
- **Islamic number theory**—Algorithms and classifications of numbers determined (beginning in ninth century)
- **Early European number theory**—Discovery of solutions to problems previously unsolved (sixteenth–eighteenth centuries)
- **Beginnings of modern number theory**—Refers to the organization of the current systematic number formulas (nineteenth century)
- **Prime number theory**—The study of the distribution of prime numbers

Factors

Factors are related to the operation of multiplication. There are generally two different factors used in a multiplication problem: one demonstrates how many sets or parts and the other represents the size of each set or part. Specifically, the factors are termed the multiplier and the multiplicand and may be used in the instruction of multiplication so children understand the difference between the two numbers.

Multiples

When computing with fractions, students may need to use the method of finding a common denominator, which is also referred to as *the multiples of*. Multiples are used to make fraction operations easier to solve. Some students have difficulty determining the multiples so they may rewrite the equation in the simpler form. They must have a good grasp of addition and multiplication, as well as division skills to figure the multiples. Practice and use of manipulatives will aid in the instruction of finding common denominators or multiples.

Variables

Variables are symbols used in problems that represent a set of numbers or objects. Young children need to understand that variables are numbers used in operations that may be manipulated. There are three different uses of variables:

- Specific unknown—Represents a place holder for a number
- Pattern generalizer—Illustrates rules or regularities in our number system
- Varying quantities—Change value within problems

In teaching variables, sometimes drawings are used to illustrate the idea and sometimes, with older students, equations help promote the concept of variable usage.

Remainders

Remainders are the result of division problems that do not result in simple whole numbers. Students should be instructed that remainders can be used in different ways depending on the context.

- A leftover quantity
- Partitioned into fractions
- Discarded
- Used to round up
- Rounded to approximation

Odd and Even

The concept of odd and even numbers is one that is often overlooked in elementary math instruction. The idea is not to simply teach that even is 2, 4, 6, 8 and so on and that odd is 1, 3, 5, 7 and so on, but to provide an understanding of the meaning of odd and even. It is clear to adults that odd numbers cannot be divided into equal parts as there is one more left over (extra) and even numbers can be divided into equal parts, but the reasoning needs to be explained and ingrained in student's minds, so they may use this knowledge in other mathematical situations. The recommended methods of teaching the concept of odd and even numbers is through oral story problems with discussion and activities using manipulatives.

Rational Numbers

As stated in the math content section 0014, rational numbers are parts of a whole, expressed as a fraction, a decimal or a percentage. These are used in daily life and are important for students to learn.

Fractions can be a difficult concept for students to master. In order to learn this math concept, it is recommended that positive initial experiences with fractions be implemented and students should be moved from a concrete to a symbolic phase very slowly, only after understanding of the concrete level. Adequate and appropriate manipulatives should be used when teaching fractions.

There are three types of manipulatives that might be used to teach fractions:

- **Region/area**—These help students to visualize fraction problems where the surface area may be divided into smaller parts. (For example, a 1,500-acre parcel of land may be visualized using patterns, blocks, geoboards, or grids.)
- **Length**—These may model a fraction situation in which dividing a line may be necessary. Use of fraction strips, number lines, and Cuisenaire rods will all help with these relationships.
- **Set**—These are related to a group of objects considered whole, and dividing a set creates fractional parts. Use of beans, small counters, and toys are useful.

In teaching fractions, students need to understand the difference between the numbers at the top and bottom. Younger students only need to know that the top number is the counting number that describes how many parts in the whole and the bottom number describes the counting in terms of the total number of parts that makes the whole. After students have a solid understanding of fractions, then they should be introduced to the terms numerator and denominator.

As the part-to-whole relationship is emphasized students develop their fraction number sense ability. In addition to counting the parts of a whole, students need to understand the concept that the more equal-sized parts in the whole, the smaller those parts will be. They may be familiar with larger numbers being bigger but that does not hold true for fractions. For example, the fraction 1/6 is not larger than 1/3, even though 6 is larger than 3.

For teaching young children to compute with fractions, Van de Walle recommends these strategies:

- Use simple contextual tasks so they understand the meaning of the task when it is structured in a story problem.
- Connect the meaning of fraction computation with whole-number computation.
- Use estimation and informal methods to develop strategies.
- Explore each of the operations using manipulatives for algorithms.

For addition and subtraction of fractions, apply the common denominator method, understand that the numerator shows the number of parts and the denominator the type of part.

For multiplication of fractions, the denominator is a divisor that allows the student to find the parts of the other factor.

For division of fractions, apply the lowest common-denominator method or the invert-and-multiply algorithm.

Decimals are important to study as they comprise our monetary system and the system of scientific measures. Students should have a solid grasp of fractions before beginning the study of decimals and understand that these are related and are not separate concepts. Manipulatives, such as a place value chart or base ten blocks, help in defining this relationship.

Percentages are a link to decimals and fractions and should be taught once students understand decimals and fractions, but not separated in the overall concept. Percentages are based on the comparison to 100. It symbolizes a fraction that has a common denominator of 100 and is indicated through the % sign. Fractions and percentages are two different ways of writing the same thing. The goal of comparing fractions and percentages is to help learners figure out how to recognize equivalencies between common fractions and percentages.

Problem Solving

According to the NCTM instructional programs from pre-K through grade 12 should enable all students to:

- Build new mathematical knowledge through problem solving.
- Solve problems that arise in mathematics and in other contexts.
- Apply and adapt a variety of appropriate strategies to solve problems.
- Monitor and reflect on the process of mathematical problem solving.

Problem solving does not just relate to mathematics, but through math education, students can learn much about developing this skill. Everyone should learn to problem solve and mathematics education can lead students from the concrete solutions to the abstract solutions, indirectly teaching them a life skill.

Several strategies are particularly helpful in the study of mathematics.

- Task analysis helps students move to a desired level of skill attainment by learning a specific skill through a series of sequential steps.
- Using guided practice at the conclusion of a lesson or period allows the students to ask questions about the concepts and algorithmic procedures. This time will ensure that students gained skills in the topic presented.
- Utilizing a closure activity, whether it is a math game, a question/answer period or a problem solving worksheet, gives students the added time to summarize what they have learned about math and which algorithms they must remember and practice before the next lesson.
- Providing homework as a form of practice for the day's math concepts reinforces the skills and mastery of the operations.
- Writing can be used for students to express themselves about what they do in math and explain their mathematical thinking. This can be completed by using student logs, expository writing, and student journals.
- Cooperative learning where students work together in assigned groups helps students to develop long term retention, increase cognitive skills, improve the ability to communicate and instills social skills, while helping one another with math concepts and activities.

Geometric Concepts

In elementary school, geometry appears to be a hands-on, exciting area of mathematics, which requires manipulatives, puzzles, and drawings to gain skills in geometric reasoning and spatial relationships. According to the van Hiele theory, there are five levels of learning geometry and they are sequential, requiring that students learn each one at their own developmental level, the final level being at the college level.

1. **Visualization**—Identify shapes and their names, according to the characteristics, and categorize them.
2. **Analysis**—Learn the classifications of shapes and their similar properties.
3. **Informal deduction**—Learn the properties of shapes and their relationships.
4. **Deduction**—Understand the theorems and axioms of shapes.
5. **Rigor**—Understand axiom systems.

Measurement

Measurement knowledge is an essential skill and the concept of measurement is complex. There are many different types of measurements. Known as attributes, these include length, weight, volume/capacity, and area. To develop conceptual knowledge of measurements, students must

- Understand the attributes to be measured.
- Realize the comparison of the attribute is a measure.
- Acknowledge the types and use of measurement tools.

Kindergarten students begin learning the concepts of measurement by comparing items to find which is longer, or which is heavier. They may use their hands or bodies to compare objects that must be measured. As students move through the grades, the concepts of measurement become more complicated and students learn to measure angles, areas, and volumes. On this journey, both informal units of measurement (hand, strips of paper) and standard units of measurement (yards, cups) are learned and utilized. Estimation is another concept used in mastering the measurement concept. Students may guess (estimate) at the size, or volume of an object and then use the proper tool of measurement to check their estimation.

Length

The first attribute learned in measurement is found by comparing how long two or more items are, using manipulatives like a rope, a string, or strips of paper to do the measuring.

Weight

This concept of measurement compares the mass of one object to another. Students may use their hands in the early stages to feel the difference of objects and whether one is heavier or larger than another one. Students may use various informal units of measure before learning to use the more standard units of measure.

Volume/Capacity

Measuring volume and capacity relates to three-dimensional objects and figures. Students may use containers to check the amount, such as cups, boxes, and bowls.

Area

This is the more difficult of the measurement concepts to learn, as it is a complex visual task. Learners may use shaped objects to compare the area measurements.

Angles

In fourth or fifth grades, students learn to measure angles through an introduction to the protractor. Instructing students on how to use a protractor will help them understand angle measurement.

Time

Measuring time indicates the duration of when something may begin or stop. Informal measures may identify the amount of time and standard measures provide the actual telling of time.

Telling time begins around late second grade and should show mastery in the fourth or fifth grade, although many students may need until seventh or eighth grade to master this skill. Students should first learn to tell time by the hour, then the half hour, and then by minutes.

- Count the days of school using a calendar or timeline.
- Select children's literature that refers to telling time.
- Sequence events that are meaningful to the students.
- Construct simple analog or digital clocks for use by students.
- Conduct research about the history of clocks and time pieces.
- Play games related to the tools of time and the telling of time.
- Use graphs and charts to indicate specific events and periods of time.

Temperature

- Include a daily time period for weather reports.
- Define the terms of weather, the seasons, and the related careers.
- Use tools associated with weather, such as a thermometer, a wind sock, and so on.
- Allow students to conduct experiments using hot, warm, cold, and cool items.
- Use charts and graphs to measure the weather over a period of time.

Money

When teaching students about money, include problems related to the properties of mathematics (addition, subtraction, multiplication, and division), fractions, percentages, estimates, and decimals as well as the concepts of earning, spending, saving, and borrowing.

- Use real coins in the classroom to do estimations and values.
- Invite a coin collector to explain the various types of coins.
- Discuss the history and current use of money and monetary systems.
- Establish a store or center that pertains to the exchange of money.
- Encourage the class to save or collect money for a donation to a charity.
- Use charts and graphs to depict the value of coins.
- Take field trips to banks, stores, financial institutions, mint, and museums.
- Describe the use of credit cards, checking accounts, and savings accounts.

Money concepts include:

Earning provides students with a sense of independence/recognition, an understanding of financial structures, instills work ethics/habits, and provides knowledge about the relationship of money, time, and work.

Spending helps students understand the difference between their desires and needs, and gives them opportunities to make decisions and be responsible.

Borrowing shows students responsibility for paying back what is owed, learning to appreciate what is earned, the consequences of using other's money, and how credit systems and interest work.

Saving instills the ideas of how to get what you want, how to plan for the future, how spending and earning are related, and how the banking savings systems function.

Probability and Statistics

Data analysis, statistics, and probability exist in our daily lives and are used in meaningful situations. Students must have opportunities to explore and experiences to practice these real-world applications. Instruction in probability and statistics should include common situations and involve the student in using reflection, guessing at chances, gathering data, and interpreting results without the structured rules and algorithms common to math. Students should participate in discussion activities about the data and the results to make the process more meaningful.

Situations of probability and statistics are much like conducting experiments and this would be an excellent topic for integrated studies with science. Developing these concept skills can be a motivational challenge for students and it increases their use of intuitive skills, critical thinking skills, and problem solving skills. Include the following when completing tasks on probability and statistics:

1. **Data analysis**—This step involves creating the questions that will be answered when the data is collected. This involves discussion, collaborative group work, or brainstorming methods.

2. **Manipulatives**—Used in data analysis, these tools can help with sorting, grouping, or classifying sets of objects. Two types of manipulatives to develop the skill of classification are: unstructured (have different attributes with various possibilities) and structured (possess a set number of attributes).

3. **Graphing data**—Once students have learned how to collect data, instruction should provide opportunities to learn how to represent the information. Often graphs are used to demonstrate and compare information. Examples of graphs include bar graphs, pictographs, tally charts, pie charts, and line graphs.

4. **Interpretation of data**—Students learn how to describe the results of the data that is graphed or charted.

Calculators and Computers

Calculators and computers are commonly used technology to support the subject of math. Many mathematics programs have commercial computer programs that coincide with the existing curriculum, and aid the teacher in remediation or enrichment of learners.

Activities to practice using a calculator:

- Have students enter meaningful numbers that they can retrieve from memory and try different operations. For example: enter their age and then add 3 years or enter their age and subtract 5 years.

- Ask students to figure out a bill from a restaurant. Bring in some menus and have the students imagine a meal they want to order. Have them enter numbers on the calculator to figure the entrée, the beverage, the dessert, and figure the tax (if developmentally appropriate).

- Suggest students compare ad prices for grocery stores. They can compare the prices across several stores to make decisions on the best selection. If older, they can also use multiple operations, memory function, and percentages.

Classroom Management

Educators will find that when math is exciting, challenging, and meaningful, students are more engaged and behavior issues are limited. Aside from students who may not understand concepts and act out, or those who are identified with learning problems, most students should be capable of mastering mathematics at some level. Making math fun for the students will be a challenge for the teacher, but well worth the effort. Using games, manipulatives, and stories will intrigue students and keep them actively involved in the lessons. The mathematical environment created in a classroom will enhance the development of students who can invent mathematics strategies they will remember throughout their lives.

Manipulatives

Manipulatives are one kind of physical tool that may be used to model mathematical concepts, considered "hands-on" learning. Manipulatives are often used at the elementary level so students can participate in their understanding of the math concepts. They should be considered concrete materials used to think about math concepts and reflect on solving problems rather than simply finding an answer. Manipulatives may be commercially made or constructed from household objects, such as popsicle sticks, buttons, and beans.

Manipulatives should not replace a student's ability to apply concepts, and must be used in developmentally appropriate and meaningful ways to be effective. Children should be allowed to maneuver the manipulatives as they need in order to understand the concept, rather than be shown how to use them, requiring that they copy a model from the teacher. This just stifles the learning that may be gained through the use of these materials. Keeping manipulatives easily accessible and in good condition helps the learner. Manipulatives are regularly used in a temporary fashion, until the student can move from the concrete to the abstract and apply the mathematical principle learned.

Content Specific Pedagogy

Pedagogy is more fully described in the "Overview" 0011 section of this study guide. Here are a few of the approaches and terms related to mathematics education.

- **Constructivism**—Individuals construct their own knowledge based on previous knowledge.
- **Conceptual knowledge**—Consists of knowledge that is understood; logical relationships and ideas.
- **Models of mathematical concepts**—Use of objects, pictures, or drawings that can represent a concept and promotes the relationship of the concept.
- **Multiple intelligences**—Specifically logical reasoning and problem solving that promotes sequential and orderly instruction within a structured environment.
- **Procedural knowledge**—Understanding of the rules, procedures, and routines and tasks of mathematics.
- **Problem-based approach**—Student-centered, which helps them create meaning from mathematics.

Assessment

As with other assessments in elementary subject areas, the purpose is to monitor student progress, make instructional decisions, evaluate student achievement, and evaluate the program. It is recommended that in mathematics, educators integrate the assessments with the instruction.

In 1995, the NCTM established six standards for assessments related to mathematics. These state that assessments should

1. Reflect the mathematics that all students need to know and be able to do.
2. Enhance mathematics learning.
3. Promote equity.
4. Be an open process.
5. Promote valid inferences about mathematics learning.
6. Be a coherent process.

In mathematics, the assessments should focus on the concepts and procedures, the mathematical processes, and the student's disposition to math. Effective assessments and evaluation strategies will allow the students an opportunity to demonstrate their skills and to obtain immediate feedback about how they are performing. Valuable to students and the teacher are assessments that require students to recall and perform the mathematical concepts and operations they have learned. These may be conducted daily, weekly, and at the end of units, as the on-going progress will be critical to on-going instruction.

Following are assessment types useful in mathematics education. (Assessment is further explained in the "Overview" 0011 of this study guide.)

- Observation
- Anecdotal notes
- Performance assessment
- Alternate assessments
- Portfolios

Mathematics Content Area Exercises (0012)

This Praxis II exam (0012) assesses an examinee's ability to apply the knowledge gained in the content knowledge section (0014) and that found in the curriculum, instruction, and assessment section (0011) to educational situations. Examinees will have 2 hours to answer four essay questions; one question will be focused on mathematics. Review the information from the Praxis II 0014 and 0011 mathematics study guide sections, as well as the "Overview" of 0011 in this book.

There are endless possibilities as to what questions may be presented on this exam, so examinees should prepare for the exam by considering how to use the mathematics information they already know. Read through the following list of questions that relate to the topic of mathematics education at the elementary level and try to answer them using a separate sheet of paper. You will notice that answers are not provided, as there are many different ways to answer these open-ended questions. A rubric is used in the scoring of the actual exam (explained in the "Overview" of 0012).

The exercises posed on this exam will test the examinees ability to prepare an extended, in-depth response to one question in the mathematics area. When preparing to answer questions on this exam, remember that some of the questions presented may have several parts and therefore require multiple answers.

1. Design an instructional activity using either of the mathematics tools (Cuisenaire rods or tens frames) to teach elementary students how to extend numbers.

2. A group of parents from your first-grade class are concerned about your instructional choice of topics in mathematics. They want you to be teaching operations and fractions to their children as they believe their children are gifted in math. You have discussed this issue with your principal who wants you to compose a letter that explains the state standards, the district's curriculum, developmentally appropriate practices, and how you might address advanced learners. Draft the letter that you will use to help parents understand the goals you have for your students and how you think you will accommodate them.

3. Discuss how to integrate mathematics at the fourth-grade level into a thematic unit about the ocean. Include two curriculum goals, three objectives related to math instruction, and list four activities that may be used in an effort to integrate math with other subjects in this unit, such as science, social studies and language arts, and then explain how to best assess students using both formative and summative formats.

4. Create a lesson plan that integrates the fine arts into teaching equivalent fractions at the 3–4 grade level, using the format of the Hunter model.

5. The 5th grade class you are teaching is studying decimals. Identify and explain three different authentic assessments that could be used to evaluate and measure a student's performance on this mathematical concept.

6. The Constructivist Theory is widely recommended in education and it especially applies to elementary mathematics education. Describe how this theory enhances the study of math and describe two learning activities that may be implemented at two different grade levels based on the application of this theory.

7. The topics of **measurement, percentages,** and **estimation** are critical topics to learn for students at the elementary level as these are foundational lifelong math skills. Using the method of instruction called *task analysis* describe how to proceed with the instruction of these math concepts.

8. Three students in your third-grade class have begun to demonstrate acting out behavior specifically during math lessons. Your class is currently studying multiplication and division. You believe the antecedents for the undesired behaviors are directly related to the students' lack of acquisition of the foundational math skills of addition and subtraction in the third grade. Identify what assessment process you could use to verify their lack of skills and knowledge in these four math operations. Then describe how you will address their behaviors and skills, and improve their attitude toward mathematics. (One of the students is also linguistically diverse.)

9. An outstanding and recommended approach for teaching geometry at the elementary level is the van Hiele theory. It is a five-level hierarchy (visualization, analysis, informal deduction, deduction, and rigor) to advance sequentially the thoughts and ideas of students regarding geometry. Identify the concept of focus on the level of visualization and construct a learning activity to promote this idea.

10. Bloom's taxonomy relates to all subject areas. Use this process to outline a lesson for a second grade class on telling time by using a standard clock.

Social Studies (0014)

The National Council for Social Studies (NCSS) has provided this statement regarding the study of social studies in the educational system: "The primary purpose of social studies is to help young people develop the ability to make informed and reasoned decisions for the public good as citizens of a culturally diverse, democratic society in an interdependent world." The NCSS created 10 standards for social studies that are used to clarify the concepts and core knowledge of this subject area.

These 10 standards are organized into themes related to social studies and include the following:

1. Culture
2. Time, continuity, and change
3. People, places, and environments
4. Individual development and identity
5. Individuals, groups, and institutions
6. Power, authority, and governance
7. Production, distribution, and consumption
8. Science, technology, and society
9. Global connections
10. Civic ideals and practices

Geography

The national standard that is reflected in this section focuses on the theme of "people, places, and environments," which helps students understand the importance of location and aids them in developing a geographic perspective so they may decipher current social situations and conditions.

Geography is the study of places that encompasses four main components:

- Physical characteristics (for example, lands and vegetation)
- Geopolitical information (such as boundaries and capital cities)
- Demographics (for example, size, density, and population)
- Economic information (that is, agricultural and manufacturing)

Approximately 15 percent of the Praxis II exam tests specific geography content knowledge that includes the following:

- Map skills and spatial organization of the world
- The places and regions of the world
- The physical and human systems
- The environment and society
- The uses of geography

Five Themes of Geography Study		
Theme	*Definition*	*Example*
Location	Where something happened; relative location (compared to another place) or exact location (latitude, longitude)	The Rocky Mountain region of the NW; latitude 55 degrees to 70 degrees north.
Place	Physical and human characteristics of a location	An arid climate in the Southwest provided few possibilities for growing crops. Therefore, the Native Americans developed irrigation devices and grew corn, also using the resources of the desert (made adobe homes and used plants) to survive.
Interaction of people and environment	People adapt, modify, and depend on the environment, which can cause changes in the environment.	People in the Northwest created dams to maintain a water source to survive, redirecting the natural flow of the rivers.
Movement	How people, goods, and ideas move around the globe	Tribes may seek relocation dependent on water sources.
Region	An area with similar characteristics	Appalachia is a region as the people have preserved traditions and culture that include folklore, foods, and language.

The World in Spatial Terms

Geographers suggest that the combination of the aspects of the earth's surface and the activities that occur on earth are considered **phenomena.** These phenomena may be physical or human related or they may occur together. Understanding and using the proper geographic terminology becomes essential for students.

Map Knowledge and Skills

A **map** is a visual representation of a particular area. A map can depict visible surface features such as rivers, coasts, roads, and towns, or underground features such as tunnels, subways, and geographical formations. Maps also show how information about physical and human features are located, arranged, and distributed in relation to one another. Maps are designed by using points, lines, area symbols, and colors.

Maps can be a mixture of objective knowledge and subjective perceptions. They can depict such abstract features as population density, lines of longitude and latitude, political boundaries, and agricultural products. They are used to analyze the spatial organization of people, places, and the environment of the earth's surface.

However, there are limitations to using maps. They cannot accurately represent a sphere on a flat surface without distortion of the distance, direction, size, and shape of water and land forms. Globes are one way to meet this problem, as they can depict the most precise representation of the earth in size, shape, distance, area, and directions.

Following are examples of map types:

- **Climate map**—Displays weather and typical climatic conditions of a region.
- **Conformal map**—Presents land masses and the retention of proper shapes, but they are often distorted.
- **Equal-area map**—Shows land areas with relatively proper sizes; however, distortion can occur.
- **Fact-book maps**—Examines the actual facts of events or activities in certain regions or specific places (for example, life expectancy rates, energy consumption).
- **Historical map**—Illustrates the people of an area and the population (such as trade routes, religions).

- **Mental map (sketch map)**—Conjures a sketch in a person's mind and is constructed mentally without any particular references; demonstrates what a person knows about locations and characteristics of places.

- **Physical map**—Reveals the features of actual geographical surfaces, like mountains or rivers, and the underlying geological structures, such as rocks or fault lines.

- **Outline map**—Shows some geographic features but does not include others.

- **Political map**—Demonstrates government boundaries and territorial borders for major countries, states, territories, provinces, and so on.

- **Relief map (topographical map)**—Exhibits a three-dimensional variation in the topography of land and water areas.

- **Thematic map**—Demonstrates the location of specific ideas or distributions (population of children, languages of the world, and time zones).

Following are some terms related to maps with which students should be familiar:

- **compass**—A tool used for determining specific direction on the Earth's surface

- **compass rose**—The precise directions on a map or globe (north, south, east, west, northeast, northwest, southeast, southwest)

- **coordinates**—Used on a map system to focus on finding specific locations

- **direction**—A concept of space and location (right-left, up-down, north-south)

- **grid**—A system on a more detailed map that shows the exact locations

- **latitude**—The horizontal lines that run parallel to the equator and measure the distance in degrees north and south from the equator

- **legend**—Explains what symbols mean on each map

- **longitude**—The vertical lines that run parallel to the prime meridian and measure the distance in degrees east and west from the meridian

- **scale**—The size of real objects represented on a map (miles, structures, and land masses)

- **symbols**—Pictures or icons representing some item on a map (land masses, population), but the same icons and pictures are not consistently used the same on all maps

Spatial Organization

Another component of geography is the ability to understand spatial relationships and the organization of people, places, and environments that exist in the world. In particular this knowledge includes knowing major areas and locations of the world and the specific terms that define examples of spatial organization.

The world is divided into sections and areas according to commonalities. This includes continents, oceans, and regional areas. Examples include the following:

- **Seven major continents**—About 30 percent of the world is comprised of land mass, which is divided into separate continents, each particular to its area and its people. These continents are large and continuous plots of land usually separated by water. They include in order of size from largest to smallest: Asia, Africa, North America, South America, Antarctica, Europe, and Australia.

- **Five major oceans**—Oceans cover 70 percent of the earth's surface and provide 97 percent of the world's water supply. These include, ranging from largest to smallest: Pacific, Atlantic, Arctic, Indian, and Southern Oceans.

- **Three major seas**—Seas are defined as a large area of water being partly enclosed by land. The three major seas include: the South China Sea, the Caribbean Sea, and the Mediterranean Sea.

- **Major deserts**—Deserts are land areas that are very dry and barren, mostly covered with sand and having specific plants and animals known only to that area. Some provide little possibility for human living conditions. The main deserts known in the world include: Arabian, Atacama, Australian, Iranian, Kalahari, Namib, North American, Patagonian, Saharan, Sonoran, Takla Makan-Gobi, Thar, and Turkestand.

Other Geographical Places

Bays	Capes	Canals	Canyons
San Francisco Bay (U.S.)	Cape of Good Hope	Panama Canal (Central America)	Grand Canyon (Arizona)
Bay of Pigs (Cuba)	Cape Horn	Suez Canal	Waimea Canyon (Kauai)
Hudson Bay (Canada)	Cape Cod	Grand Canal of China	Chaco Canyon (New Mexico)
Bay of Banderas (Mexico)	Cape Morris-Jessu		Bryce Canyon (Utah)
Chesapeake Bay (U.S.)			Zion Canyon (Utah)
Bay of Bengal (India)			Copper Canyon (Chihuahua, Mexico)
			Hell's Canyon (Idaho)
			Canyon de Chelley (Arizona)
			Yarlung Tsangpo (China)
			Cotahuasi (Africa)
			Black Canyon (Colorado)
			Cheddar Gorge (England)

Gulfs	Islands	Lakes	Mountain Ranges
Persian Gulf (Saudi Arabia and Iran)	Greenland	Great Salt Lake (Utah)	Kangchenjunga
Arabian Gulf	Great Britain	The Great Lakes (U.S.)	Rockies
Gulf of California (U.S.)	New Zealand	Caspian Sea (Iran)	Alps
Gulf of Mexico (U.S.-Mexico)	Aleutian Islands, Alaska	Victoria Lake (Africa)	Mount Everest
Gulf of Aden (between Red Sea and Arabian Sea)	Hawaiian Islands	Tangan Yika (East Africa)	Sierra Nevada
	Philippine Islands (7,100 islands)		Appalachian
	Venice Italy (built on 118 islands)		K–2
	Caribbean Islands		Mount McKinley
	Falkland Islands		Matterhorn
	British Isles		Mount Cook
	Japan		Kilamanjaro
	Azores		Cascades-Mount Rainier

Penisulas	Seas	Waterfalls
Florida	Arabian Sea	Niagara Falls (U.S.-Canada)
Italy	Black Sea	Angel Falls (Venezula)
Panama	Coral Sea	Barron Falls (Australia)
Baja (CA-MX)	Greenland Sea	Victoria Falls (Africa)
	Red Sea	Yosemite Falls (U.S.)
	Sea of Japan	
	Tasman Sea	

- **People**—The people of the world are diverse and offer a rich contribution to global unity. They live throughout the regions of the earth's surface and sometimes are the primary means to defining an area. People are categorized in many ways in order to better describe them as related to their characteristics. Knowing information about the people will help in understanding their relationships to the spaces of the world.

  Tribes (Navajo, Inuits, Aborigines, and so on)

  Cultures of people (Appalachians, and so on)

  Regions of people (Texas ranchers, Florida citrus farmers, and so on)

  Defined countries or states of people (French, Hawaiians, Filipinos, and so on)

Following is a list of individuals who study geography:

- **Anthropologist**—A person who studies the history of people such as culture and language
- **Cartographer**—A person who studies the science or practice of map drawing
- **Geographer**—A person who studies land formations and the earth's composition
- **Meteorologist**—A person who studies climates and the affects on the earth
- **Sociologists**—A person who studies the behaviors of people and how they impact the world
- **Topographer**—A person who designs, describes, and develops maps

Places and Regions

Both human and natural resources exist in different forms across the world, but are not evenly distributed. Land masses may be separated into enormous areas (places and regions) which espouse specifically defined characteristics. These two important features of geography help students learn about the world one area at a time.

The more generalized areas can be divided into specific **regions,** which are used to organize and identify the overall earth's surface. These regions exude unique and distinct attributes related to both the people who live there and the land forms that are present. For example, a region may be a combination of the parts of two continents, two or more countries, several cities, or extended territories.

Regions may be described according to three types:

- **Formal**—Defined in two ways through either common human features such as language, religion, nationality, and culture (example: the cattle ranches of Texas, and the Four Corners region) or common physical features such as climate, landform, or vegetation (example: the Mediterranean climate and the Wine country of California)
- **Functional**—Organized around a central hub with the surrounding areas connected to the center by transportation systems, communication systems, manufacturing, or trading. The most common functional region is a metropolitan area. For example: Sydney, Australia is linked by an established harbor area with commuting patterns, trade flows, TV and radio broadcasting, newspapers, travel, and goods commencing in this one region.
- **Perceptual**—Constructed around human feelings and attitudes of the area, these regions are defined by peoples' subjective images of an area and can be based on bias and stereotypes which may be incorrect or inappropriate. An example: The Appalachian Region of the United States, which is perceived as an isolated rural area, where the people are modest and promote oral traditions and strong religious beliefs.

According to the United States Embassy, there are six regions of the United States. **Regions** are cultural groupings not dependent upon government or political rule. They are formed by a common history and geography as well as shaped by economics, literature, and folklore. Within each region, there are unique demographics, dialects, language, and attitudes based upon heritage and geography. Several states comprise each region with special landforms, people, climates, and resources.

- **New England**—Connecticut (CT), Maine (ME), Massachusetts (MA), New Hampshire (NH), Rhode Island (RI), Vermont (VT)
- **Mid-Atlantic**—Delaware (DE), Maryland (MD), New Jersey (NJ), New York (NY), Pennsylvania (PA)
- **The South**—Alabama (AL), Arkansas (AR), Florida (FL), Georgia (GA), Kentucky (KY), Louisiana (LA), Mississippi (MS), North Carolina (NC), South Carolina (SC), Tennessee (TN), Virginia (VA), West Virginia (WV)
- **The Midwest**—Illinois (IL), Indiana (IN), Iowa (IA), Kansas (KS), Michigan (MI), Minnesota (MN), Missouri (MO), Nebraska (NE), North Dakota (ND), Ohio (OH), South Dakota (SD), Wisconsin (WI)
- **The Southwest**—Arizona, (AZ), New Mexico (NM), Oklahoma (OK), Texas (TX)
- **The West**—Alaska (AK), Colorado (CO), California (CA), Hawaii (HI), Idaho (ID), Montana (MT), Nevada (NV), Oregon (OR), Utah (UT), Washington (WA), Wyoming (WY)

Places are also large sections but they are human created areas which are a part of the earth's surface. Each place has a certain bordered area whether specific or imaginary and the place has been given meaning according to the humans who live there. A place may be a continent, an island, a country, a state, a territory, a city, a province, a neighborhood, or a village. Each place has a name and a boundary with a specific set of characteristics to help set it apart from other places. Places can change as a result of alterations in human characteristics as well as the restructuring of the physical characteristics of the area. Since places are human-generated, people gain a sense of self based on where they live.

The two types of characteristics used to define a place or region are based on physical and human traits. **Physical characteristics** can include water systems, animal life, plant life, landforms, and climate. **Human characteristics** can consist of values, religious beliefs, language systems, political structures, economic methods, and socioeconomic status.

Physical Characteristics

Physical characteristics include elements found on the earth in natural form such as animals, plants, and landforms. Following is a list of terms students need to know to study landforms.

- **archipelago**—A chain or group of islands in a sea or ocean
- **atoll**—A ring or partial ring of coral that forms an island in a sea or ocean
- **bluff**—A cliff
- **butte**—A high isolated flat top rock or hill with steep sides formed by the impact of tectonic plates
- **canyon**—Deep valley carved by a river with very steep sides includes a deep gorge with a running stream or river
- **cape**—A narrow pointed piece of land that juts out from a coastline into a body of water
- **cave**—A large hole or hollow in the ground or side of a mountain
- **cavern**—A cave especially large and dark
- **cliff**—A steep face of rock and soil
- **col**—A mountain pass; a depression in the summit line of a chain of mountains
- **continent**—A large mass of land, of which there are seven, that covers a specific area of the Earth's surface.
- **delta**—Silt, sand, and rock which is low watery land formed at the mouth of a river and often shaped like a triangle
- **desert**—A very dry barren area with little to no rainfall, mostly sand covered
- **dunes**—A hill or ridge made of sand and shaped by wind
- **equator**—An imaginary circle around the earth half way between the poles that divides north and south hemisphere
- **hill**—A raised area or mound of land smaller than a mountain
- **island**—A small area of land surrounded on all sides by water
- **isle**—A small island or peninsula
- **islet**—A small island usually isolated
- **isthmus**—A narrow strip of land connecting two larger pieces with water on two sides
- **mesa**—An isolated land or hill usually in a dry area with a flat top and steeply sloping sides
- **mountain**—A very tall high natural place on earth that rises above the surrounding levels of land
- **peninsula**—A body of land surrounded by water on three sides
- **pinnacle**—The highest point of rock, ice, or land
- **plains**—Flat lands with very small changes in elevation most often a level track of treeless country
- **plateau**—High flat area of land higher than the surrounding area
- **prairie**—Wide, flat area of land with grasses and a few trees
- **summit**—The highest point of a mountain
- **tundra**—A cold, treeless area, considered the coldest biome
- **valley**—A low place between mountains
- **volcano**—A mountainous vent of the earth's crust where lava, steam, or gases may erupt in intervals
- **wetland**—A damp area of land often with wet soil that is low in oxygen (swamp, riparian, bog, moor, peatland, mire, Delmarva, fen, marsh, slough)

Following is a list of terms students need to know about water:

- **bay**—An area of water partly enclosed by land and smaller than a gulf
- **canal**—An artificial waterway constructed for irrigation, drainage, river overflows, water supplies, communication, or navigation
- **channel**—A body of water that connects two larger bodies of water
- **cove**—A horseshoe shaped body of water along the coast surrounded by land formed of soft rock
- **estuary**—The location where a river meets the sea or ocean
- **fjord**—A long narrow sea inlet bordered by steep cliffs
- **geyser**—A natural hot spring (Old Faithful in the United States)
- **glacier**—A slow moving river of ice
- **gulf**—A part of ocean or sea that is partly surrounded by land, larger than a bay
- **lagoon**—A shallow body of water located alongside of a coast
- **marsh**—A freshwater, brackish water, or salt water wetland found along rivers, ponds, lakes, and coasts with plants growing out of the water
- **ocean**—A large body of salt water that surrounds a continent
- **pond**—Smaller than a lake it is surrounded by land on all sides
- **river**—A large flowing body of water that empties into a sea or ocean
- **sea**—A large body of salty water connected to an ocean, partly or completely surrounded by land
- **sound**—A wide inlet of sea or ocean that is parallel to the coastline; it separates coastlines from nearby islands
- **strait**—A narrow body of water that connects two larger bodies of water
- **swamp**—A type of freshwater wetland that consists of spongy, muddy land full of water
- **tributary**—A stream or river that flows into a larger waterway
- **waterfall**—The waterway created when a river falls off a cliff or falls steeply

Climate is the long-term pattern of weather in a specific area on earth. Climate determines what plants and animals will survive in a region. There are five primary climates:

1. **tropical**—High temperatures year round with large amounts of rain
2. **dry**—Limited rain with huge daily temperature ranges (semi-arid and arid)
3. **temperate**—Warm and dry summers with cool and wet winters
4. **cold (continental)**—Seasonal temperatures vary widely and overall precipitation is not high; found on the interior of large land masses
5. **polar**—Extremely cold with permanent ice and tundra present

A **biome** is a large geographical area of distinctive **plant life and animal life** groups, which have adapted to that particular environment. A region's biome is determined by climate and geography. There are nine major biomes:

Name	*Climate*	*Description*
Alpine	Snow, high winds, ice, and cold	Mountain regions around the world with an altitude of 10,000 feet or above and lies below the snow line of a mountain.
Chaparral (deserts)	Hot and dry (fire and droughts are common)	Located on most continents (west coast U.S., west coast of South America, Cape Town region of South Africa, western tip of Australia, and the coastal area of the Mediterranean) with flat plains, rocky hills, and mountain slopes.

Name	Climate	Description
Deciduous forest	Four separate seasons-spring summer, fall, and winter	Generally located near an ocean, which aids in the wind and precipitation. Found throughout the world (eastern half of North America, Central Europe, Southeast Asia, southern part of South America, southeast coast of Australia, all of New Zealand).
Desert	Two types: a) hot and dry with little rainfall b) extreme cold and snow, mostly barren	a) Located in the Tropic of Cancer and the Tropic of Capricorn b) Found near the Arctic
Grasslands	Two types: a) tall grass, humid, and very wet b) short grass, dry and hot summers, with cold winters	With large rolling terrains of grasses, flowers and herbs, also known as prairies; located in the interior of continents and in the middle latitudes.
Rainforest [Rainforests produce 40% of the earth's oxygen.]	Year round warmth and high rainfall levels	Almost all lie near the equator, located in northern South America, central Africa, and southern Asia
Savanna	Warm temperatures year round with two seasons a) winter (long and dry) b) summer (short and wet)	With rolling grasslands and scattered shrubs and isolated trees (near the equator and around the edges of tropical rainforests) found in Africa, (Serengeti Plains-Tanzania) South America, northern Australia, and India.
Taiga (boreal forest) [the largest biome in the world]	Winters are cold with much snow and summers are warm, humid, and rainy	With a needle leaf forest that is cold and barren, stretches across northern Europe to northern Asia and northern North America (Alaska and Canada), located at the top of the planet just below the tundra biome.
Tundra [world's coldest and driest biome]	Cold, dark winter with a soggy, warm summer in which the sun shines 24 hours each day	A vast and treeless area covering the northern part of the world from latitude 55 degrees to 70 degrees north; located in the northern hemisphere, the ground is permanently frozen and trees cannot grow.

Human Characteristics

Human characteristics can consist of values, religious beliefs, language systems, political structures, economic methods, and socioeconomic status. Human characteristics may be impacted by a particular area. In specific regions and places this may include the clothing, diet, shelter, transportation, monetary use, social organization, and employment of the people.

For example: The Inuit people of the Arctic North America (Canada, Greenland, and Alaska) traditionally are of short stature, and wear heavy clothing made of thick animal skins and furs. They live in homes made of ice blocks or stone covered with moss. They must hunt for food, and eat fish, seal, and walrus and they travel by kayak, dog sled, and by foot. The monetary system consists of the trading of furs, ivory, and arts and they have a social organization that is comprised of strong family structure of multiple generations in the same homes. Employment for the Inuits is limited.

Physical and Human Systems

A **system** is a set of connected parts functioning together. There are two systems that are critical to the earth: physical systems and human systems.

Physical Systems

Physical processes that shape the Earth's surface and interact with plant and animal life to create, maintain, and change the ecosystems. For example, changes in the earth's surface may occur due to these physical system conditions: tsunami, earthquake, volcano, typhoon, hurricane, water or wind erosion, and weathering.

There are five concepts that explain the interaction and impact of physical processes on the earth: system, boundary, force, state of equilibrium, and threshold (point of change). The interdependency of the physical systems and human systems affect the earth's environment.

For example, the Water Cycle (system) occurs between the hydrosphere and atmosphere (boundaries). Gravity (force) pulls the water down to the earth's surface. Friction (force) erodes the earth's surface causing new land forms. After the water evaporates it condensates in the atmosphere and is released back to the earth (equilibrium). When the condensation that saturates the atmosphere is too much, the atmosphere releases the water (threshold is reached). After the rain, the Cycle begins again (equilibrium).

An ecosystem is a key element in the viability of earth as a home. Populations of different plants and animals are called a community. When a community interacts with three components of a physical environment it is called an ecosystem, which is an interwoven infrastructure that produces and consumes energy.

The physical, chemical, and biological cycles, functioning within an ecosystem, form the different environments on earth. When changes occur to one ecosystem, other ecosystems may be drastically affected, positively or negatively. Ecosystems can maintain a natural stability and balance when left to function on their own. However, the balance of an ecosystem can be significantly changed by natural events, such as flooding or fire. When they are transformed, ecosystems can either recover and flourish or diminish and disappear.

The primary change an ecosystem experiences is through the impact of the human factor. For example: Glen Canyon Dam reduced the amount of water flow and sediment that the Colorado River carries, thus destroying the ability to arrive at the delta in the Gulf of California. Before the dam, the water was warm and muddy with bottom feeding fish. With the dam, the river is clear and cold with trout which caused the migration pattern of the bald eagle to change. Non-native species of animals and plants have been established which adversely affected native wildlife.

There are four physical processes that mold the shape of the earth's surface. The earth's landscape is constantly reshaped by this complex group of symbiotic physical processes.

- **Atmosphere** (air)—Climate and meteorology
- **Lithosphere** (ground and surface)—Rock formation, soil formation, plate tectonics, and erosion
- **Hydrosphere** (water)—Water cycle, currents of rivers, and tides of oceans
- **Biosphere** (life)—Ecosystems, habitats, and plant and animal realm

Human Systems

People affect the planet's topography, soils, vegetation, and ecosystems as well as the available natural resources. Humans rarely live isolated away from other humans. It is the human condition to organize groups of others to live and function within settlements. These settlements focus upon economic, communication, transportation, political, and cultural systems. Settlements are not the same around the world and represent cultural differences across the earth's surface. Spatial organization is essential to these units, the most familiar being a *city*.

There are three primary ways that humans impact earth:

1. by consuming natural resources and changing natural patterns
2. by building structures
3. by competing for control

This planet has a limited amount of resources that are not available on every continent. No one country is able to produce all of the resources necessary to survive. Due to this lack of natural resources, continents, regions, and countries must communicate and trade with one another. They promote the **consumption of natural resources** from one area to use in another **changing the natural patterns** on the earth. Meeting resource demands in the world causes a great toll on the physical systems.

As humans began to interact and live together, large settlements sprouted which led to the increased need for economic activity. These settlements were based on the specific region that was important to the natural resources, transportation or the cultural systems. **Building structures** were developed to establish settlements conducive to meeting human needs. This created a change in the earth's surface and impacted a variety of ecosystems. For example, the increase in construction causes deforestation, an overuse of a natural resource that destroys a natural land form (a forest area) and the entire ecosystem (deciduous forest-animals-lands-weather).

The third way that humans have influence upon the earth is through their participation in conflicts. As they **compete for control,** conflicts often revolve around the management of resources, the acquisition of land, the organization of transportation and migratory routes, and power over other people. These conflicts very often result in the division and the destruction of the earth's surface.

The results of these three methods of interaction are seen in

- Population growth
- Urbanization increases
- Consumption of natural resources (oil, gas, water, coal)
- Migration of humans (reshapes landscape and modifies cultures)

Environment and Society

An environment impacts and affects human society as well as has influences on itself. Natural disasters are not caused by humans but can have harmful consequences for humans and the environment. Volcanoes, earthquakes, floods, tsunamis, forest fires, tornadoes, insect plagues, and hurricanes are mostly unpreventable and unpredictable. The harmful impacts these natural disasters have upon humans can be lessened through improved construction design, public education, warning systems, and regulations of land usage. Environments have a carrying capacity. Each environment or region differs in its capacity to withstand and sustain use. Environments like ecosystems must have equilibrium and balance between consumption and production.

Humans play an essential role in the structure and transformation of the environment in which they live. Human interactions have intended and unintended repercussions on earth. This may include deforestation, loss of wildlife habitat, redirection of water to arid lands, transplantation of non-native vegetation, depletion of the ozone layer, and reduction of air pollution in some regions.

However, human survival depends upon the environment. Using and adapting the environment to meet human needs modifies nature's balance. The physical environments can bring prosperity to a region but also crisis and environmental conflicts. Making decisions based on these relationships will be developed through geographical knowledge of the opportunities and limitations of the earth's surface. For example: Damming a river for settlement and agriculture can bring homes, livelihood, and mobilization of populations to an area while at the same time alter the physical systems, wildlife, and vegetation. As population increases, the physical systems must cope with accommodating and absorbing human by-products (trash, pollution, waste, and overuse).

In order for humans to live in a variety of environments, technologies and adaptations must be employed. This also encompasses special organization of an environment which utilizes the resources provided by the earth. For example: New Orleans was originally developed on the natural levies or high ground along the Mississippi as a port city and a hub for the slave trade industry. It was originally established on high ground and inland to reduce its vulnerability to hurricanes and flooding. In the early twentieth century, engineers developed a pump system which allowed the city to further expand into the low lying areas, placing the city several feet below sea level.

Resources are **any** physical materials that make up part of the earth that people need, value, or want. The three basic resources are land, water, and air. Consumption and value of resources increase as humans seek them (oil, coal, metals, and minerals).

The results of how people and resources interact:

- Location of resources causes population movement and settlement
- Location of resources causes activity (employment and technology)
- Demand of resources causes economic development
- Consumption of resources are caused by wealth
- Lack of resources causes conflict

Following are three types of resources:

- **Renewable**—Resources that can replenish themselves after they are used (example: animals and plants)
- **Non-renewable**—Resources that can be cultivated and used only once (example: minerals, oil, natural gas, coal)
- **Flow**—Resources that must be used when, where, and as they occur (example: water, sunlight, wind)

Uses of Geography

Students must be able to use geography to analyze the causes, meanings, and influences of the physical and human events that take place on the earth's surface. The uses of geography imply that students have learned the content in such a way that they may apply their knowledge to the past, present, and future in relation to this subject.

World History

The national standard that is reflected in this section focuses on the theme of "time, continuity, and change," which aids students in gaining knowledge about the significance of place and they may develop a geographic perspective on the social aspects of the world. The Praxis II assesses specific content knowledge of a subject area. In this section of the guide the content includes information about the history of the world:

- Early and classical civilizations
- European and non-European civilizations
- Twentieth century developments and transformations
- European exploration

Use the historical timeline of events presented at the end of this book as a quick reference and study aid.

Prehistory and Early Civilizations

The prehistory period was a time of unwritten records, so knowledge of the time and the gains that were made are only evident through the existence of continued achievements.

Early civilizations brought the following:

- Basic achievements: wheel, alphabets, math, time measurements
- Art and architecture
- Alphabetic writing
- Defined religion
- Commonality and diversity (separate geographically and culturally but all developed trade, writing, cities)

Neolithic Revolution—10,000 B.C.E.

- Developed agricultural societies
- Rise in economic, political, and social organizations
- Began in Middle East and spread into India, North Africa, and Europe
- Gave humans the ability to remain settled permanently

Civilization—6,000 to 3,500 B.C.E.

- Developed alongside major rivers for agricultural production ("river-valley")
- Created basic set of tools
- Introduced writing, mathematics, and politics

Tigris-Euphrates Civilization—3,500 B.C.E.

- Originated in valley of Tigris and Euphrates rivers in Mesopotamia
- Started from scratch with no model or examples (Sumerian people)
- Created cuneiform (earliest form of writing)
- Developed astronomical sciences, religious beliefs
- Established political system with a king and organized the "city states"
- Improved agriculture through fertilizer
- Used silver to conduct trade and commercial trade
- Developed procedures for law courts and property rights
- Focused on a standard legal system

Egyptian Civilization—3,000 B.C.E.

- Emerged along Nile River in northern Africa
- Modeled trade on Mesopotamia
- Built impressive architectural structures (pyramid and sphinx)
- Produced mathematical achievements
- Ruled by Pharaohs
- Established effective government, defense, monetary, and transportation systems
- Centralized the community to meet needs of citizens

Indian and Chinese River Valley Civilization—2,500 B.C.E.

- Developed along the Indus River
- Prospered in urban civilizations
- Traded with Mesopotamia
- Developed well-defined alphabet and artistic forms
- Maintained and regulated irrigation system
- Created advanced engineering and architectural technology
- Developed impressive intellectual establishments
- Constructed massive tombs and palaces
- Invaded and destroyed by Indo-Europeans

Classical Civilizations

There were three recognized classical civilizations that contributed to the present day organization. Each of these major civilizations

- Expanded trade and provided other influences to areas outside their own borders
- Re-evaluated and restructured key institutions upon the decline and fall of empires or rules, policies, and values
- Created new and various religions
- Increased agricultural options and opportunities
- Extended the territories
- Integrated the people and societies (social cohesion)

The Civilization of China (1029 B.C.E.)

The China Civilization was the longest lasting civilization in world history and one of the most influential. They established the model for global trade. They had three dynastic cycles: Zhou, Qin, Han, all of which developed strong political institutions, created active economies and promoted central tax systems. As one dynasty began to falter, the next rose and developed through a prominent general, peasant or invader who took the lead role.

China Civilization Major Accomplishments	
Political	Began bureaucracy training
	Established a system of tax collection
	Promoted mandatory labor services
Religion and Culture	Developed Confucianism and Daoism
	Promoted personal ethics of acting with self-control, humility, and respect
	Embraced harmony in nature
	Stressed details in art and craftsmanship
	Encouraged geometrical and decorative arts
	Developed accurate calendars
	Studied mathematics of music
	Studied science for the practical uses
Economy and Society	Established three main social groups: upper class, laboring peasants, unskilled laborers
	Excelled in technologies
	Promoted trade as essential
	Encouraged tight-knit family unit
	Instilled patriarchal society (women subordinate to men) and demanded arranged marriages

The Civilization of Greece and Rome (800 B.C.E.)

Greece and Rome were both extremely powerful and influential throughout the world and they created a rise in city-states. The Greeks set up large expanding colonial and trading systems or webs. Rome gained territory and power by acquiring lesser developed cultures, causing it to grow into an empire.

Greece/Rome Civilization Accomplishments	
Political	Emphasized aristocratic rule but democratic elements also present
	Formed democracy in Greece
	Promoted intense loyalty to state
	Created uniform legal principles

(continued)

Greece/Rome Civilization Accomplishments *(continued)*	
Religion and Culture	Taught moderation and balance (Aristotle and Cicero)
	Taught followers to have conventional wisdom using rational inquiry (Socrates)
	Excelled in sculpture, architecture and plays (Greeks)
	Promoted geometry and anatomy (Greeks)
	Made the greatest contribution to science — engineering (Romans)
Economy and Society	Developed systems for agriculture (farming)
	Participated in extensive trade by using a structure of slavery
	Promoted a unified family structure
	Instilled a patriarchal community, although women could own property

The Civilization of India (600 B.C.E.)

India's civilization was shaped by its topography as it is partially separated from Asia by its northern mountain range. Most agricultural regions were along the Ganges and the Indus Rivers. Rule in India was sporadic and divided into widespread empires (invaders) to small kingdoms. During both types of rule, culture and economics advanced. The Mauryn and Gupta were the two most successful dynasties and managed completely by Indians. India's culture spread widely due to its extensive trading practices which allowed the open acceptance of outside influences. Buddhism crossed cultures and became a world religion.

India Civilization Accomplishments	
Political	Practiced diversity and regionalism (still today)
	Established caste system (social classes)
	Utilized a variety of languages
Religion and Culture	Promoted Hinduism and Buddhism
	Taught religion, medicine and architecture in universities
	Excelled in science and mathematics
	Developed concept of "zero," Arabic numerals, and decimal system
	Created lively and colorful art
Economy and Society	Established extensive internal and external successful trade practices
	Promoted patriarchal society (dominance over women)
	Emphasized family, group or government, not individuals
	Utilized a non-opposed social hierarchy (caste system)

The Rise of Non-European Civilizations

A selection of civilizations began during this period with the following five being the most prominent contributors to the present day.

- **Mayans**—Astronomy and mathematics, elaborate written language system, architecture, and art
- **Mongolians**—Nomadic society with law code unification, strong military, but transmitted diseases across continents
- **Muslim/Islam**—Islamic religion, chemistry advances, high-quality maps, influential arts and sciences
- **Africa**—Stateless societies
- **Inca**—Artistic pottery and clothing, metallurgy, architecture, irrigation, road systems, supreme military organization, and agriculture

The Rise and Expansion of Europe

Movement in Europe is associated with a shift in life from the Mediterranean to the Atlantic Coast. European countries crossed oceans in search of fertile lands to use for agriculture and for international trade. This curbed the conquest of the new world and the discovery of America to occur. The establishment and colonization of new areas overseas caused migration of populations. As expansion increased improvements were made in communications and means of transportation.

United States History

The national standard that is reflected in this section focuses on the theme of "time, continuity, and change" which aids students in gaining knowledge about the significance of place and they may develop a geographic perspective on the social aspects of the world. The Praxis II tests specific content knowledge of a subject area. In this section of the guide the content includes information about the history of the United States.

European Exploration and Colonization

There were a variety of reasons that early settlers came to the United States looking for a new homeland; to escape religious persecution, to develop business ventures, to promote personal/economic gain, and for political reasons. Those people who made the pilgrimage from England to the new land brought with them horses, cattle, hogs, and diseases.

English investors often financed the building of a colony for profit; however, when profits were slow to return or did not return at all, investors often pulled out of the venture leaving colonists to build their own lives, communities and economies.

Most settlers and colonists did not rely upon imports but were instead self-sufficient. They were proficient in fur trading, trapping, fishing and farming. By the eighteenth century, the colonists had created regional patterns in colonial development:

- New England—Relied on ship building, sailing, and fishing
- Maryland, Virginia, South Carolina, and North Carolina—Grew tobacco, rice, and indigo
- New York, Pennsylvania, New Jersey, and Delaware—Shipped crops and traded furs

The colonists set high standards of living for themselves which surpassed the standards of living in England. Entrepreneurship was highly popular in this New World. By 1770 the colonies were economically and politically ready to become a self-sufficient entity. Disputes arose with England over taxation and control.

Mounting frustrations and quarrels grew and blossomed into turmoil. In 1775, the American Revolution began with the colonists rallying "unalienable rights to life, liberty, and property" (John Locke's *2nd Treatise on Civil Government*).

The **13 Colonies** began with the founding of Jamestown (1607); Plymouth (1620); and Massachusetts (1629). In 1773, these were the established **13 Colonies**: New Hampshire, Massachusetts, Rhode Island, Connecticut, New York, New Jersey, Pennsylvania, Delaware, Maryland, Virginia, North Carolina, South Carolina, and Georgia.

Following is a list of famous explorers with which all students should be familiar:

- **1450–1499, John Cabot**—English explorer and navigator who explored the Canadian coastline looking for a north west passage to Asia.
- **1451–1506, Christopher Columbus**—Italian explorer took a voyage across Atlantic Ocean in 1492 hoping to find a route to India. He sailed his three ships, the Nina, Pinta, and Santa Maria, and discovered North America.
- **1454–1512, Amerigo Vespucci**—Italian explorer was the first person to realize that the Americas were separate from Asia. He was the first person to state that the Americas were not the East Indies and in 1507 a map maker named the Americas after him.

- **1458–1521, Juan Ponce de Leon**—Spanish explorer and soldier who discovered the Gulf stream and was the first European to set foot in Florida, while searching for the Fountain of Youth.

- **1485–1547, Hernan Cortez**—Spanish conquistador who wiped out the Aztec Empire and claimed Mexico for Spain.

- **1491–1557, Jacque Cartier**—French explorer who discovered Canada. He paved the way for French exploration of North America.

- **1496–1542, Fernando De Soto**—Spanish explorer who explored Florida and the Southeastern United States. He is credited with the discovery of the Mississippi River.

- **1510–1554, Francisco Vasquez de Coronado**—Spanish conquistador who explored the American Southwest (AZ, NM, TX, OK, KS). He killed many Native Americans because they would not convert to Christianity.

- **1552–1618, Sir Walter Raleigh**—British explorer, poet, historian, and soldier who established English colonies in the Americas. He named the state of Virginia after Queen Elizabeth.

- **1565–1611, Henry Hudson**—English explorer who explored the Arctic Ocean and northeastern North America. The Hudson River, the Hudson Strait, and the Hudson Bay were named after him and he is credited with founding New York.

- **1580–1631, John Smith**—Captain in English military who founded Jamestown, Virginia. He explored Chesapeake Bay and the New England coast.

- **1681–1741, Vitus Bering**—Dutch explorer who explored Alaska and Siberia. The Bering Strait bears his name.

- **1728–1779, Captain James Cook**—British explorer and astronomer who led expeditions to the Pacific Ocean, Antarctica, the Arctic, and around the world. He is credited with discovering Hawaii.

- **1755–1806, Robert Gray**—The first American-born explorer to circumnavigate the globe. He also explored the northwestern United States and helped obtain the Oregon territory.

- **1734–1820, Daniel Boone**—American pioneer, explorer, trapper, mountain man, and soldier who founded the first U.S. settlement west of the Appalachian Mountains. He also explored the Kentucky wilderness.

- **1774–1809, Merriweather Lewis and 1770–1838 William Clark**—They explored and mapped the American west. They traveled through the Louisiana Territory (Missouri to Oregon Coast) and were led by Sacagawea.

- **1798–1831, Jedediah Smith**—American mountain man, hunter, and fur trapper who was the first person to travel from New York to California through the Rocky Mountains and the Mohave Desert. He was also the first person to cross the Great Basin Desert via the Sierra Nevada Mountains and the Great Salt Lake.

- **1809–1868, Kit Carson**—American explorer, guide, trapper, and soldier who explored the southwest and western United States with John Fremont. In 1863 Carson destroyed the Navajo settlement in Canyon De Chelley and forced Native Americans on the "long walk."

American Revolution and the Founding of the Nation

The founding of the nation took shape in the last half of the eighteenth century. Prior to that, settlers and colonists were under English rule (Great Britain) rather than being an autonomous society.

In 1775, the 13 British colonies in North America rebelled against the British rule because the people did not want continued taxation and government rule from England. Britain imposed a series of taxes upon the colonies and the colonists had no representation in the British parliament. The British colonists did not believe that Great Britain represented their needs nor could govern them from across the ocean.

As frustrations mounted, and tensions grew, colonists began forming militia in preparation for the impending fight for freedom. The American Revolution was triggered by an event that occurred in April, 1775. The government of England sent soldiers to the colonies to maintain order and gain control. British soldiers collided with colonial militiamen in Concord, Massachusetts during a raid on a colonial arms depot. When a shot was fired, the eight year Revolutionary

War began. The American Revolution, which lasted from 1775–1783, was a civil war between the Kingdom of Great Britain and the 13 British colonies for their independence.

When foreign nations (France, Spain, and the Dutch Republic) became allies with the revolutionaries, the war became an international conflict. The writing of the Declaration of Independence, in 1776, was a turning point in the formation of the nation. The Treaty of Paris, signed in 1783, ended the war and recognized the sovereignty and the independence of the United States of America and by 1787, the American government was formalized by the development of the U.S. Constitution.

Major Battles of American Revolution (The America War of Independence)

- Battle of Lexington and Concord, April 9, 1775
- Battle of Bunker Hill, June 17, 1775
- Battle of Princeton, January 2, 1776
- Battle of Brandywine, September 11, 1777
- Battle of Yorktown, October 19, 1781

Important Government Actions

- **1765, Stamp Act**—First direct tax placed on the colonies and all printed media were required to have stamps
- **1767, Townshend Act**—Placed a tax on essential goods (paper, glass, tea)
- **1773, Tea Act**—Tax break to East India Company
- **1773, Boston Tea Party**—A protest of the Tea Act by American colonists
- **1774, Intolerable Acts**—Massachusetts Government Act; Administration of Justice Act, Boston Port Act; Quartering Act
- **1776, The Declaration of Independence**—Adopted by a 13 colony vote, which led to an alliance with France, followed by alliances with Spain and the Dutch province

Important Documents in United States History

- **The Magna Carta (1215)**—The clauses of this document (63 total) explained and restricted the rights of the monarch.
- **The Mayflower Compact (1620)**—This compact, signed en route on the Mayflower, established a temporary majority-rule government for the Pilgrims.
- **The Declaration of Independence (1776)**—The principles set forth in this document justified the separation of the 13 American colonies from Great Britain and provided responsibilities to individuals, with a government ruled by the people.
- **Articles of Confederation (1781)**—The first constitution of the 13 American states, was later replaced in 1789 by the Constitution of the United States.
- **The Federalist Papers (1787–1788)**—This group of 85 articles was published in the New York newspapers to influence the decision to ratify the Constitution and even today help to explain the intent of the Constitution.
- **The U.S. Constitution (1787)**—The document that established the basic principles of the American government.
- **Emancipation Proclamation (1865)**—Issued during the Civil War, President Lincoln ended slavery in the Confederate states.
- **The Pledge of Allegiance (1892)**—An oath of confirmation, written by Francis Bellamy, to support the nation.

United States Presidents			
1789–1797	George Washington	1889–1893	Benjamin Harrison
1797–1801	John Adams	1893–1897	Grover Cleveland
1801–1809	Thomas Jefferson	1897–1901	William McKinley
1809–1817	James Madison	1901–1909	Theodore Roosevelt
1817–1825	James Monroe	1909–1913	William Taft
1825–1829	John Quincy Adams	1913–1921	Woodrow Wilson
1829–1837	Andrew Jackson	1921–1923	Warren Harding
1837–1841	Martin Van Buren	1923–1929	Calvin Coolidge
1841	William Harrison	1929–1933	Herbert Hoover
1841–1845	John Tyler	1933–1945	Franklin D. Roosevelt
1845–1849	James Knox Polk	1945–1953	Harry S. Truman
1849–1850	Zachary Taylor	1953–1961	Dwight D. Eisenhower
1850–1853	Millard Fillmore	1961–1963	John F. Kennedy
1853–1857	Franklin Pierce	1963–1969	Lyndon B. Johnson
1857–1861	James Buchanan	1969–1974	Richard Nixon
1861–1865	Abraham Lincoln	1974–1977	Gerald Ford
1865–1869	Andrew Johnson	1977–1981	James Carter
1869–1877	Ulysses S. Grant	1981–1989	Ronald Reagen
1877–1881	Rutherford B. Hayes	1989–1993	George H.W. Bush
1881	James Garfield	1993–2001	William (Bill) Clinton
1881–1885	Chester Arthur	2001–2009	George W. Bush
1885–1889	Grover Cleveland	2009–	Barack H. Obama

Growth and Expansion of the Republic

The proclamation of 1763 restricted American movement across the Appalachian Mountains. Colonists ignored this and traveled westward. This led to expansion of the United States and further migration across North America. The original territorial boundaries of the United States were between Canada (north), Florida (south and controlled by Spain), Atlantic Ocean (east), and the Mississippi River (west). These boundaries were established with Great Britain and defined by the Treaties of November 30, 1782 and September 3, 1783.

Difficulty arose when the colonies began claiming the unoccupied territory between the original 13 colonies and the Mississippi River. Due to conflicting claims and the realization of impending conflict the Continental Congress passed a resolution (1779) recommending the territories in dispute be ceded to the government. This land included the total area that is now known as Ohio, Indiana, Illinois, Michigan, Wisconsin, Minnesota, Alabama, and Mississippi. When this was one large territory, the government held title to the lands and administered the laws upon them.

The original colonial territories began relinquishing boundary lines and control so new states could form. Once this occurred, the vast area west of the colonies to the border of the Mississippi River began forming as states. The majority of the remaining states had their boundaries defined in the Enabling Acts (an act of Congress) which admitted them into the Union.

After exploration moved westward, the remaining land areas were divided into states and ratified and admitted into the Union. Additions to the original territory such as the Louisiana Purchase (from France–1803), the Purchase of Florida (from Spain–1819), the Annexation of Texas (1845), the acquisition of the Oregon Territory (1846), the Mexican Cession (1848), the Gadsden Purchase (from Mexico-1853), the purchase of Alaska (from Russia–1867), and the Annexation of Hawaii (1898) all brought forth the expansion of our country to its present boundaries.

Wars

- **American-Indian Wars (1587–1890)**—The struggles in which European settlers and the colonies defeated Native Americans and tribes to expand their ownership of land resulted in the placement and confinement of Native Americans on reservations.

- **American Revolution (1775–1783)**—The struggle of how the United States won independence from Great Britain.

- **War of 1812 (1812–1814)**—Congress declared war upon Britain which resulted in increased national patriotism, united the states into one nation, built confidence in U.S. military strength, and brought forth the Star Spangled Banner.

- **Civil War (1861 to 1865)**—The two factions of the new nation, the North (Union) and the slave-owning states of the South (Confederacy), fought until the succession of the south was squelched, slavery was abolished, the federal government gained great power and united the country.

- **World War I (1914–1918)**—Great Britain, France, Russia, Belgium, Italy, Japan, the United States, and other allies defeated Germany, Austria-Hungary, Turkey, and Bulgaria overthrew four empires (German Empire, Hapsburg Empire, Turkish Empire, Russian Empire) which resulted in the birth of seven new nations.

- **World War II (1939 to 1945)**—The struggle in which Great Britain, France, the Soviet Union, the United States, China, and other allies defeated Germany, Italy, and Japan. Two atomic bombs were dropped to end the war (Hiroshima and Nagasaki). Of the many outcomes of the war there are a few to note: Germany was divided into 4 parts and controlled by the allied powers, geopolitical power shifted away from western and central Europe, United States and Russia became known internationally as the superpowers, new technologies appeared (computer, jet engine, nuclear fission), and many global organizations sprouted (United Nations, World Bank, World Trade Organization, International Monetary Fund).

- **The Korean War (1950–1953)**—The struggle between North Korea (communist) aided by China and USSR, and South Korea (non-communists) aided by the United States, Britain, and the UN, resulted in the same boundaries between the North and South.

- **The Vietnam War (1956–1975)**—A long conflict in which North Vietnam (communist) was supported by China and the Soviet Union and tried to take over South Vietnam (non-communist), supported by the United States which resulted in the take over of South Vietnam implementing a socialist republic where the communist party now governs.

- **Persian Gulf War (1990–1991)**—The United States led a coalition of forces and destroyed much of Iraq's military forces, resulting in driving out the Iraqi army from Kuwait.

- **The Iraq War (2003–present)**—The struggle in which the United States and Great Britain led a coalition of forces against Iraq to expel Saddam Hussein.

Twentieth Century Developments and Transformations

The twentieth century has provided humankind with many advancements and technologies. From radios to cell phones to artificial intelligence, the developments of the twentieth century have been overwhelming. These developments and technologies have both improved our lives and placed lives in peril.

Developments of the Common Era January 1, 1901 to December 31, 2000			
Automobile	Radio	Missiles	Personal computer
Transistor	Laser	Electric refrigeration	Chemical weapons
Television	Wireless technology	Manned space flight	Quantum Physics
Airplane	Radar	Magnetic tape	Theory of Relativity
Plastics	Air conditioning	Global networks	Xerography
Atomic bomb	Artificial intelligence	Fiber optics	Internet

Political Science

The primary goal of political science programs is to promote citizenship education, so students may make informed decisions that improve and enhance society. The National Standards for Civics and Government suggest five elements of citizen education which form the basic content knowledge for political science that will be assessed:

- The nature and purpose of government
- The forms of government
- The United States Constitution
- The rights and responsibilities of citizens
- State and local government

The national standards reflected in this section focus on the themes of "power, authority, and governance" and "civic ideals and practices" which provides students with knowledge about the forms of government and the importance of community participation in a society.

The Nature and Purpose of Government

Formal governments have been around for more than 5,000 years and the aspects of their function are about the same as those today. Governments were established to protect individual's liberties, properties, and lives from other people. Societies developed as people joined together to establish consistent ways to protect their rights as human beings.

Therefore, the most important function of the government is to provide laws or rules. These are essential to prevent conflicts between individuals, and the groups who reside in the same country or land. Not only does the government make the laws but it must enforce them. The government also establishes procedures to settle conflicts and some create government bodies to manage the people. By using established laws the government can focus on order and provide security for its people, with the ultimate goal being peace between and among its constituents.

Depending on the size of a country or state, there may be several levels of government, which might include governments of local, county, district, state, regional, and national origin. Each provides services and order critical to its area and its people.

The Forms of Government

The form of the United States government is a democracy. However, there are many other forms of government unlike that of the United States throughout the world. The main systems of government include the following:

Systems	Description	Examples
Anarchism	A form of government in which the people hold beliefs and attitudes that reject compulsory government.	Isocracy and Tribalism

(continued)

Systems	Description	Examples
Authoritarianism	A form of government that demonstrates strict control and may coerce and use oppressive measures to ensure obedience.	Autocracy, Communism, Oligarchy, Aristocracy, Dictatorship, Monarchy, Fascism, and Tyranny
Democracy	A form of government in which the people hold certain liberties and freedoms and retain the power and rule either directly or through representatives.	Republicism, Parliamentary system, and Democratic Socialism

Within these main types of government there are a variety of other more specific ruling entities. There is no inclusive list of the many forms of government, as there may be new types developing as countries change and borders are moved. This list describes the basic guidelines of rule. A government may have one or more types of rule as its basis. For example, the United States is considered a democratic republic.

Anarchy	Rule by no one
Autocracy	Rule by one
Oligarchy	Rule by minority
Republic	Rule by law
Democracy	Rule by majority
Socialism	Rule by all

These are just a few specific forms of government that are practiced around the world. (This is not a comprehensive or complete list.)

- **Communism**—A type of government in which the state designs and controls the economy under the power of an authoritarian party and eliminates private ownership of property or individual capital in order to create a classless society where all goods are shared equally by all individuals.

- **Dictatorship**—A type of government in which a single ruler or small group have absolute power, not restricted by constitution or law, where citizens have no choice in the leadership.

- **Monarchy**—A type of government in which supreme and absolute power resides in the hands of a single monarch who rules over the lands for life through hereditary right.

- **Theocracy**—A type of government in which a Deity is the ruler and the laws are interpreted by religious clergy.

- **Totalitarian**—A type of government that controls all political aspects, economic matters, attitudes, values, and beliefs of the population keeping the individuals subordinate to the state.

The U.S. Constitution

The U.S. Constitution was written by the "founding fathers" in order to avoid the power of one single figure and to create a strong centralized government away from Great Britain. The **founding fathers** were delegates to the Constitutional Convention in Philadelphia in 1787. These writers utilized the concept of the separation of powers and created three branches of government, each with their own purpose and responsibilities. The writing of the Constitution, the world's oldest constitution, was completed by 1787.

These three branches work together, creating a system of checks and balances, ensuring that the rights of citizens and the management of the country are all considered in the decisions. The three branches of government are as follows:

- **Executive**—This branch of the Government ensures that the laws of the United States are followed. The head of the executive branch is the President of the United States who also commands the military. The President has assistance from the Vice President, Cabinet members, Department members, and agencies all of whom help in carrying out policy and providing special services.

- **Legislative**—This branch of government is comprised of Congress and government agencies that provide support. Congress has the power to make laws for the United States and is divided into two parts: House of Representatives and Senate. The Senate allows for two representatives of each state and the House permits representatives from the states based on population, with 435 seats.

- **Judicial**—This branch of government contains the court system. The highest court in the land is the Supreme Court and included in the system are the Federal courts. The Courts must ensure that the rules of the Constitution are upheld, so members of the Courts interpret the meanings of laws, and how they should be applied.

The components of the U.S. Constitution include a preamble, seven original articles, twenty-seven amendments, and certification of the enactment.

The Preamble

"We the People of the United States, in Order to form a more perfect Union, establish Justice, insure domestic Tranquility, provide for the common defense, promote the general Welfare, and secure the Blessings of Liberty to ourselves and our Posterity, do ordain and establish this Constitution for the United States of America."

The Bill of Rights

The first 10 amendments ratified in 1791 are considered the "Bill of Rights." It outlines the rights of citizens and visitors, according to the law of the land, expressing the freedoms and culture of this country.

An **amendment** is a modification, addition, or deletion of a law or bill; amendments are incorporated into the meaning of the Constitution. The first 10 amendments are listed here.

Amendment 1—Freedom of Religion, Press, Expression

Amendment 2—Right to Bear Arms

Amendment 3—Quartering of Soldiers

Amendment 4—Search and Seizure

Amendment 5—Trial and Punishment, Compensation for Takings

Amendment 6—Right to Speedy Trial, Confrontation of Witnesses

Amendment 7—Trial by Jury in Civil Cases

Amendment 8—Cruel and Unusual Punishment

Amendment 9—Construction of Constitution

Amendment 10—Powers of the States and People: The Body of the Constitution

When this country broke away from the rule of England, and established the first 13 colonies, the people wanted order and freedom from strict monarch rule, so they created the Articles of Confederation (1777–1787). They wrote a document outlining the rights and responsibilities later known as the Constitution, which was majority ratified and implemented by 1788. It outlines the three branches of government, their powers and the rights of its citizens.

The seven articles (principles) of the Constitution are as follows:

1. Legislative Power (Popular Sovereignty)
2. Executive Power (Republicanism)
3. Judicial Power (Federalism)
4. States' Powers and Limits (Separation of Powers)
5. The Process of Amendments (Checks and Balances)
6. Federal Powers (Limited Government)
7. Ratification (Individual Rights)

The Rights and Responsibilities of Citizens

The first founding document of the United States of America that dissolved any connection of the 13 colonies with Great Britain is the **Declaration of Independence,** adopted on July 4, 1776 (now called Independence Day). It led to the development of the Articles of Confederation and later the U.S. Constitution, both of which serve to outline the rights and responsibilities of U.S. citizens. The Constitutional Amendments further outline the various rights of citizens. In the Gettysburg Address of 1863, the United States President Abraham Lincoln summarized the basic premise of the Declaration: "Four score and seven years ago our fathers brought forth on this continent, a new nation, conceived in liberty, and dedicated to the proposition that all men are created equal."

The United States federal system of government and democracy focuses on the right to life, liberty and the pursuit of happiness; promoting equal opportunities; addressing the common good; and seeking truth and justice. In the democratic society, the government has limited powers. It is the people who have the ultimate authority which is exercised through elections and government representation, chosen by the people. Final decisions are based on majority rule.

Citizenship is defined as the way we act and live our lives. It includes how an individual makes decisions that may affect others and how individuals demonstrate their concern about the community and nation. The two social science disciplines included in citizenship education are Civics and Government. Civics portrays the rights and responsibilities of people and their relationship toward others and the government. Information about the political and legislative institutions of a certain place is included in instruction about government.

Three components are important to citizenship education:

- **Content**—Knowledge that helps promote good citizenship
- **Values**—Set standards of human behavior
- **Processes**—The practice of citizenship through activities and opportunities

State and Local Government

After the victory of independence resulting from the Revolutionary War, the 13 colonies became 13 states and formed a league in which they could work together. This system of cooperation between states was outlined and established through the Articles of Confederation. In this type of government, the national body was very weak and retained little power, whereas the individual states held the majority of the power. However, this lack of unity in overall governing left the nation weak and non-cohesive, so the Founding Fathers wrote the Constitution to replace the Articles of Confederation. The Constitution divided the power between the national government and the state governments, outlining responsibilities of each and creating a federalist system.

Federalism—The sharing of power between the national government and the individual state governments.

State governments have their own Constitution, similar to the U.S. Constitution, but the laws of the individual states cannot conflict with the federal Constitution. Every state constitution reflects its individual history, needs, philosophy, and geography and is uniquely different from all other states.

When the United States first formed it embraced the type of governing called **dual federalism**. Dual federalism is when the states govern the people directly and the national government governs foreign affairs. This type of governing eventually led to the Civil War as there was a disagreement as to division of powers. As a direct result of the Civil War a series of Amendments were passed which outlined the federal government's authority over social and economic policy and the protection of citizen rights. These included the 13th, 14th, and 15th Amendments.

Dual federalism continued until the Great Depression of 1930. During this time, states were ill equipped and unable to deal with the economic troubles within the country. President Roosevelt's *New Deal* brought forth a system of cooperative federalism in which national, state, and local governments would work together on programs rather than assigning specific functions to each level.

Distribution of Power in the United States		
National Government	*Both (State and National)*	*State Government*
Declares war	Create and enforce laws	Oversees export and import within its boundaries
Manages foreign relations	Set taxes	Manages public health and safety
Oversees international, foreign, and interstate trade	Borrow money	Ratifies amendments
Mints money in a treasury		

The interaction between state, local, and national governments is complex, yet clearly and concisely outlined in the Constitution in order to maintain a productive and democratic country.

Students should be familiar with the following political science terms:

- **amend**—To change the wording or meaning of a motion, bill, constitution, and so on by formal procedure.
- **alien**—Resident of another country who has not yet become a citizen of the country where s/he now lives.
- **census**—Periodic, official count of the number of persons living in a country.
- **checks and balances**—Limits imposed on all branches of government by giving each the right to amend acts of the other branches.
- **citizen**—Member of a state or nation who owes allegiance to its government and is entitled to its protection.
- **congressional district**—Division or part of a state; each district elects one person to the House of Representatives.
- **constituent**—Person who is represented by an elected official.
- **civil**—Relating to citizens, occurring within the community.
- **delegate**—Person who acts for or represents another or others.
- **immigrant**—Person who moves from one country to another to live permanently.
- **indictment**—Formal accusation through a legal process.
- **national**—Citizen of a nation who is entitled to its protection.
- **separation of powers**—System of dividing the powers and duties of a government into different branches.
- **veto**—Cancel or postpone a decision, bill, and so on.

Anthropology, Sociology, and Psychology

The Praxis II exam tests specific content knowledge of this subject area according to

- Social institutions and cultural changes
- Socialization and acculturation
- Human growth and development

The national standards that are reflected in this section focus on the themes of "culture," "individual development and identity," "individuals, groups, and institutions," and "global connections," which guides students in learning about the characteristics of cultures around the world, how cultures shape personal identity, what institutions influence lives, and how global connections affect societies.

The study of anthropology is divided into two major divisions:

- **Physical anthropology**—The study of physical characteristics and differences between groups of people.
- **Cultural anthropology**—The study and comparison of ancient and modern cultures and groups of people, which should include:
  - Food getting structures
  - Economic systems
  - Social stratification

143

- Patterns of residence
- Political organizations
- Religions
- Arts

Social Stratification and Cultural Changes

Social stratification is the distribution of rights and obligations, power and authority, and goods and services within a society. There are five main topics of social stratification:

1. **Family**—Families exist in every society in every part of the world in one form or another. Every human being is or was a member of a family. There are many different definitions of a family (biological, psychological, and social). Biologically, everyone has a mother and a father. Psychologically, people can identify with someone they define as a parent (grandparent, uncle, aunt, brother, or sister). Socially, people can identify with other individuals or other groups of people as a "family" such as a friend or work place peers. There are a variety of family types, with the most common being the *nuclear family* which consists of any two or more people related to each other by blood marriage or adoption and who share a common residence. Anthropologists and sociologists depict families as structural institutions that exist to help the continuation of a society.

2. **Norms**—The general rules by which a society exists. These define the patterns and structures of family, kinship, and marriage within a society.

3. **Marriage**—All societies recognize and permit marriage in one form or another. The most predominant form of marriage in the world is monogamy (exclusive relationship between two people), and it is a universally recognized norm.

4. **Residence**—When people marry, they decide where to live, which is dependent upon the societal norms and conforms to one of three patterns.
   - **Neo-local**—Couples choose a place of residence separate from either set of parents (most common in the West).
   - **Matrilocal (Uxorilocal)**—The couple lives with or near the family of the wife. For example, Hopi, Pueblo, Amazon, !Kung.
   - **Patrilocal (Virilocal)**—The couple lives with or near the family of the husband. For example, Turkey, Igbo.

5. **Authority**—Rules of authority are often dependent on gender in most societies and the two different types of authority include:
   - **Patriarchal**—The male has the power and authority demonstrated in personal as well as governmental law. For example, Japan, Iran, Thailand.
   - **Matriarchal**—The female has power and authority, often times being the oldest maternal figure. For example, Mosuo of China, Nair of South India, Wemale of Seram.

There are also three types of societies based on authority:

1. **Egalitarian**—No one social group has greater access to economic resources, power, or prominence than another. Economic differences hold no bearing upon prominence within the society. For example, a cook and a doctor have equal access to societal possessions.

2. **Rank**—Economic resources and power are equal to all social groups, but prominence is unequally distributed. Often a ruler or chief maintain the highest prominence and status.

3. **Class**—There is unequal distribution in economic resources, power and prominence among social groups. It can be a closed system (no ability to move into a higher rank) or an open system (the ability to move into a higher rank).

Socialization and Acculturation

- **Socialization**—The acceptance and practice of the behavior patterns of a culture (following the norms).
- **Acculturation**—The modification and adaptation of an individual or a group as a result of contact or interaction with another culture. It can also be the manner by which an individual learns a culture.
- **Stereotypes**—Unsophisticated and strongly held beliefs about the characteristics of a group of people.

Human Development and Behavior

The three main psychological models of development are as follows:

1. **Piaget**—He believed there are structural schemas in which we fit our experiences through assimilation.

   sensori-motor (birth–2 yrs.) Experience through action; grabbing, looking, touching.

   pre-operational (2–7 yrs.) Thinking is concrete, egocentric, and language develops.

   concrete operations (7–11 yrs.) Thinking is logical, mathematics develops, classification of objects begins.

   formal operational (12 yrs. and above) Thinking can handle abstract concepts.

2. **Freud**—His theory revolved around sexual development and reflects five stages:

   oral (infancy)

   anal (1 to 3 yrs.)

   phallic (3 to 5 yrs.)

   latency (6 to puberty)

   genital (after puberty)

3. **Erikson**—He further developed Freud's theories into 8 "either/or" stages.

   Trust versus Mistrust (birth to 1.5 yrs.)

   Autonomy versus Self-Doubt (1.5 yrs. to 3)

   Initiative versus Guilt (3–6 yrs.)

   Competence versus Inferiority (6-puberty)

   Identity versus Role Confusion (adolescence)

   Intimacy versus Isolation (early adult)

   Generativity versus Stagnation (middle adult)

   Ego-Integrity versus Despair (later adult)

Anthropology has helped establish that gender or sexual inequality is not a biological fact but rather a cultural and societal one. Gender role is a task or activity that a culture or society assigns to the different sexes.

Economics

Economics is one of the social sciences and is defined as the study of the production, distribution, and consumption of goods and services. Together, three organizations promote economic education and have developed national content standards for economics: the National Council on Economic Education, the Foundation for Teaching Economics, and the National Association of Economic Educators.

An economic system is the organization in which a state or nation allocates resources or apportions goods and services to the community. The society must follow the set principles and abide by guidelines pertaining to economic resources.

The following basic economics content knowledge will be assessed on the Praxis II:

- Key terms and major concepts of the economic market
- Economic effects on population and resources
- Impact on individuals and the government
- Economic systems
- Economic influences on technological developments
- International economics

Key Terms and Major Concepts

The National Content Standards in Economics recommends 20 standards with benchmarks for grades 4, 8, and 12. These are summarized here as a short list.

- Resources are limited, so individuals must make choices.
- Costs and benefits must be analyzed when making economic decisions.
- Economic systems are complex and involve several institutions.
- Economic systems have a specific nature.
- Supply and demand plays a major role in the market.
- Profits, incentives, and prices support the market system.
- Private and public economic sectors are different.
- Employment opportunities are specialized.
- Exchange or money use has various forms.
- Income is determined by market conditions.
- Investment and entrepreneurship are complex topics.
- Government policy affects a market system.

Economic theories include the following:

- **Anarchist**—There is no established control or guidelines.
- **Capitalism**—Property is privately owned and goods are privately produced.
- **Communist**—Endorses the establishment of society based on common ownership of the means of production.
- **Industrialism**—Uses large industries rather than agriculture or craftsmanship to create a system.
- **Laissez-faire**—Promotes private production to maintain freedom, security, and property rights.
- **Mercantilism**—Defends that a nation must depend on its capital and that the world market is unchangeable.
- **Socialist**—System of social control regarding property and income rather than individual control.

Students should be familiar with the following economic terms:

- **budget**—Management of current money that requires choices and analysis of the situation
- **black economy**—An unreported sector of the primary economic system in which transactions are handled in cash only
- **consumption**—The use of resources
- **depression**—A long period of financial and industrial decline
- **fiscal policy**—A way to regulate the economic activity
- **inflation**—Increase in overall prices for products and services
- **microeconomics**—How specific markets function involving consumers and businesses
- **macroeconomics**—How the national economics function (income, consumption, and investment)
- **monetary policy**—The way government controls the money supply, such as interest rates
- **recession**—Period of slow economic growth plagued with high unemployment and minimal spending
- **supply and demand**—The amount of goods and services is directly related to the request for them (When the request (demand) goes up, the amount (supply) must go up, and therefore, the price goes up.)
- **value**—The basis for economics and used to describe and measure what is occurring in the market

The Individual and the Market

The *basic law of economics* is that of supply and demand, and individuals must often make choices based on the availability of the resources and their ability to obtain them.

Every individual is affected by economics on a daily basis. Learning economics helps an individual better understand their role in relation to local, state, nation and international policies. Citizens become better informed of issues, more involved in changes, and could be influenced to vote.

Economic decisions are made by individuals based on the costs and benefits to them personally. Choices may be restricted or affected by laws and regulations. Individuals have a "say" in the amount of products produced and the costs, which is based on their rate of spending and desire for the items. This creates competition and promotes the issue of supply and demand.

Effect on Population and Resources

A free market economy, like that of the United States, is based on two premises, that of **competition** and **supply and demand.** This type of economy allows the businesses and consumers to decide what should be produced, what employees should be paid, how much product or service should cost, and how much should be provided for the population.

According to the United Nations, it reports that the global population will be greatly reduced and the aged population will increase. These two factors will cause for change in the culture, health care systems, and economic systems of this nation. They estimate that the rising numbers of people, primarily in underdeveloped countries, will cause a drastic drain on resources. The acceleration of resource usage and the impact on the environment are primarily the result of the growing populations in China and India and our natural resources are diminishing. It is believed that food, shelter, water, and other natural resources will be greatly affected and that the need for increased plans to address poverty, disease, and conflicts are necessary.

It is believed that to eliminate the economic burden, people will work longer and investigate other options of working situations, as well as to impose the same plans worldwide to reduce population growth as was implemented for developing countries in previous years. Without careful planning and serious considerations, resources will be greatly diminished, migration will occur and economies will be strained.

Government's Role

Most economic decisions in the country are based on consumers and producers of products. The government often refers to the "free enterprise system" as being the most positive for the state of the economy. Debates about government involvement in economic efforts abound. Yet, the government plays a role in the economic development and process in four areas: fiscal policy (taxes), regulation, spending, and monetary policy (credit).

Stabilization and growth are of primary concern and therefore the government attempts to guide the economic activities in the country, which includes employment rates, prices and overall growth. When the government adjusts the fiscal level, manages the supply of money, or controls the credit rates, the economy changes (up or down depending on the intervention).

Spending and taxes can be controlled by the President and Congress, which changes the status of the economy in the country and may influence economies abroad. The government's monetary policy is directed by the nation's central bank, the Federal Reserve Board, with involvement from the President and Congress.

Other types of economic government interventions are termed: **capitalism** (mostly private owned for profit), **laissez-faire** (strict free market, with absence of government involvement), **anarchism** (self-regulated market with voluntary trade), and **socialism** (cooperative and labor managed).

Economic Systems

An economic system pertains to a specific group of social institutions and people dealing with the production, distribution, and consumption of goods, services, and resources in the society.

The general economic systems are as follows:

- **Autarky economy (Closed economy)**—Self-sufficient system that limits outside trade, relying on its own resources.
- **Dual economy**—Two systems (local needs and global needs) within one country, occurs mostly in under developed countries.

- **Gift economy**—Believes that goods and services should be given without specific reason such as for generosity.

- **Market economy**—Functions through the exchange in the "free market." It is not designed or managed by a central authority, but through privately owned production, in which the revenue is distributed through the operation of markets.

- **Mixed economy**—Considered a compromise system, as it allows publicly and privately owned companies or businesses to operate simultaneously.

- **Natural economy**—Operates on a bartering or trade system rather than a monetary foundation for the exchange of goods and services.

- **Open economy**—Allows export and import from the global market.

- **Planned economy** (directed economy)—Is designed and managed through a primary authority.

- **Participatory economy**—Guides the production, consumption and allocation of resources through participatory decision making of its society members.

- **Subsistence economy**—Is one in which the output of services and goods meets only the population consumption of the area and resources are renewed and reproduced.

Impact of Technology

As technology increases we see changes in the local as well as global economies. In the past, vast improvements were made in transportation of goods (by automobiles, trains, boats, planes). Most recently, immense strides have been made in communications enabling products and services to be more widely distributed. The use of computers and the world wide web has dramatically increased the abilities of economies to interact with one another. Now a small t-shirt manufacturer can reach international customers more rapidly by creating a website and placing order forms online. Customers around the world may shop and browse online, place orders, and pay from the comfort of their own homes.

International Economics

International economics is the interaction of economic practices and factors between countries. It includes the production of items, international trade (import-export), and investments. International economics influences labor standards, the monetary exchange rates, outsourcing of work, and resource policies (based on supply and demand). It may also affect wages and incomes for the people of the various countries. Globalization of the economy, in some areas of the world, causes conflicts and issues of safety for its people.

Another factor in the status of international economics is the establishment of the International Monetary Fund (IMF) which allocates short-term credit to countries who need to pay off a debt. They may do so by taking a loan, using reserves, or increasing exports. Countries generally need assistance from the IMF when their economy is out of balance.

Introduction to Curriculum, Instruction and Assessment (0011)

The National Council for Social Studies (NCSS) states, "the primary purpose of social studies is to help young people develop the ability to make informed and reasoned decisions for the public good as citizens of a culturally diverse, democratic society in an interdependent world." They strongly promote "citizenship education" through social studies in order to preserve the democratic way of life. They believe that when students understand the concepts of social studies, the historical events, the functions of government, and the practice of economics they can become independent and informed citizens as they become adults managing their lives in a changing society.

The NCSS convened a task force in 1989 to develop the taxonomy of social studies thinking skills. They organized these skills from simple to complex critical thinking skills which resulted in these categories being the essential outcomes for students of social studies education:

- Classify information
- Interpret information

- Analyze information
- Summarize information
- Synthesize information
- Evaluate information

The social studies portion of the Praxis II 0011 exam assesses an examinee's knowledge on teaching strategies and activities related to curriculum components, social organizations, human behavior, social structures, history, geography, government, classroom management and content specific pedagogy. In this section of the study guide, examinees will find information specific to social studies topics and the more general elementary practices are found in the "Overview" to 0011 at the front of the study guide. Use both of these sections to study for this exam.

A portion of the 0011 exam evaluates how well an examinee understands how to promote learning based on social studies content knowledge. This exam utilizes examples of classroom situations through multiple choice questions so the examinee may select answers based on knowledge of curriculum, the methods and strategies of instruction, and the assessment of students. This section of the study guide includes the information necessary for the examinee to clearly utilize the content of 0011 in the implementation of curriculum and instruction and the use of evaluations for the following areas:

- Curriculum components
- Social organizations and human behavior
- Social structures
- History
- Geography
- Government
- Classroom management
- Content specific pedagogy

Being familiar with standards is the first essential step a teacher should take in developing curriculum and activities that promote effective instruction. Instructional activities should be designed to meet student needs while also addressing the required standards and skills to be mastered in social studies.

Curriculum Components

Basic elements of instruction and development of the curriculum are found in the "Overview" of 0011 section of this book. It includes curriculum components such as scope and sequence, appropriate materials, technology, and learner objectives. This information is used in all elementary subject areas and can be adapted and modified for social studies. The content in this portion of the study guide is more specific to social studies topics for 0011.

Curriculum should be carefully designed for the specific grade level and aligned with state and national standards. The content of the social studies curriculum should be integrated with other social sciences as well as other academic subjects and the arts. The scope of the curriculum should establish perimeters of the topics covered and the material should be sequenced logically with discussions, projects and authentic activities available to solidify concept acquisition and skill mastery. The social studies curriculum should be enhanced using a wide variety of instructional resources as these are more interesting for the student and will support universal design in classrooms.

Social Organizations

This section focuses on social organizations, citizenship, and human behavior in society such as that related to an individual, a family, a community.

Citizenship

The National Center for Civics Education has proposed standards for Civics and Government to implement in school programs. They suggest that teachers provide students with information about

- What a government is and does
- The basic premises and values of American democracy
- The role of the U.S. Constitution
- The relationship of the United States to other nations
- The roles and responsibilities of United States citizens

Teachers should include activities for the practice of being a good citizen (citizenship) and not just conduct readings from social studies texts. Books present facts, but may not provide opportunities for students to observe and apply what they have learned to become strong citizens. Educators should also provide activities to engage students in learning about civics, and the government as well as practice strong citizenship skills.

Ways to encourage citizenship include the following:

- Conduct school service projects.
- Develop a class newsletter.
- Establish a classroom management system.
- Encourage individual service projects for the school or community.
- Read about and discuss public issues.
- Visit local government agencies and speak with government officials.
- Join in local community service groups and community activities or services.
- Participate in elections and practice voting.
- Work on school councils or government.
- Be involved in community groups that represent citizenship (Scouts, YMCA).
- Use participatory writing activities.
- Create a logo, motto, or rules for class or school.
- Promote involvement in school based decisions and resolving problems.

Understanding the values, principles, and beliefs of a democratic government and practicing the positive aspects of each is what creates a citizen of the United States. Different perspectives on citizenship education affect the delivery of instruction. Educators have personal and varying viewpoints, sometimes in combination, which may lead them directly toward teaching citizenship in various ways. Two models of instruction are debated in current citizen education: **transmission** and **transformation**.

These two models and their perspectives include the following:

Transmission

Transmission is the learning of government function and following the rules as set forth. The two perspectives are

Legalistic—Focuses on following the laws explicitly and acknowledging the rights and responsibilities

Assimilationist—Promotes the values of society

Transformation

Transformation is the analysis of information, the formation of opinions and the actions taken. The two perspectives are

Critical thinking—Encourages open-minded thoughts, views, and values, and questions authority

Cultural pluralism—Provides students with a range of values and ideals and provides information about diversity and other governments

Anthropology, Sociology, and Psychology

The social sciences have become part of the general social studies curriculum and include: anthropology, sociology, psychology, economics, political science, and most recently global education, environmental education, and current events. Knowledge of these areas helps students understand their world and how they should function within it. Each of the social sciences is defined by the content knowledge and its individual processes.

Anthropology is the study of the cultural traits and the physical characteristics of people. The focus of the content should be on archaeology and prehistory, human evolution, defining culture, comparing different cultures, and identifying cultural changes. Elementary studies focus on the cultural aspects of anthropology and these studies should include: daily living, economic systems, social classes, housing, political structures, the arts, religion, and recreation.

Key points to remember in the study of people are as follows:

- Avoid stereotypical content.
- Specify historical periods.
- Use a variety of resources.
- Include diverse information.

Methods/activities to pursue anthropological study:

- Simulate research and archaeology activities.
- Visit museums.
- Conduct library research.
- Study artifacts.
- Utilize online content and other media services.
- Focus on native cultures.
- Identify examples of cultural conflicts.
- Include storytelling.

Sociology and **psychology** together comprise the study of humans, society, behavior, and relationships. These subject areas provide opportunities for students to investigate their personal identities, compare their families, study peoples' interactions, share experiences about others, and research the institutional influences and relationships.

Sociology content includes information about institutions, primary and secondary groups, social change, communication, social problems, and relationships within and among groups of people. Activities should

- Focus on group membership.
- Involve community studies.
- Identify social problems.
- Investigate communication.

Psychology content includes individual differences, perceptions, and behaviors. Some activities that specifically relate to this topic are

- Observe people.
- Identify and compare groups of people.
- Research human emotions.
- Study human development.

Methods and activities that will stimulate the study of sociology and psychology include the following:

- Read biographies.
- Write autobiographies.

- Use photographs and pictorial histories.
- Create family trees.
- Conduct surveys and interviews.
- Identify roles and responsibilities.
- Establish rules of behavior and interactions.
- Study social tensions and issues of history.
- Visit the community to learn about social organizations.

Social Structures

This is comprised of information regarding communication, transportation, industrialization, technology, and economics. Students need to be educated about how the relationships of these primary entities affect the management of a society.

The movement of people, the import and export of goods, and the use of mass communication all contribute major roles to shaping the world. People must interact. They do so through movement, through travel, trade, information flow, and political events. People live unevenly in many different parts of the world and use transportation, industrialization, technology, and economic systems to function within their villages and in the larger society. They live in a global community and must function in a global economy.

Activities that enhance this topic include

- Use of field trips to community entities and businesses.
- Use of various types of technology.
- Study of economic systems (household, school clubs).
- Build skills in area of communication (speeches, presentations).

Economics

Under this topic of social studies, students are expected to acquire basic economic knowledge and to perform economic analysis. They do not develop economic reasoning or abstract knowledge for all concepts at the same time. Children's development of concept knowledge and their understanding of economic factors move from the more complex and the more abstract as they mature.

Important to the development of economic reasoning are both skills and content. Learning how to use reason regarding economic issues is important because the analytic approach to economics differs from approaches used for other related subjects such as history and civics. Economic analysis helps students examine many questions in history, politics, business, and international relations.

The key skills students must develop include the ability to

- Describe economic problems, alternatives, benefits, and costs.
- Examine economic situations.
- Identify the consequences of changes in economic policies.
- Analyze economic evidence.
- Compare benefits and costs.

Students should be able to

- Understand basic economic concepts and key issues.
- Recite economic facts about the United States (unemployment, inflation, and so on).
- Explain historical events from an economic perspective.
- Use economic reasoning to evaluate policy proposals for contemporary issues like unemployment and pollution.
- Trace historical economic patterns.

- Compare economic systems in the world.
- Identify issues related to economics.
- Study economic policies and current status.
- Make decisions and realize that decisions affect self and others.
- Understand that not all trade is volunteer and that choices have future impact.

Activities that help in the study of economics include the following:

- Create classroom societies that reflect real-life situations in which students can develop rules and laws, establish a government, and plan the economic system.
- Study the market and seek information on products, compare prices, and analyze advertising.
- Work at an individual level to prepare personal budgets, show ways to economize, and select necessary goods and services based on the budget.
- Workforce education in which students learn about careers, gain knowledge about the requirements and responsibilities of contemporary jobs, conduct career research, make career choices, hold career days/fairs, and allow career shadowing.

History, Geography, and Government

This section includes information about the history, geography, and government of states, regions, the United States, and the world.

United States and World History

Students are very capable of learning history and related concepts if the instruction is clear, appropriate, and meaningful. Learning about the history of the world, the United States, a specific state, community, a school, or a family all help students learn their place within the world. To aid students educators may use the following:

- Developmentally appropriate concepts
- Contextual support
- Multiple lesson formats
- Cooperative learning activities
- Critical thinking activities
- Discovery-based learning opportunities
- Motivational hands-on activities
- Inquiry-based learning projects
- Assignments where the students are historians
- Variety of resources

Political Science

The primary educational component of social studies that helps to produce a reliable citizen is the knowledge of Civics, and Government. **Civics** is the study of people and their relationships with government and other people in their county. The Center for Civic Education promotes instruction of basic values of American democracy. **Government** is the study of the legal and political institutions in the world, specifically that of the nation's democratic status.

In this content area, students should learn

- What a government is and how governments function
- How rules are made and enforced
- How rules affect family, community, local, state, national, and international places

- Why government is necessary and how power and authority is utilized
- The democratic values and beliefs of civic life

Educators should teach the basic structures of political science and the rights and responsibilities of its citizens. They must help students understand that this nation is comprised of groups of different ethnicity, race, religion, class, language, gender, or national origins and it is because of these factors that the United States has a diverse population. They need to know that the set ideals of a nation have not always been fair or achieved.

To plan effective instruction in political science, educators should become familiar with the national content and state academic standards. Classroom activities and learning opportunities may then be developed and designed to address the proposed skills. Consider students with a wide range of abilities and acknowledge cultural diversity in all activities. Include discussions on controversial issues and decision making to encourage thoughtful consideration of values topics.

Students should learn the components of decision making which support governmental studies and citizenship education:

- How to identify and define a problem
- How to identify and define values
- Predict consequences or outcomes
- How to reach decisions
- How to justify decisions
- How decisions can be altered

An example of a curriculum plan focus in political science studies for specific grades includes the following:

- K–2—Families, schools
- 3—Cities
- 4—State
- 5—Federal government
- 6—Ancient and foreign governments

Citizenship

Educators should want students to become good citizens who are informed voters, who promote positive values, and who perform community services. They should understand the democratic ideals and realize that they have not always been practiced.

Citizenship education should teach students

- About how government works, so they can follow rules
- Ways to change society for the better
- Value-based decision making
- Analyze social settings and conditions
- Define key political issues and to develop personal perspectives
- Forms of civic participation

Activities that enhance citizenship education include

- Going on field trips to government facilities and historical museums
- Creating situations in which students may practice their citizenship skills
- Developing scenarios for useful problem solving practice
- Discussing and debating current events

Geography

Geography is only one component of the subject of social studies; but it is as significant as the study of history. Students need a broad base of geographic knowledge as they grow and develop into an ever changing global society. Just knowing where places are on earth is not enough in our current world. The basic areas students need to know in geography are as follows:

- Map skills and spatial organization of the world
- The places and regions of the world
- The physical and human systems
- The environment and society
- The uses of geography

Students need to

- Understand the relationships of places to one another and how the people who exist across the world interact and affect each others' communities.
- Investigate the distribution of resources and products throughout the world.
- Comprehend how the use of these goods influence the people who consume them and what the impact of these resources is on the environment.
- Have a clearer understanding of how decisions that people make in their environments not only shape the present, but also the future.
- Know how places change over time and what their own role will be in the world.

The primary components of learning geography are: pattern, regularity, and the reasons for spatial organization. Students must become adept at reading maps and demonstrate knowledge about the spatial relationships of people, places, and environments and the events that alter them.

The World in Spatial Terms

According to the nationally recommended standards for geography, students must become "geographically informed" and learn how to organize information about the world in a spatial context. Becoming geographically aware and thinking in **spatial terms** means that students gain the ability to describe and analyze the presented spatial organization around the people and environments found on the earth's surface. Students who acquire a strong foundation of geography vocabulary, map terms and spatial organization phrases will be better equipped to learn the major concepts, and apply their knowledge of this subject area.

Pertaining to the development of map skills and understanding spatial organization, examinees must be capable of aiding students in learning the following concepts of geography.

- The key concepts and legends that refer to pictorial or semi pictorial symbols.
- The relationships of geographical information and how places change over time.
- How to produce maps of geographical information.
- To show spatial relationships and influences of the people, places, and environment on one another.
- About the various types of reference works that are available.

Places, People, and Regions

The ability to function in the world is dependent upon the understanding and appreciation of similarities and differences of various places and regions in the world. Students must learn

- The physical and human characteristics of certain places and specific regions.
- The human relationships that exist and how these function in places and regions.

- The various regions and places to gain their ability to function within the world.
- To understand and appreciate the similarities and differences of the diverse places and regions across the continents.

Physical and Human Systems

Since this area overlaps with science, it lends itself to instruction as a topic for integrated study. Students must learn how **physical systems** shape the earth's surface and understand the concepts related to ecosystems and how they affect the world. They must gain knowledge about how to maintain and modify the earth's environments as these are critical to all human activity. By understanding how physical systems affect the earth, students will begin to understand how the earth serves as a home to plants and animals. Equally important is the history of **human systems,** which can be influenced and shaped by understanding geography. It is important for students to understand the historical and geographical values of human development. Viewing the past from both a historical and a geographical aspect aids in the understanding of physical and human events.

Students must learn

- Events (past and present) are formed by human perceptions of places and regions.
- To answer complex questions such as:

    What was the purpose of the Alaskan pipeline?

    Why was the Berlin Wall constructed?

- The events of the past provide many insights into climate, resources, ecosystems, and migration of human ancestors.
- To explain why certain events happened in a certain way.

Environment and Society

Humans are instrumental to the continuation of the environment, yet can be the destructors of certain environments, thus altering the world. Students must gain a sense of the interactions of humans and the environment in order to understand how the world changes and what their role will be.

Students need to understand

- Consuming resources and altering natural patterns have consequences.
- Building structures that are a part of the earth's surface changes the region.
- The reasons that people compete for control of the earth.
- Modifying the natural environment causes changes in ecosystems.
- The relationships of nature and people.
- How physical systems alter people's construction of their environment.
- The opportunities and constraints the environment offers and the costs of such properties/characteristics.
- There is a carrying capacity for the environment.
- The intended and unintended repercussions of human interaction with the earth.
- How to synthesize and evaluate the ways that humans have used and adapted the environment to meet needs.
- To develop skills to interpret, evaluate, analyze, and synthesize the impact of humans on the environment and vice versa.

Concepts and Skills

Students need to develop appropriate concepts and skills under the subject of social studies, which includes: organizing data, problem solving, comparing and contrasting, model building, planning, forecasting, and decision making.

Reference Works and Resources

Students need to know the various types of reference works that are available to them to find geographical information. These include such materials as encyclopedias, computer-based programs, almanacs, atlases, gazetteers, geographical dictionaries, statistical abstracts, and data compilations. Students will improve their ability to understand geographic information if they know where to find these tools, learn how to use them efficiently, and determine how to gauge the accuracy and reliability of the resources. Students also need to learn how to apply and interpret the information they seek, such as changing the information found on charts and graphs into a written form.

Classroom Management

Overall classroom management, motivation, participation, inclusion, organization, fairness, and expectations in social studies is much the same for other subject areas. Strategies for establishing environments, developing and presenting lessons, managing behaviors, and accessing activities and materials all pertain to classroom management and essentially affect instruction. These are further reviewed in the "Overview" of 0011 portion of the study guide.

Social studies teachers can weave lessons into classroom management and structure that cover topics such as laws and regulations, citizenship and individual rights, government and control. Incorporate classroom systems where students

- Work together to problem solve
- Develop rules and guidelines
- Make democratic decisions

Content Pedagogy

This section relates to map and globe skills, inquiry based instruction, decision making, and models. Additional information regarding pedagogy may be found in the overviews.

Map Knowledge and Map Reading Skills

Maps are an essential component to learning the subject of geography. Maps require the use of different types of skills, both in language and reading. Map reading skills can be developed through **direct instruction** and **repeated practice**. Helping students to move from concrete to abstract concepts and promoting practice from the simple to more complex tasks will be valuable for successful student achievement.

The three stages of map reading skill development according to Piaget:

- **Topographical stage**—The ability to understand different areas, but no specific place.
- **Projective stage**—The ability to locate an object or place in relation to self.
- **Euclidian stage**—The ability to use strong spatial relationship skills.

Students need skills on how to read and understand the **symbols** and **key concepts** of maps. They need to learn how to view certain maps and to determine which maps to use when searching for specific information. They must be able to create a representation of information on a map, know if the properties depicted are correct, and understand which properties are misshaped. Critical to map reading is the ability to read the legends, understand the symbols, use the scales, determine directions, and comprehend the details.

Reading maps requires specific skills and the following strategies may assist students in acquiring these important life-long competencies. For example, they must be able to understand the scale or units of measurement being used (inches, meters, and so on). Some strategies that will help are

1. Use simple maps to begin instruction (map of class, student's house, school, community, 50 states).
2. Instruct on the simple symbols used (direction, landmark, grids).
3. Require students to construct a map or 3-D model.

Geographic Representations

When students learn how to produce maps of geographical information, they are able to make sense of the world. Map studies are often focused in the 3rd grade, but can begin earlier with simple maps and continue with reading, studying, and creating more complex maps as students move past the 3rd grade. In order to become proficient at map usage, they must feel comfortable with the four aspects of maps: symbols, scale, directions, and grid.

Knowledge about geographic representations help students make sense of the world and they learn to store and recall information about shapes, and patterns of physical and human features of the earth. Students internalize one or more aspects of the earth's surface based on previous knowledge and new concepts.

Geographic representations may be constructed of maps, globes, graphs, tables, diagrams, aerial photos, and satellite images. These tools provide valuable information on spatial terms and relationships, and can be used as supplements to the existing classroom materials. However, there are some limitations: they may not be understood by students; certain lessons on the content and use may need to be developed on these specialized mapping tools; and they may be difficult to access depending on the location.

Uses of Geography

The Joint Committee on Geographic Education proposes that students learn this specific set of geographic skills.

- Ask geographic questions.
- Acquire geographic information.
- Organize geographic information.
- Analyze geographic information.
- Answer geographic questions.

Applications of Geography	Concepts and Skills Mastered
Spatial Organization	patterns and reasons movement between places and regions local, national, and global interactions diversity of areas and people systems in locations
Ecological Focus	patterns and processes ecosystems and biomes physical connections—local and global environments human impact and relationship to environment
Geographical Understanding	analyze and make informed decisions gain knowledge about destinations ability to function at home and abroad predict consequences of interactions

Instructional Strategies for Social Studies

There are three types of essential lessons used for social studies:

1. **Utilize primary sources**—Includes actual items from the period or place studied, such as original documents, artifacts, maps, newspaper articles, photos, clothing, music, and tools.
2. **Incorporate fiction**—Includes the use of books, stories, and integrated readings, such as the use of oral traditions or storytelling and the outline of events.

3. **Use of timelines**—Depicts the dates and sequential order of events such as those specific to an area, certain historical events, or people.

Following are strategies and techniques for use in the realm of social studies:

- Multiple lesson formats.
- Cooperative learning sessions such as group projects, interview projects, and think-pair-share activities.
- Inquiry learning periods aid students in developing problem solving skills, using reflective thinking skills, and learning through discovery. It is particularly useful in social studies, as it supports students in learning to use resource materials. In order to pursue inquiry learning, students may need access to resources such as atlases, encyclopedias, almanacs, magazines, newspapers, and electronic media.
- Group investigation strategy is the use of both cooperative learning and inquiry learning.
- Scaffolding instruction and small or large group work.

Following are suggested activities to enhance social studies education:

- Consider historical investigation.
- Use of diagrams, charts, maps, graphs, dioramas, and tables.
- Debate team topics.
- Critical thinking activities.
- Group models, presentations, and reports.
- Partner or team activities.
- Provide current event topics and study.
- Learn to use the newspaper and gather information from media news.
- Establish career days or job shadowing opportunities.
- Identify types of work and monetary use around the world.

Social Studies Assessment

The purpose of assessment is the same in all subjects and there are many different types of assessments used in elementary education. The details of the topic of assessment are further explained in the "Overview" of 0011 in this study guide.

Conducting assessments help teachers to determine the performance levels of their students and aids in developing the social studies curriculum to provide appropriate activities to the students. When assessing for social studies, a teacher should seek to collect data on students from a variety of sources (quizzes, homework, presentations) in different formats (group projects, individual research) and collect the data regularly.

Authentic assessments for use in social studies may include

- Complete a project (use a criteria form).
- Make a presentation (use a rating scale).
- Submit a research paper (use for portfolio collection).
- Maintain a journal (use an evaluation rubric).
- Homework or essay (set criteria).
- Non-written project such as developing a chart or maps (observation or rubric).

Social Studies Content Area Exercises (0012)

This Praxis II exam (0012) assesses an examinee's ability to apply the knowledge gained in the content knowledge section (0014) and found in the curriculum, instruction, and assessment information (0011). Examinees will have 2 hours to answer four essay questions; one question may be focused on social studies. Review the information from the Praxis II 0014 and 0011 social studies study guide, as well as the "Overview" of 0011 in this book.

There are endless possibilities on what may be presented on the exam, so examinees should prepare for this exam by considering how to use the social studies information they already know. Read through the following list of questions that relate to the topic of social studies education and try to answer them using a separate sheet of paper. You will notice that answers to these are not provided, as there are many different ways to answers these open ended questions.

The exercises posed on this exam will test the examinees ability to prepare an extended, in-depth response to one question in the social studies area. When preparing to answer questions on this exam, remember that some of the questions presented may have multiple parts.

Following are samples of possible Social Studies essay questions:

1. As an elementary teacher, you have just completed a unit of study on exploration and the explorers of North America. Explain three informal assessment techniques and three authentic assessment techniques that you would use during this unit to evaluate student comprehension and retention. Explain why these types of assessments help evaluate student understanding better than giving a 100-question multiple choice question test.

2. While studying Native American tribes and cultures, your fourth-grade class asks whether they can design a school wide Native American festival to show everything they have learned. Explain the student objectives/goals for a project of this magnitude and write an outline of three activities that could be included in the festival.

3. Explain how an elementary teacher should integrate poetry into the study of U.S. history in a fifth-grade classroom.

4. Describe how an elementary teacher would integrate math and science into a unit of study on the classical civilizations during world history.

5. It is a presidential election year and as an elementary teacher, you are teaching topics in political science to your class. Write a lesson plan on the electoral process. Include learner outcomes, materials, and assessment techniques.

6. Economics can be a difficult topic to cover for elementary students. Identify at least five activities that will help promote an interest in this topic and explain why these would be motivational to the students.

7. Incorporating children's literature to support social studies instruction is an effective method for this topic. If you, the elementary teacher, were to develop a unit on transportation for a second-grade class, how would you utilize children's literature? Provide examples and indicate how you would address diversity.

8. A primary goal of social studies is to teach students positive citizenship and community participation. Create a community service project that your third-grade class may use to improve their knowledge about the community and work toward gaining skills that support good citizenship.

9. Howard Gardner recommends that educators utilize the nine intelligences when creating lessons for students. Identify four of the nine intelligences and explain how you would include them in a lesson on map reading skills.

10. An elementary class has just completed the study of famous inventors, from the mid 1800s to the mid 1990s. Using a cooperative learning approach, what are some of the project possibilities for students to complete as a form of authentic assessment? Describe two different assignments and identify the objectives, the process, and the materials needed.

Science Content Knowledge (0014)

The National Science Teachers Association (NSTA), an organization of science teachers, formed the National Commission on Science Education Standards and Assessment (NCSESA) to develop national standards related to science education. Although available, these are not federally mandated nor are they part of any national curriculum. This organization produced a document that outlines the perimeters of science to ensure that students receive the proper instruction and benefits from science education programs. Their primary goal states:

> "All students regardless of age, sex, cultural or ethnic background, disabilities, aspirations, or interest and motivation in science should have the opportunity to obtain high levels of scientific literacy."

Several principles guide the science standards set forth by the NCSESA:

1. Science is for every student.
2. Learning science requires an active process.
3. Science education should emulate the intellectual and cultural traditions of contemporary science.
4. Education reform should include the improvement of science education.

The NCSESA, supported by NSTA, created eight recommended student outcomes for science at the elementary levels (K–4, 5–8) and the secondary level (9–12). The content includes the following:

1. Unifying concepts and processes in science
2. Science as inquiry
3. Physical science
4. Life science
5. Earth and space science
6. Science and technology
7. Science in personal and social perspectives
8. History and the nature of science

Note: **These are explained more fully in "Science (0011)."**

Prominent Scientific Laws

Many important laws and theories govern science. A **scientific law** is some statement of fact that is proven time and time again. A **scientific theory** is a statement, which is based upon educated observations, tested, and may be proven. Educators should be knowledgeable about the laws and theories that support the processes and concepts of science.

Although these laws may not be formally taught in the early elementary grades, the general science concepts and instruction at that lower elementary level will lead to the understanding of these laws when they are more formally taught in upper elementary and secondary programs. Here is a list of prominent laws of science and their explanations that you will need to be familiar with in order to be well versed in elementary science.

I. **Conservation Laws**—Fundamental laws of all science.

Conservation of Mass/Matter—Matter cannot be created or destroyed but can be rearranged.

Conservation of Energy—Energy remains constant in a system and cannot be recreated, but can change forms.

Conservation of Momentum—Total momentum remains the same unless acted upon by an outside force (p=mv).

Charge Conservation—Electric charge can neither be created nor destroyed but is always conserved.

II. **Gas Laws**

Boyle's Law—For a specified amount of gas kept at a specified temperature, pressure and volume are inversely proportional (while one increases, the other decreases) (PV=*k*).

Ideal Gas Law—The state of an amount of gas is determined by its pressure, volume and temperature (PV=*n*RT).

III. **Einstein's Laws**

Mass-Energy Equivalence—When a body has a mass it has a certain energy even if it is not moving (E=mc^2).

General Relativity—Gravitational attraction between masses is a result of the nearby masses. Gravity has waves.

IV. **Newton's Laws**

First Law: Law of Inertia—An object will remain at rest or in motion unless acted upon by an outside force.

Second Law: Law of Acceleration—An object will move in the direction of the force applied to it. The object's acceleration is proportional to the force applied to it and inversely proportional to the mass of the object.

Third Law: Law of Reciprocal Actions—For every action there is an opposite and equal reaction.

Fourier's Law (Law of Heat Conduction)—The transfer of heat moves through matter from higher temperatures to lower temperatures in order to equalize differences.

General Law of Gravitation—Describes the gravitational attraction between two masses; gravitational force between two objects is equal to the gravitational constant times the product of the two masses divided by the distance between them squared $F = G\dfrac{m_1 m_2}{r^2}$

V. **Electromagnetic Laws**

Ohm's Law—Measures voltage and current in electrical circuits; states that the current going through a conductor is equal to the voltage divided by the resistor. (I=V/R)

Faraday's Law of Induction—Explains the ways that voltage can be generated; any change in the magnetic environment of a coil of wire will cause voltage to be produced. (EMF)

VI. **Darwin's Laws**

Natural Selection—Individual organisms with favorable traits are more likely to survive and reproduce.

Evolution—The world is in a constant state of change.

Common Descent—Every group of living organisms on earth descended from a common ancestor.

Multiplication of Species—Species split into or produce other species depending on geographical location.

Gradualism—Changes occur through the slow gradual change of population, not through fast sudden production of new beings.

VII. **Kepler's Laws (Planetary Motion)**

Law of Ellipses—The path of the planets around the sun is an elliptical shape with the center of the sun being at the focus.

Law of Equal Areas—The speed of the planets' is constantly changing. A planet moves fastest when it is near the sun and slowest when it is further away.

Law of Harmonies—Compares the orbital period and the radius of the orbit of a planet to the other planets; provides an accurate description of the time and the distance for the planets' orbit around the sun.

Earth Science

This area of science examines the structure and function of the earth. It also extends studies into space and the universe. Earth science is important to understand as it directly relates to human actions and behaviors. Within this section are topics such as structures of the Earth, processes of the Earth, Earth history, universe, and interactions of the earth and universe.

Structure of the Earth System

The Earth is comprised of many complex systems. These systems make up the various components and layers of the Earth, both on the surface and above the Earth.

The following four principle components of the Earth must work together in a constant complex system.

- Atmosphere (air)
- Lithosphere (land)
- Hydrosphere (water)
- Biosphere (life)

There are five layers that comprise the atmosphere.

- Exosphere (from 300–600 miles to 6,000 miles)
- Thermosphere (includes ionosphere) (265,000–285,000 feet to 400+ miles)
- Mesosphere (160,000 feet to about 285,000)
- Stratosphere (23,000–60,000 to about 160,000 feet)
- Troposphere (23,000 to 60,000 feet)

The Earth's structure is composed of four concentric spheres. These layers of the Earth include:

- **Crust**—5–30 miles thick, not fixed, a mosaic of moving plates, outer shell
- **Mantle**—1,800 miles thick, plasticity (ability of solid to flow), circulating currents, causing the plates to move
- **Outer core**—1,300 miles thick, viscous liquid, the Earth's magnetic field originates here
- **Inner core**—800 miles to the center of the earth, a solid

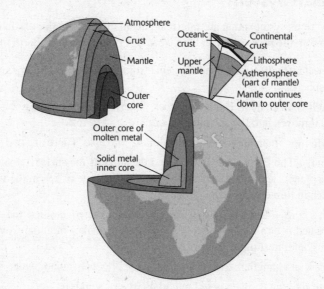

Plate Tectonics

The Earth's crust is divided into plates (about 20). Each plate varies in size and thickness. These plates continually drift and shift. Plates are found under continents (continental plates) and beneath the ocean (oceanic plates).

Plate Movement

There are three types of plate boundaries.

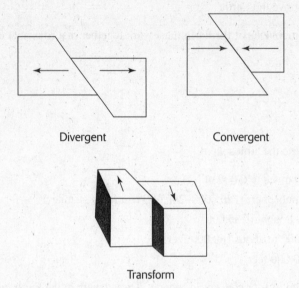

Divergent   Convergent

Transform

Convergent (collision)   results in   mountains, volcanoes, ridges, recycling of crust

Transform (rubbing)   results in   earthquakes

Divergent (separating)   results in   new crust, rivers, oceans, lakes

Processes of the Earth System

The Earth functions through various systems that are interrelated and affected by their individual processes. Plants, humans, heat, weathering, erosion, the rock cycle, and the weather cycle impact the Earth in various ways.

- **Plants** (biosphere) pull water (hydrosphere) and nutrients from the soil (lithosphere) and release oxygen and water vapor into the air (atmosphere).

- **Humans** (biosphere) built Glen Canyon Dam using rock materials (lithosphere) to control a lake (hydrosphere); as the water evaporates, it moves into the air (atmosphere).

- **Heat** influences the Earth more than any other process in the universe. There are two sources of heat.

  1. **Solar Energy** (the sun)—The Earth is on an axis, and the sun hits the surface at varying angles causing the major climates of the planet. The sun affects and influences the type of life in the various regions. It affects Earth's weather, which in turn affects vegetation and erosion.

  2. **Radioactivity** (Earth's core)—Radioactivity is responsible for plate tectonics, most volcanoes, and earthquakes, which are located near plate boundaries. Radioactivity makes mountains, valleys, ocean basins, lake beds, islands, trenches, and most other land forms.

- **Weathering**—The process of changing structures through the effects of wind, water, ice, sun, and gravity.

- **Erosion**—The process of moving the weathered materials (rivers, winds).

- **Rock cycle**—All rocks come from the mantle (except limestone).

Following are three types of rocks:

- **Igneous**—Forms when magma cools (for example, granite, pumice)

- **Sedimentary**—Forms when layers of sediments are compressed (for example, sandstone, limestone, coal, shale)

- **Metamorphic**—Forms through the transformation of igneous and sedimentary rocks through heat and pressure (for example, marble, slate, quartzite)

The **weather cycle** occurs in the troposphere. There are three contributing factors to weather:

1. Solar radiation: heat energy (infrared radiation) from the sun that hits the Earth's surface is changed into heat.

2. Earth movement: the seasons are caused by the orbit around the sun and the rotation of Earth upon its axis.

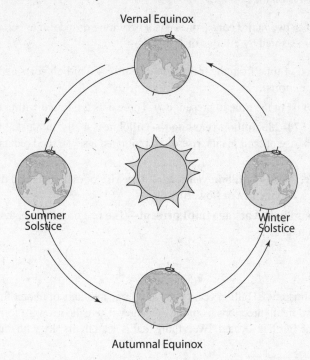

3. Water Cycle: a natural process in which water evaporates, condensates, and precipitates.

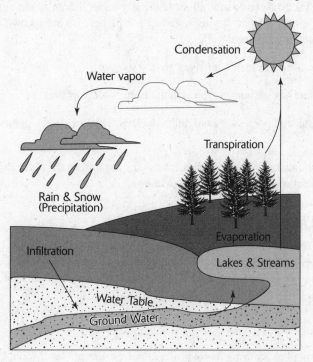

Earth History

The Earth is almost 5 billion years old. Currently, we know that 71 percent of the Earth's surface is ocean and 97 percent of the Earth's water is also ocean. The Earth's plates move 2–5 cm. per year. A type of science, geological history, investigates how the Earth and its life-forms have developed over time.

- **Principle of Uniformitarianism**—The scientific laws that govern Earth today are the same since the beginning of time. ("The present is the key to the past.")
- **Law of Superposition**—The oldest rocks and events are found at the bottom of formations, and the youngest are found at the top. (The past is on the bottom.)

The geologic time scale describes two major **eons**. An eon is a very long or indefinite period of time that explains the age of the universe and can be measured by billions of years.

- **Precambian Eon**—Period of time from the formation of Earth (4.6 billion years ago) to the rise of life-forms (similar to present day life forms).
- **Phanerozoic Eon**—The rest of the time to present day. Three eras are found within the Phanerozoic Eon:
  - **Paleozoic: early life, 570–286 million years ago**—Trillobites, shells, mollusks, brachiopods, echinoderms, rise of first vertebrates, rise of land plants, rise of amphibians, insects, seed plants, and trees, and rise of reptiles.
  - **Mesozoic: middle life, 245–144 million years ago**—The rise of mammals and dinosaurs, the rise of birds, the extinction of dinosaurs, and the rise of flowering plants.
  - **Centzoic: late life 66 million years ago until present**—The rise of primates, the rise of horses, the rise of hominids and modern man.

Earth and Universe

The universe originated approximately 20 billion years ago from large amounts of matter that experienced a catastrophic explosion, which spread outward in all directions from the epicenter. The galaxies were formed into galactic clusters. The **Milky Way Galaxy** is where the Earth is located. Everything that is seen in the sky with the naked eye belongs to this galaxy.

The sun and all bodies that revolve around it comprise our **solar system.** There are **nine planets:** Mercury, Venus, Earth, Mars, Jupiter, Saturn, Uranus, Neptune, and Pluto (currently under debate as the ninth planet). Each planet revolves around the sun in an elliptical orbit at varying speeds. Each planet also has its own moon(s) that revolve around the planets', caught in the planets gravitational pull.

A **meteoroid** is a stony or metallic particle that revolves around the sun.

A **meteor** is created when meteorites are burning through the Earth's atmosphere.

A **comet** revolves around the sun and possesses a tail and a nucleus. The tail always points away from the sun due to the solar wind.

Constellations are a type of boundary system astronomers use for organizing the night sky. There are 88 constellational regions. Each region is named for a group of stars found within it.

The Earth within the Universe

Earth has one moon, which takes one lunar month to revolve (28 days) around the Earth. The moon does not emit its own light but rather reflects the sun's light. The moon rotates upon an axis just like Earth, at exactly the same period and speed. Therefore, the same side of the moon is seen at all times. The moon phases are caused by the position of the moon relative to the sun.

Moon Phases

The moon exhibits five different phases during its rotation around the Earth: New Moon, Crescent Moon, Quarter Moon, Gibbous Moon, and Full Moon.

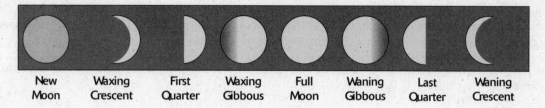

| New Moon | Waxing Crescent | First Quarter | Waxing Gibbous | Full Moon | Waning Gibbous | Last Quarter | Waning Crescent |

During a **lunar eclipse,** the moon is blocked by the Earth's shadow.

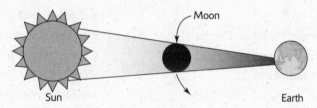

Lunar Eclipse

During a **solar eclipse,** the moon casts a shadow upon the Earth.

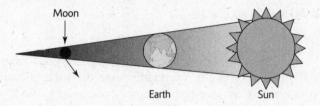

Solar Eclipse

Life Science

This area of science studies living things and their characteristics. It encompasses both plants and animals, the structure of the cell, reproduction and propagation of the species, physical structure, behavior within environments, adaptations, and interdependence of species. Millions of species exist and there are newly identified organisms each year. These living things are categorized according to kingdoms.

There are five known kingdoms based in biology:

- **Monera**—Single-celled organism without nuclei (bacteria)
- **Protista**—Single-celled organism with nuclei (algae, protozoans)
- **Fungi**—Single-celled and multi-celled organisms (mushrooms, mold, yeast, lichen)
- **Plantae**—Multi-cellular plant organisms (moss, fern, pine, flowering)
- **Animalia**—Multi-cellular animals (10–21 phyla)

The organization of living things is further studied as a ladder or a pyramid. Within the traditional Linnean classification system, there are seven major levels or categories that are classified according to shared physical characteristics:

- **Kingdom**
- **Phylum**
- **Class**
- **Order**
- **Family**
- **Genus**
- **Species**

The organization is further explained here. Each **kingdom** is broken down further into smaller categories named phyla. A **phylum** contains organisms that are genetically related through common ancestry. Each phylum is then broken down into separate classes. A **class** is a more specific breakdown of organisms in which the group shares a common attribute, characteristic, or trait. Classes are further divided into orders. **Order** then specifically divides the class into smaller shared characteristics. Order then splits into smaller units called **family** in which organisms have multiple traits in common. Family is broken into **genus** where the organisms show many common attributes. The last break is into **species** in which organisms can interbreed and produce offspring that can propagate the species.

There are many mnemonic devices used to remember this breakdown of categories. Here are a few that may help you and your students:

> **K**ing **P**hillip **C**ame **O**ver **F**or **G**ood **S**paghetti
>
> **K**ids **P**laying **C**hicken **O**n **F**reeways **G**et **S**mashed
>
> **K**ids **P**refer **C**heese **O**ver **F**ried **G**reen **S**pinach
>
> **K**ings **P**lay **C**hess **O**n **F**ine **G**lass **S**urfaces

Carolus Linnaeus was an 18th-century Swedish botanist who developed the system of binomial nomenclature used for naming the various species. Each species is given a two-part Latin name, formed by affixing a specific label to the genus name. The genus name is capitalized, and then both the genus name and specific label are italicized (for example, common dog is *Canis familiaris*).

Following are examples of specific classifications:

Human	**Giant Panda**
Kingdom: Animalia	**Kingdom:** Animalia
Phylum: Chordata (animals with backbones)	**Phylum:** Chordata
Class: Mammalia (with hair, female makes milk)	**Class:** Mammalia
Order: Primate (apes and monkeys)	**Order:** Carnivora
Family: Hominadae	**Family:** Ursidae
Genus: *Homo*	**Genus:** *Ailuropoda*
Species: *Homo sapiens*	**Species:** *Ailuropoda melanoleuca*

Structure and Function of Living Systems

The living systems include the plants and animals that inhabit the Earth, and characteristics of living things include:

- Made of protoplasm
- Organized into cells
- Use energy
- Capable of growth
- Have definite life spans
- Reproduce, give rise to similar organisms
- Affected by the environment
- Adapt to the environment
- Respond to the environment

Cells

A **cell** is the fundamental unit that composes the structure and function of life. All living things are made up of cells. Following is the breakdown of a living body:

> A group of similar cells = **tissue**
>
> A group of tissues working together = **organs**
>
> A group of organs working together = **system**
>
> A group of systems = **organism**

Functions of a cell:

- Manufacture proteins and other materials for building cells
- Manufacture energy
- To reproduce

Plant cells manufacture their own food from water, minerals, and carbon dioxide.

Parts of a Cell-Animal and Plant	
Cell membrane	Made of lipids, permits inward passage of needed items/outward passage of waste
Nucleus	Control center of cell; "the brain" that contains DNA
Cytoplasm	All materials outside of the nucleus
Endoplasmic reticulum (ER)	Transport canals that travel from the nucleus to cytoplasm
Ribosomes	Manufacture proteins
Mitochondria	Releases energy to cell through chemical reactions
Lysosomes	Hold enzymes to breakdown molecules
Golgi apparatus	Packages the proteins and transports them through the cell
Vacuoles	Store food, water and minerals

In addition to those parts listed in the previous chart, plants also include the following:

Cell wall	Made of cellulose, provides rigid structure for plant, permits passage in and out of cell
Chloroplasts	Plastids that contain chlorophyll

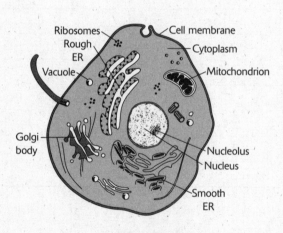

Animal Cell

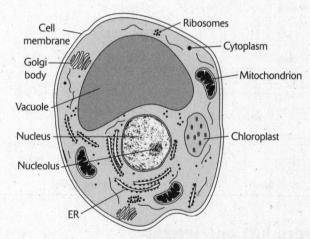

Plant Cell

Structure and Function of Plants	
Part	*Description/Purpose*
Roots	The anchor/absorbs water and minerals
Stem	The transport/taking nutrients to the leaves
Leaves	The builder/manufactures food for the plant
Flower	Sexual organs/reproduction site of the plant
Fruit	The ripened ovaries of flowers

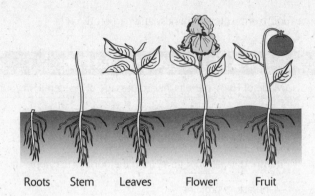

Roots   Stem   Leaves   Flower   Fruit

Flowers are the reproductive organs of plants. Insects and birds are attracted to the petals and help transport and disperse pollen for cross-fertilization. The stamen, the male reproductive organ, manufactures the pollen. The pistil, the female reproductive organ, has multiple parts: a stigma, which is the sticky top that captures pollen; styles that transport the pollen to the ovary; and an ovary that makes the ovules. When pollen joins the ovule, fertilized seeds are the outcome.

Structure and Function of Animals

For animals to live and survive as a species, they must grow, reproduce, and interact with the environment. Animals must have systems that support each of their individual cells.

There are eight basic functions of animals:

Functions	System
Nutrition	Digestive
Respiration	Respiratory
Response	Brain and nervous system
Regulation	Glands and hormones
Excretion	Kidneys and other organs
Circulation	Circulatory
Movement	Nervous system and brain
Reproduction	Sexual and asexual

Reproduction/Heredity

Reproduction facilitates organisms to grow and to continue their species. There are two types of organisms:

- **Asexual**—A cell that creates two identical pairs of chromosomes, splits, and forms nuclei around the chromosomes. The way cells divide is called **mitosis**. New cells are created using only one "parent" (for example, algae, bacteria, sponges, mold, fungi).

- **Sexual**—Requires the union of a male gamete and female gamete (gamete is a reproductive cell). Meiosis is when the gametes form. Each gamete has 1/2 the chromosomes needed for reproduction. When the two gametes combine, they each donate 1/2 of the chromosomes to the new nucleus. When combined, the egg is fertilized with a full chromosome count.

DNA (deoxyribonucleic acid) carries the code of protein production, which is the code of life. **Chromosomes** are made of genes that are comprised of strands of DNA. Chromosomes come in pairs with a gene for each trait on each part of the pair and traits can be dominant or recessive.

DD	Dominant trait appears in organism.
DR	Dominant trait appears in organism, but organism carries recessive trait and can pass it on to its young.
RR	Recessive trait appears in organism.

Examples of these traits follow:

- D traits—brown eyes, curly hair, widow's peak, ability to curl tongue, freckles, unattached earlobes, dimples
- R traits—blue or green eyes, straight hair, cannot curl tongue, no freckles, attached earlobes, no dimples

Biological Evolution

Genetically, most offspring mirror their parents; however, abnormalities can sometimes occur. Abnormal genes (mutant) occur by mistakes in DNA duplication. This usually results in a non-fertilized egg. However, occasionally these mutations allow fertilization and in fact make the offspring more able to prosper or have a better chance of reproduction than offspring without the mutation. When this happens, eventually most of the species will possess the mutation.

Biological evolution is a scientific process in which inherited traits of organisms change from one generation to the next. There are two major beliefs in biological evolution:

- **Natural selection**—Producing and passing on traits that are helpful and necessary for survival of the organism.
- **Adaptations**—Large changes that occur after successive, small, and random changes in traits. Through natural selection, the best traits for the specific environment are kept or propagated forth.

The basic principles of ecological evolution are as follows:

- **Survival of the Fittest**—Organisms best adapted to an environment will generally produce the most offspring. Offspring that pose the more favorable traits will survive and reproduce. For example,

  Polar bears are best suited to the cold region of the world and continue to populate there.

  Mountain lions (cougars) are adaptable to most regions of the world.

- **Natural Selection**—This is the process in which individuals with favorable traits survive and reproduce. It shows how organisms become better adapted to survive environments while the organisms with less favorable adaptations or traits die out. For example,

  Camouflaged brown lizards living in the desert are more apt to survive than if they were black.

  An Arctic fox with white fur is more likely to survive the Arctic climate and its predators than a fox with black or brown fur.

Interdependence of Organisms

Since there are numerous organisms that inhabit the Earth, they must learn to adapt and function in diverse environments located on the Earth's surface. In general, on the Earth,

- Atoms and molecules cycle through the living and nonliving components of the biosphere.
- Energy travels through the ecosystem in a specific direction (the food chain cycle: photosynthetic organisms – herbivores – carnivores – decomposers).
- Organisms cooperate and compete within the ecosystem.
- Living organisms have the ability to produce populations of unlimited size; however, environments and resources are limited, and this interaction has significant effects on how the organisms react.
- Human beings live within the world's ecosystems and alter them by such things as population growth, technology, and consumption.

- **Ecology**—The study of the interaction of organisms within their environment and with one another.
- **Biosphere**—The environment in which living things exist (land, air, water).
- **Ecosystem**—The community of living things and the non-living environment. An ecosystem has energy flow and recycling of minerals. They can be large (desert or ocean) or small (pond or backyard).

There are three key characteristics of a balanced ecosystem:

1. Constant source of energy (sun-solar energy).
2. Energy is converted to glucose (needed by all living things).
3. Organic nutrients and matter are recycled successfully.

The **food chain** is the primary way ecosystems transmit and disperse energy.

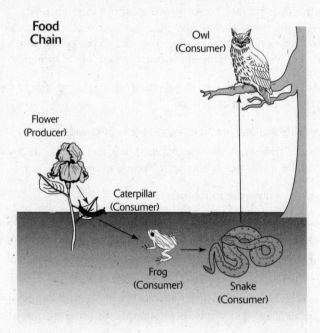

Ecosystem balance depends upon species interactions. The interdependence of organisms maintains a healthy world. Some conditions that change an ecosystem's balance include the following:

- Supply of energy changes
- Food cycle interrupted
- Organic matter and nutrients increase or decrease
- Natural disasters (floods, earthquakes, tornadoes, erosion)
- Natural phenomena (el niño)
- Human contributions (air or water pollution, raw material usage, increase production of carbon dioxide, radiation, mining, deforestation)

Life Cycle

Every living organism moves through these stages:

1. Come into being (sometimes a larvae state)
2. Grow
3. Metamorphosis
4. Mature
5. Reproduce
6. Die

Some lower species exhibit additional juvenile and larvae stages, and these occur in order to develop into adults (for example, frog). In higher species, the fertilized egg develops directly into the adult (for example, monkey, dog, human).

Physical Science

This is the first domain of science in which the tangible and material world is studied. Instruction should focus on facts, concepts, principles, theories, and models of science. Following are physical science components:

- Structures and properties of objects, materials, and matter
- Motion and force
- Light, heat, electricity, magnetism
- Energy (transfer, consumption, production)

Structure and Properties of Matter

Materials found on Earth include elements, compounds, and mixtures.

- **Atom**—Something so small it can no longer be divided. It is the basis of chemistry as atoms make up all matter. An atom has a **nucleus** (protons and neutrons) and seven shells (orbiting electrons). An atom is comprised of **neutrons** (no charge), **protons** (positively charged), and **electrons** (negatively charged). The atomic number is the number of electrons. The atomic mass is figured based on the total number of protons and neutrons. Bohr discovered the structure of the atom and developed the Bohr diagram.
- **Nucleus**—Has a positive charge (+). The center of the atom, it contains neutrons and protons.
- **Proton**—Located in the nucleus, it has a positive (+) charge. It is symbolized by 'p.'
- **Electron**—Located in the shells that orbit an atom's nucleus, it has a negative (−) charge. The symbol is 'e.'
- **Neutron**—Located in the nucleus, it has no charge, and the symbol is 'n.'

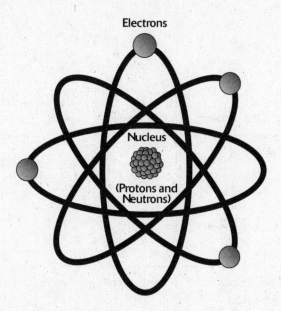

Chemistry

An **element** is matter that cannot be separated into different kinds of matter.

Common elements to know:

H=Hydrogen	O=Oxygen	He=Helium
C=Carbon	Cu=Copper	Ag=Silver
Au=Gold	Ni=Nickel	Sn=Tin
Fe=Iron	Al=Aluminum	N=Nitrogen
S=Sulfur	I=Iodine	K=Potassium
Ca=Calcium	Na=Sodium	Mg=Magnesium

A **compound** is the chemical bonding of two or more elements.

Common compounds to know:

H_2O=water	CO_2=carbon dioxide	CO=carbon monoxide
NaCL=table salt	$NaHCO_3$=baking soda	SiO_2=sand or glass

Three Forms of Matter: Gas, Liquid, Solid

State of Matter	Definition of Type of Matter	Shape of Container	Example	Graphic Representation
Gas	Has weak molecular forces with no shape, color, or volume and can expand infinitely	volume	air	**Gas** Shape of container Volume of container
Liquid	Takes on the shape of the container that holds it and has definite volume with molecular forces weaker than a solid	fixed volume	milk	**Liquid** Shape of container Free surface Fixed volume
Solid	Has defined shape and definite volume with strong molecular forces, and holds a shape	fixed volume	wood	**Solid** Holds shape Fixed volume

As a matter of fact, all matter can move from one state to another. This can be accomplished through temperature changes and pressure.

Solid   Decrease pressure → Increase energy →   **Liquid**   Decrease pressure → Increase energy →   **Gas**

States of matter include the following:

Name of State	Starts from	Changes to
melting	solid	liquid
freezing	liquid	solid
boiling	liquid	gas
condensation	gas	liquid
sublimation	solid	gas (skips liquid stage)
deposition	gas	solid (skips liquid stage)

Energy

Energy is necessary to do work.

- **Work** (w)—When an object is moved through a distance in response to some force; energy is transferred from one object to another (w = fd means work = force × distance).
- **Power**—The rate of doing work.

There are two types of energy.

- **Potential energy**—This is energy that could do work if released. For example, a ball resting at the top of a steep hill is in the potential energy position.
- **Kinetic energy**—This is energy that is doing work or is occurring. For example, a ball rolling down a steep hill is displaying kinetic energy.

Interactions of Energy and Matter

The Law of Conservation of Matter states that matter can neither be created nor destroyed. Einstein created the formula of $E = mc^2$ to show the relationship between energy and matter. E is the amount of energy, m is the given mass, and c is the speed of light (300,000 km/s). It was discovered that particles of matter can be made to go fast enough that they will gain in mass.

The Law of Conservation of Matter and Energy states that the sum of the matter and the energy in the universe remains the same.

- **Heat energy and states of matter**—The motion of particles within a substance causes heat.

  All objects are made up of atoms and or molecules that are in a constant state of motion.

  The cooler an object is, the slower the motion of particles.

  The hotter an object is or becomes, the faster the motion of particles.
- **Melting**—When a solid reaches a point at which its particles move so rapidly that they escape their boundaries and begin to move more freely (liquid).
- **Vaporization/evaporation**—When the particles in a liquid are heated to such a temperature as to make then uncontainable within liquid boundaries, then they escape into a gas.
- **Diffusion**—The movement of particles from a high concentration to an area of low concentration. In a system, diffusion occurs until the concentrations in all areas is the same. This is called *a state of equilibrium*.

Most solids, liquids, and gases expand when heated (due to the increase in the motion of particles) and contract when cooled (due to the decreased motion of particles). For example, tire pressure increases as a person drives a vehicle on the road. Friction causes heat, but it decreases if the car is left in the shade (cooling off of air particles).

Little known fact: Ice is the exception to this rule, as it expands as it cools, due to the molecules of water arranging themselves into a crystalline matrix that occupies more volume as a solid than a liquid.

Force and Motion

Forces that cause changes in the motion of objects (Newton's First Law) are gravity, friction, air resistence, pushing, pulling, and throwing.

- **Gravity**—Acceleration of objects toward the center of the earth.
- **Inertia**—The state of an object remaining at rest or in motion.
- **Friction**—The force between any two objects that come into contact with one another. Friction cannot be eliminated. For example, parachute and air, socks on a tile floor, and bicycle wheel on a road.

Energy and Matter

The universe is comprised of things made from energy and matter. **Energy** that cannot be created or destroyed can be defined by separating it into seven categories which relate to the forms of physical science: **heat, sound, light, magnetism, mechanical, electric, chemical,** and **nuclear.** All these forms of energy can be changed into another form without the loss of any energy. **Matter** that can not be created or destroyed can be converted into another form without losing its mass. Einstein created the law of relativity which verified the laws of energy and matter, previously thought not to be possible.

Heat can be produced in many ways, all of which cause an increase in the motion of particles of a substance.

Types of heat movement follow:

- **Conduction**—Heat moves from warmer areas to cooler areas along materials that conduct heat (wire and rod).
- **Convection**—Heat is transferred through collisions of molecules and occurs only in liquids and gases as they circulate.
- **Radiation**—Heat is transmitted in the form of infrared radiation and occurs only in gases and empty space.

Sound is controlled by vibrations. The speed of sound depends upon the space between the molecules. It travels quickest through solids and slowest through gas.

Rules of sound:

- The more rapid the vibration, the higher the pitch.
- Sound travels through solids, liquids and gases.
- Objects produce sound by causing a series of compressions and rare fractions (wave) of molecules.

A **wave** is a longitudinal movement in which the compressions and rare fractions travel spherically outward from the source. A **wavelength** is the distance between two successive compressions or two successive rare fractions.

The characteristics of sound are as follows:

Characteristic	Definition	Cause
Pitch	How high or low the sound	Rate of vibration
Amplitude	Loudness or volume of the sound	By force used to create the sound (the greater the force, the louder the sound)
Quality	A distinctive timbre	Source of the sound

Light travels through anything that is transparent or translucent. Following are four rules of light:

- Travels in rays (straight lines).
- The more dense the object or medium, the slower light travels.
- Travels in transverse ways.
- Is an electromagnetic wave that is created by causing the electrons to move rapidly and emit energy.

A **transverse wave** has a series of crests and troughs; like dropping a pebble into still water.

A **wavelength** is the distance between the crest or the distance between the troughs.

Reflection is caused by light rays bouncing off of a surface.

Refraction is caused by the bending of light rays as they passed from one medium to another.

Magnetism involves magnets, which have two poles (North and South). The rules of magnets are

- Similar poles repel (N-N, S-S)
- Opposite poles attract (N-S, S-N)

Electric energy can be found in different forms. Electricity is a kind of energy that can produce light, heat, motion, and magnetic force. Electricity flows through a conductor as current.

Laws of electric energy include:

- Like charges repel one another (+ +, − −).
- Opposite charges attract one another (+−, −+).

Electric current contains an electrical energy and a conductor.

A **conductor** is a material that allows electric current to flow through it (for example, copper, gold, aluminum, silver).

Insulators are material that does not allow electric current to flow through it (for example, wood, rubber, plastic).

Voltage is the amount of force of the current.

Amperage is the amount of electricity that flows through a conductor.

Resistance causes electron flow to do the work and decreases flow of amperage in a circuit.

Circuit is the path that an electric current flows. Two types of circuits are as follows:

- **Series**—The resistances are connected to one another, one following another. If one resistance is disconnected, the circuit fails to work.
- **Parallel**—Each resistance is connected to the main circuit with its own connection. If one is disconnected the others still work.

Static electricity is a result of the accumulation of electric charges.

Mechanical energy relates to that action or power created by use of machines.

A **simple machine** is a tool with few or no moving parts that does work. There are six types of simple machines.

Machine	Purpose	Illustration
Lever	Magnifies force, increases speed, or changes directions and is used to lift things. Three types of levers follow: • 1st class (fulcrum is in the middle or between the effort and the load). For example, scissors and seesaw. • 2nd class (fulcrum is at one end, so the load is between the fulcrum and the effort). For example, stapler, wheelbarrow. • 3rd class (fulcrum is at the end, and the effort is between the fulcrum and the load). For example, tweezers, fishing rod.	**Class 1** Load ... Effort ... Fulcrum **Class 2** Load ... Effort ... Fulcrum **Class 3** Effort ... Load ... Fulcrum
Wedge	Magnifies force, used to push things apart, or secure things together.	Wedge
Incline Plane	Magnifies force and distance increases. Is used to help move things up and down, and reduces the force needed.	Inclined plane
Pulley	Reduces force needed to move an object, but increases the distance. Is a wheel and a rope that moves things up and down, and changes the direction of force.	Pulley

Machine	Purpose	Illustration
Wheel & Axel	Increases speed, facilitates motion, and movement of objects.	Wheel & Axel
Screw	Magnifies force by increasing distance.	Screw

The Law of Simple Machines—The force put into the machine (effort force) times the distance the effort moves equals the output force from the machine (resistance) times the distance the resistance moves.

Chemical energy is the result of the materials found on earth interacting with another material. Materials are elements, compounds, or mixtures. An element is a simple form of matter and everything in the universe is made of some element. There are 92 known elements naturally found and 21 known that are manmade (all radioactive). A **compound** is the result of a chemical reaction of two or more elements. When two or more elements combine without a chemical reaction, it is known as a **mixture.**

In **nuclear** energy, the nucleus of the atom forms a different kind of element producing increased energy. This change or disintegration of the nucleus represents the half life of the substance. Radioactivity is a form of nuclear energy that can be used in the field of medicine, creating electricity, or powering generators.

Two kinds of nuclear reactions are known:

- **Fission**—When the nuclei of atoms are disintegrated (for example, nuclear reactors or atomic bomb)
- **Fusion**—When two or more nuclei are smashed together with increased force to form a different kind of nucleus (for example, the sun or a hydrogen bomb)

Science as Inquiry

Science is the process of obtaining and verifying knowledge. The subject of science permits educators to allow children to be curious, ask questions, discover information, and explore possibilities. When it is studied as inquiry, it supports skill development in critical thinking and learning scientific reasoning. When children are involved in seeking the answers, as the constructivist theory emphasizes, the results have more meaning. It is recommended that science be inquiry-based as this promotes the basic principles of organization and knowledge of science. Cognitive development and the acquisition of knowledge are enhanced through this process. **Scientific concept** includes the process of producing knowledge.

Features that exhibit sound and valuable science inquiry:

- Identify and control of variables.
- Collect data using various instruments.
- Interpretation of data through reliable and valid reasoning.
- Formulate and test hypotheses.
- Communicate procedures, methods, results, and interpretations.

According to Niels Bohr:

> *"The task of science is to both extend the range of our experience and reduce it to order."*

Twelve Processes of Science

Scientific theory includes the following processes in order: observation, question, theory, experiment, data, results, and conclusion. **Processes** are a systematic chain of actions directed toward a conclusion, usually in the form of steps that clarify the concepts. These processes are the fundamental building blocks of science:

- **Observation**—Uses the five senses to watch the world and the movement within it
- **Classification**—Uses commonalities of objects to logically group items
- **Communication**—The ability to share findings and results with others
- **Measurement**—The ability to use appropriate tools
- **Prediction**—Uses prior knowledge and experience to foresee what may occur
- **Inference**—Uses prior knowledge and experience to state why something may occur or why it is the way it is
- **Variable identification/control**—To determine the factors and stabilize all but one
- **Formulation of hypothesis**—Develops an assumption based on variables
- **Interpretations of data**—Uses gathered information and constructs it in charts, graphs, or narration to provide reasonable results
- **Define operations**—Applies mathematical equations and principles
- **Experimentation**—Uses prior knowledge and the hypothesis to try different solutions
- **Constructing models**—Identifies the need for a model and creates an accurate and appropriate model

Science in Personal and Social Perspectives

This specific area of science helps students learn to connect with their world. They focus on the study of personal health, environmental issues, and science/technology, and the greater society.

History and Nature of Science

This is an area of science education that enhances the study of nature and includes history in science to promote an understanding of inquiry, science in society, and human relationships within science.

Science is the process for producing knowledge, and according to David Jerner-Martin, there are six characteristics of science.

1. **Science rejects authority and authoritarianism**. Most science is working to disprove hypotheses by not proving them correct. Elementary science should focus on trying to contradict theories which in turn all prove and affirm knowledge.
2. **Science is honest.** The scientific method and steps for experiments allows others to duplicate and disprove or prove theories. Flawed research will lead to failed theories.
3. **Science rejects supernatural explanations for observed phenomena.** Science looks for natural explanations for phenomena that can be tried, retried, and tried again.
4. **Science is skeptical.** There is always some degree of uncertainty in the natural world; there is no "absolute truth."
5. **Science is parsimonious**. The simplest explanation of an observation is always chosen. Science should focus upon quality of understanding rather than quantity of information presented.
6. **Science seeks consistency**. There are basic rules for the natural world and events will occur in consistent patterns.

Science produces products such as jet engines, medical advances, cell phones, computers, draught resistant crops, ethanol, and so on. Technology and science go hand in hand. However, technology is defined as the means by which humans control or modify their environment. Technology has helped humans adapt to their world and environment, creating more sophisticated methods to meet their needs; metal tools instead of stone tools, cars for transportation rather than horses, email for communication rather than telegraphs and so on.

Careers

Working with elementary students to excite them in the area of science, as well as technology, engineering, and mathematics (STEM), should include the study of various careers in the field. Students should be provided with information about the many types of science careers in the many different categories of science: health sciences, space sciences, environmental sciences, science education, ocean sciences, and so on. Acknowledging that not all science careers require significant study of science and that there is a focus on gender equity in the field may help to entice diverse learners into the field. Providing school and community activities, descriptions of specific careers and guest speakers will help establish the many possibilities of science as a career.

Systems, Order, and Organization

Science is reflected in its systems and the order and organization of information. Establishing a method of arranging and categorizing data is a fundamental practice in science. There are universal methods to maintain organization of science data collection and information. Some methods are listed in the following table.

Systems	Examples	Purpose
Small units of the natural world to investigate Organized groups of related parts, objects, and components that form a larger whole Have boundaries, input and output, parts and reactions Two types: closed (not affected by external forces) open (able to be affected by external forces)	machines education organisms transportation numbers galaxy	Keeps track of organisms, energy, mass, and events Develops understanding of regularities, commonalities, reactions, and equilibrium Extends knowledge of law, theories, and models
Order	Examples	Purpose
Statistically describes the behavior of matter, organisms, events, and objects	probability	Develops knowledge of factors influencing matter, organisms, events, and objects Promotes improved and increased observations Creates advanced exploratory models
Organization	Examples	Purpose
Various types and levels Gathering, grouping, and structuring of systems and information	Food Pyramid Periodic Table of Elements Organism Classification	Provides useful ways of thinking about the world Shows interaction of systems Demonstrates hierarchy

Measurement is a process (method) in science to describe length, distance, volume or capacity, mass, and temperature.

Distance	Volume	Mass	Temperature
inches feet yards miles league meters (cm, mm, Km)	ounces cup quart gallon liter (mL, cL, KL)	pounds grams (mg, cg, Kg)	Fahrenheit Celsius

Tables of Measurement Conversions

Length is the distance between two points.

Standard or Conventional measure	Metric measure
12 inches (in) = 1 foot (ft)	100 centimeters (cm) = 1 meter (m)
3 feet = 1 yard (yd)	1,000 millimeters (mm) = 1 meter (m)
5,280 feet = 1 mile (mi)	1,000 m = 1 kilometer (km)
3 miles = 1 league	2.54 cm = 1 inch (in)

Volume is how much space something takes up.

Standard or Conventional measure	Metric measure
8 ounces (oz) = 1 cup (c)	1 liter (L) = 1,000 milliliter (ml)
4 cups = 1 quart (qt)	1 liter (L) = 100 (cl)
4 qts = 1 gallon (gal)	1 ml = 1 cubic centimeter (cc)

Mass versus Weight

Mass is the amount of material in something.

Weight is the pull of gravity on something, and the amount depends on the strength of gravity.

Metric Prefixes Chart						
Milli-	Centi-	Deci-	Unit-	Deca-	Hecto-	Kilo-
1/1000 or .001	1/100 or .01	1/10 or .1	1	10 times	100 times	1000 times

Science Introduction to Curriculum, Instruction, and Assessment (0011)

Science is everywhere in the world. Students are exposed to it on a daily basis and its concepts reach far beyond the academic subject. The attitudes people gain about science are based on the knowledge and experiences they have. To help children develop strong, positive attitudes about science concepts and applications, educators must provide them with successful experiences and exciting opportunities to study, research, investigate, think about, ask questions, and draw conclusions.

What children learn about science is influenced by how it is taught. The key to acquiring scientific knowledge is for children to "do" science and by doing it, they will learn. Children move from the concrete level of science knowledge to the abstract level as they mature and understanding is actively constructed through individual and social processes. Furthermore, multidisciplinary and integrated approaches need to be utilized to further increase science comprehension (history of science, reading science).

The National Science Standards (see "Science (0014)") are available for review and provide educators with an overall view of the needs of students in this academic area. Each standard assumes the knowledge and skills of the other standards. The National Science Teachers Association (NSTA), is involved with science education transformation in this country. The NSTA has two primary goals:

1. Master scientific literacy for all.
2. Strengthen the supply of scientists, engineers, and science teachers.

Other organizations related to science education expound upon the beliefs that children should be provided with less scientific content and more opportunities for discovery. Children should be allowed to investigate, study, gain access through interdisciplinary topics, be offered inquiry, and be stimulated not only by the topics of science, but through the methods of science instruction.

The American Association for the Advancement of Science promotes the advancement of science and human progress. This organization published a document that is utilized by many schools in science education programs, as it outlines what students should know in the areas of science, mathematics and technology at the grade levels: K–2, 3–5, 6–8, and 9–12. It is an aid to teachers in the development of science curriculum.

The National Science Education Standards and Assessment created a document that outlines the standards and describes the expectations for student knowledge and achievement. Additionally, the National Association for the Education of Young Children provides guidelines for developmentally appropriate practices for children ages 3–8 years and is a resource to consider when developing a science program.

Other organizations helpful in securing information about science education are as follows:

- The National Institute for Science Education (NISE)
- The Council for Elementary Science International (CESI)
- National Institute of Health Office of Science Education (NIHOSE)
- The National Center for Science Education

The science portion of the Praxis II 0011 exam assesses an examinee's overall knowledge and application of information regarding curriculum, instruction, and assessment, specifically the unifying concepts and processes, inquiry, technology, health principles, and pedagogy. In this section of the study guide, examinees will find content specific to these science topics and the more general elementary practices are found in the Overview to #0011 at the front of the study guide. Use both of these sections to study for this exam.

The 0011 exam measures how well an examinee knows how to develop and deliver instruction based on science content knowledge. This exam employs examples of elementary situations through multiple choice questions. This section of the study guide includes the information necessary for the examinee to clearly utilize the content of 0014 in the implementation of curriculum and instruction and the use of assessments in science education.

Curriculum Components

The more basic elements of instruction and curriculum design are found in the "Overview" of 0011 section of this book. It includes curriculum components such as scope and sequence, appropriate materials, technology, and learner objectives. This information is used in all elementary subject areas and can be adapted and modified for science. The content in this portion of the study guide is more specific to science education topics.

Curriculum must be carefully addressed at the specific grade level and aligned with state and national standards. The content of any science curriculum should be integrated with other academic subjects and the areas of fine arts. The scope of the curriculum should establish parameters of the topics covered and the material should be sequenced logically to promote concept and skill acquisition. Inquiry-based learning and authentic assessments are critical to science education at the elementary level.

The disciplines of science are vast and comprehensive and each discipline depends on another discipline. For this reason, many science educators and researchers believe that sciences should be taught using the STS or science-technology-society perspective. This is the integration of all areas of science. Science-technology studies endorses the study of social, political, and cultural values and their impact on scientific research and technological innovation as well as society, politics, and culture as a whole.

Curriculum Content	
Approach	**Description**
Historical	Studies the history of science at a human level
Philosophical	Studies the nature of science and the different viewpoints
Issues-Based	Studies the factors of science that affect the environment and society

Yet, many educators also believe that science instruction must integrate not only the areas of science, but other academic areas as well. Incorporating language arts, mathematics, social studies, and fine arts into science education provides a rich curriculum for elementary children. It provides a more realistic view of the world and the situations they will face in the future.

Most educators who teach science believe that it is better to teach the processes than just the products of science. The laws, facts, and content of science are best discovered through learning the processes.

Strategies and Activities

The majority of elementary science teachers use a combination of methods, strategies, and activities for science instruction. A highly recommended format, **inquiry-based learning,** is being utilized across the country. It leads students towards mastering higher level analysis skills and using logical thinking skills. Many publishers of science materials are incorporating this type of format in their printed materials.

Science educators refer to an instructional cycle and a series of steps that may be followed with students as active learners. This series of steps aligns with the EEI model of instruction (defined in the "Overview" section).

Following is the outline of the instructional cycle for science instruction:

- **Discrepant event**—An unusual phenomenon is demonstrated or described to students. This aids students in developing the hypothesis and experimental design.
- **Question**—A question that integrates the variable for the selected investigation. Example of question format: When does (*independent variable*) impact (*dependent variable*)?
- **Inquiry**—Experiments may be constructed by the students based on the investigated variable. The format may be question/answer, collection of more data, or by inferences/comparisons. The experiments should follow an outline:
    - State the question that will be investigated.
    - Formulate a hypothesis.
    - Describe the independent (condition to be changed) and dependent variables (what is being measured, with suggested tool).
    - Indicate the controls; identify the constant variables.
    - Collect data; organize and carefully gather data to ensure accuracy of results through use of tables, charts, graphs.
    - Organize and correlate the data to determine how to present the gathered information. The use of line or bar graphs and solid communication helps students learn the presentation skills regarding experimentation results.
    - Use mathematical applications; science and math terminology may be used, as well as math equations and tools.
    - Conclusion—Present summary of the experiment, the process, and the results.
    - Include enrichment activities. For some learners an extension of the basic experiment may be quite beneficial. It may include readings, additional research, further experiments, or a project to enrich their knowledge base.

Several methods of instructional delivery are utilized by science teachers in classrooms, according to the specific topic and the students. It is valuable to educators to vary the presentation of science as it helps in the coverage of the content and the motivation of the students. Some of the more common methods:

- **Demonstration**—This provides young students with models or visual examples of the information. It may precede an experiment or inquiry-based activity or it may be incorporated into a lecture or group presentation.

- **Lecture**—The teacher imparts the information to the students and may use multimedia to deliver the content. It is a structured format generally not recommended for elementary students, as inquiry-based learning is not represented.

- **Inquiry-based or inquiry-guided learning**—Evidence of high retention rates, this format is often facilitated or guided by the teacher. The process of learning is given to the students, so it is often used for small group projects. It may be used for experimental investigations and gathering data regarding a hypothesis.

- **Cooperative learning activity**—Group activity using homogeneous or heterogeneous combinations of students, selected by the teacher. Aids students in gaining problem-solving, communication, and critical thinking skills.

- **Small group instruction and presentations**—Students work in groups of 2, 3, or 4 to gather information and develop a presentation that is then made to the whole group. Students take on roles in the small group, such as presenter, recorder, defender, organizer, researcher, and so on.

- **Whole group discussion**—Similar to the lecture format, but here students are doing more of the talking. They are responsible for regurgitation of the information learned, while also analyzing the content, thereby presenting opinions or asking questions of others. The teacher often facilitates and manages the discussion.

- **Laboratory-Experimentation**—Sometimes used from those provided in a textbook or experiment manual or ideas collected from teacher experience. This is a large group activity as everyone does the same experiment, so inquiry is not a part of the learning process.

- **Research projects**—Can be part of the overall assignments for the class or used as enrichment for students who might need additional and extended content information.

- **Literature review**—Either used as a whole class project, or for individual assignments, students use additional resources besides the textbook, by selecting books and materials via the library, the Internet, or classroom.

Unifying Concepts and Processes

These concepts provide students with the knowledge, procedures, and ideas of how the natural world works. These concepts are carried out and repeated throughout the other standards. NSTA states: "In early grades, instruction should establish the meaning and use of unifying concepts and processes-for example, what it means to measure and how to use measurement tools. At the upper grades, the standard should facilitate and enhance the learning of scientific concepts and principles by providing students with a big picture of scientific ideas—for example, how measurement is important in all scientific endeavors."

Unifying processes include the following:

- Systems, order, organization
- Evidence, models, explanation
- Change, constancy, measurement
- Evolution, equilibrium, cycles
- Form, function, structure

Science as Inquiry

Inquiry takes the student a step beyond science as a process. Inquiry introduces students to science skills such as observation, inferences, and experimentation. Students should be engaged in scientific reasoning and critical thinking during this period. Inquiry activity involves the student and teaches him to ask questions, plan and conduct investigations, use tools and techniques to gather data, draw conclusions between evidence and explanation, construct and evaluate alternate explanations, and to form and communicate scientific arguments.

Inquiry should promote the following:

- Comprehension of scientific concepts
- Appreciation of history of scientific knowledge
- Understanding the nature of science
- Acquisition of the skills needed to become independent thinkers of the natural world
- Increasing the tendency to use the skills, abilities and attitudes associated with science

Physical Science

This is the first domain of science in which the tangible and material world is studied. Instruction should focus on facts, concepts, principles, theories, and models of science. Physical Science includes properties of objects, materials, matter; motion and force; light, heat, electricity, magnetism; energy (transfer, consumption, production).

Life Science

The second domain of science examines the existence of organisms. Instruction should focus on facts, concepts, principles, theories, and models of science. Life Science includes characteristics of organisms, behavior and regulation, diversity and adaptation; life cycles, reproduction, heredity; structure and function in living systems; organisms and environments, populations, and ecosystems.

Earth and Space Science

This is the third domain of science in which properties and the structure of the Earth are studied as well as the universal structures. Instruction should focus on facts, concepts, principles, theories, and models of science. Earth and Space Science includes properties and structure of Earth systems; Earth's history; Earth within the solar system; objects in space; changes in Earth and space.

Science in Personal and Social Perspectives

This area helps students obtain the tools and understanding to act on personal and social issues. These perspectives promote, encourage, teach, and allow them to develop decision-making skills. They also incorporate the technology of science in which students will learn the process of design in science and how science is intertwined with technology. Students will gain strong foundations on which to base decisions they will encounter as citizens. Science in personal and social perspectives includes personal health; populations, resources, environments; natural hazards, local challenges, risks, and benefits; science and technology, technological design, artificial versus natural designs.

History and Nature of Science

Students must recognize and understand the symbiotic web of science and history. Science reflects history and is a continual and every-changing enterprise. This standard examines the role science has played in the development of various cultures and the human aspects of science. History and Nature of Science includes science as a human endeavor; nature of science; history of science.

Use of Materials and Technology

Use of science materials in elementary classrooms is an area educators should evaluate. Storage is a critical need, as the materials vary for the topics covered, some being of large and multiple parts. Using inexpensive, safe, and easily obtainable materials for experiments will enhance the instruction. Equally important is to obtain science tools that will withstand multiple uses, even though they may be more expensive (microscopes, thermometers).

Technology is a strong component of a science education program. It is one of the disciplines of science and can be utilized to enhance student achievement. Students must be proficient in their use of technology tools and methods in order to sufficiently use them as a benefit to their instruction.

Technology encompasses the media (films, videos, audio recordings), 3-D hard copies (charts, displays, models, manipulatives), electronic tools (calculators, lab equipment), and computers (databases, distance learning opportunities, software). Information is easily accessible and areas of science may be reachable throughout the world. Six reasons for the use of computers and technology in an elementary science education program are:

1. Computers are available and used throughout the world.
2. Students are comfortable with electronic equipment and media.
3. Information is readily available and new information is constantly obtainable.

4. Electronic equipment provides opportunities for investigation and research not before possible.

5. Students' learning needs may be addressed by use of technology.

6. Technology is a vehicle of science that scientists use.

Model Building and Forecasting

Models in science provide a concrete, visual representation of something that cannot otherwise be seen, such as the solar system. Building models helps students comprehend the size and use of an object or process in the field of science. Students can investigate scientific phenomena to create or build a model that represents the object or process based on their research. They learn observation, measurement, comparison, and investigative skills.

Spatial relationships is the most difficult aspect of building models, as most models are based on science objects or processes that are incomprehensibly large or so minute that they cannot be seen without powerful microscopes. It becomes a mathematical challenge to replicate it with some accuracy, although with some models that is not possible.

Forecasting consists of discovering, simplifying, and applying patterns in scientific discovery. Students need to learn how to proceed with finding, collecting, and using data about the patterns they find, specifically in the natural and manufactured worlds. This act of forecasting is a process of prediction and students may use graphs, charts, or equations to communicate the findings. This skill is used in weather reporting, the aviation field, and in studying the Earth.

Analysis of Work-Assessment

The NSES establishes assessment standards that include evaluation of the process skills, assessment of inquiry, evaluation of attitude, and the evaluation of content.

For most educators, the assessment of content is primary to their instruction. Teachers probably agree that in order to proceed with next stage concepts in any subject, students must demonstrate that they comprehend and can utilize the recently presented information. It is essential in science that students are able to show their knowledge base of one concept before moving on to the next concept, as many of the concepts are interrelated and dependent upon the prior information. Teachers should be able to assess a classroom of students quickly each day to ensure the grasp of critical concepts.

Naturally, quizzes and tests are used in all subjects and provide some benefit in science education. These may even be required by the state, district, or school as a measure of accountability regarding the standardization of the materials and instruction. However, there are other assessments (alternative and authentic) that will be useful for science education. These may include the following:

- Presentations
- Research papers
- Literature reviews
- Laboratory use and techniques
- Discussion format
- Science project
- Homework

- Games
- Journal
- Interview
- Small group discussions
- Checklists
- Portfolios

Note: **Common types of assessments used for other subject areas are explained in the "Overview" of 0011.**

In addition to the content knowledge of science, an **evaluation of the process skills** is ultimately important to students' overall abilities to master science topics. When children perform these skills, teachers may observe the **indicators** to evaluate their mastery. Helpful to teachers in identifying indicators is the use of a checklist, observation, or interview as not all indicators are required at every grade level. Identifying the expectations for the age group, and the grade are necessary in determining student proficiency.

Process indicators at the elementary level may include:

observing	classifying	communicating
measuring	predicting	inferring
identifying content	controlling variables	formulating hypothesis
interpreting data	researching information	experimenting
constructing models	using math operations	presenting findings

Another area of assessment critical to science education is the student's **proficiency of the inquiry method.** When a teacher provides an open-ended task, students must use their skills in investigation, communication, and processing data to complete the activity. Teachers generally develop a list of the inquiry indicators that suit the class, the age, and the content. Some specific skills to evaluate include

initiates investigation	presents ideas and findings	exhibits self-evaluation
investigates questions	challenges ideas	uses prediction
discusses processes	uses variety of resources	applies learning to life

Since one of the primary goals of elementary science education is for students to become more interested in the subject and perhaps select a science related career for this fast paced world, an assessment of the student's **attitude about science** will relay critical information to the teacher about how well the student is performing or will perform. The indicators to assess in the area of attitude are based on the student's characteristics, the program available, the community resources, and the existing attitudes. Some indicators include

enjoys science and the investigation process	curious about the topic or activity
participates in additional science activities	displays verbal skills
inquires about science related topics	wants more time to participate

Basic Principles of Health Education

Health education is an important topic in the science curriculum. Not only will the student benefit from the instruction, but families, communities, and environments will improve. The primary goal is for students to attain and maintain a healthy lifestyle, and while in school, good health impacts student learning and achievement.

School health education should utilize community resources to promote educational opportunities, establish an environment conducive to appropriate health practices, empower students to demonstrate effective healthy routines, work with families to encourage change for health benefits, and maintain health messages that ultimately motivate students to adopt healthy habits.

When educators develop the health education program, it is essential to focus the curriculum on the following:

- Behaviors and conditions that ensure proper health, reducing at-risk behaviors
- Instilling skills to use the behaviors or establish the conditions in personal lives
- Teaching attitudes, values, and knowledge of the behaviors and conditions
- Providing opportunities to practice and acquire the skills

The health education curriculum is sometimes taught separately and oftentimes integrated into subjects or classes, like science, physical education, consumer education, or social studies. Integrating the health content is particularly beneficial at the elementary level. It offers a more meaningful and detailed study of the concepts and students are more apt to retain the critical information and make changes to their habits.

Content Specific Pedagogy

Research demonstrates the effectiveness of promoting the concept of scientific products first before teaching the scientific processes at the elementary level. Selecting those products of most interest to elementary students is the recommended method for then teaching the processes. When children are active participants in scientific exploration they arrive at their own conclusions which become more meaningful.

Two of the most recognized theories useful to the instruction of science include

1. Constructivism
2. Inquiry-based learning

Constructivism is based on Piaget's work where the student constructs his own learning by using existing knowledge to create new knowledge. It is closely related to inquiry-based learning. Science is the process of construction and reconstruction, so students study existing knowledge and reconstruct their idea base when new information is discovered. A basic premise of science education is that children learn science best when they construct meaning by merging prior information with new information, as they must observe, think, infer, and process the information.

Inquiry-based learning is at the forefront of contemporary science education programs. Research demonstrates that when students are involved in hands-on tasks, active in discovery, and participate in their own learning, they will retain knowledge for longer periods of time. If learning makes more sense to the student, it drives the learner toward higher levels of participation and achievement.

Three methods of imparting scientific knowledge to young children include

1. Expository method
2. Free-discovery method
3. Guided inquiry method

The **expository method** is completely a teacher dominated and directed way to instruct children. The teacher may manage the science classroom by providing lecture, delivering demonstrations, or imparting explanations of science topics. Some topics in science may require the expository method as the information and presentation may be standardized for all children. Delivering concepts, explaining procedures, demonstrating experiments, describing safety procedures, and distributing content information are all examples of topics which may require the expository method. Usually a summary of the information and an evaluation are included in the expository method.

Challenges which may be encountered while using the expository method include

- Motivation and attention of students may wane
- Opportunities for differentiated instruction are limited
- Pacing of instruction and that of student learning stilted
- Some topic discussions may not be relevant to all students
- Application of knowledge may not be available

The **free-discovery method** is based on child-directed topics and direction of the inquiry and knowledge acquisition where students may be involved and motivated in the learning process and the use of materials. Children create the situation of learning that is meaningful to them and where they may better apply the knowledge they have absorbed.

There are advantages and disadvantages of the free-discovery method according to educators. The advantages are in the use of the constructivist model and how the children may be actively engaged in the learning. The disadvantages include the appearance of lack of structure or organization, the need for additional time, materials, equipment and resources, and the need for implementation of strong classroom management principles.

Guided inquiry is on the continuum between the expository and free-discovery methods. In guided inquiry, the teacher may choose the topic of study and identify the process, by delineating questions and activities, while allowing students to construct their own investigation, determine their needed resources, find the answers to their questions, and organize the information. The teacher facilitates the children in experimentation, investigation, and exploration of teacher selected topics, by encouraging students through use of inquiry and open-ended questions based on the activity. The teacher guides the students in the direction of their findings yet permits them to be the "doers" of science.

Other concepts pertinent to the instruction of science at the elementary level are: universal design, blending integrated subjects and interdisciplinary studies, incorporating the multiple intelligences, and including literature studies.

Universal design should be utilized in addition to inquiry or constructivism, as it provides accommodations to diverse learners, which are necessary to meet each student's needs as related to science and the activities.

Integrated subjects and interdisciplinary studies focus on including other academic areas and other disciplines in the study of science. Because the world is not fragmented into separate subjects, it is recommended that science education be delivered in elementary classrooms as a broad approach to learning. For example: When studying the Water Cycle (science), students may construct a poster to advertise a movie about the cycle (art and language arts).

Multiple intelligences were first identified by Gardner who believed that humans have at least nine intelligences (more defined under "Overview" 0011) and these intelligences are demonstrated differently in each student. Therefore, teachers should create a variety of activities and utilize different instructional methods to address every student in the classroom, which focuses on each student's areas of strength. Students may use a combination of the intelligence strands to be successful in school and teachers should challenge students to utilize the less used intelligence areas by combining them randomly in their lessons.

Instructional styles to recognize in the area of science include

1. **Inductive** (from specific to general)—in which instruction begins with a study of the more finite information on which to base general conclusions or make broad generalizations about the subject or item.
2. **Deductive** (general to specific)—in which instruction begins with the study of the broad topic of information and then focuses down to the more detailed information on the subject

Note: **Additional pedagogy is outlined in the "Overview" of 0011 for elementary education.**

Science Content Area Exercises (0012)

This Praxis II exam (0012) assesses an examinee's ability to apply the knowledge gained in the content knowledge section (0014) and found in the curriculum, instruction and assessment information (0011). Examinees will have 2 hours to answer four essay questions; one question may be focused on science. Review the information from the Praxis II 0014 and 0011 science study guide, as well as the "Overview" of 0011 in this book.

There are endless possibilities on what questions may be presented on the exam, so examinees should prepare for this exam by considering how to use the science information they already know. Read through the following list of questions that relate to the topic of science education at the elementary level and try to answer them using a separate sheet of paper. You will notice that answers to these are not provided, as there are many different ways to answer these open ended questions. A rubric is used in the scoring of the actual exam (explained in the "Overview" of 0012).

The exercises posed on this exam will test the examinee's ability to prepare an extended, in-depth response to one question in the science area. When preparing to answer questions on this exam, remember that some of the questions presented may require multiple answers.

1. As the elementary teacher of a first-grade class you are planning instruction about plant growth and want to include experiments in your unit. Write a learner goal for the class on this topic. Explain and outline an experiment you would conduct with your students to help them achieve the learner goal.

2. Explain when and how to use manipulatives in science at the elementary level. Provide specific examples for two different science topics.

3. The second-grade class you are teaching is studying biomes. Explain five specific authentic assessments that could be used to evaluate and measure the students' comprehension and retention of the subject information.

4. Using Bloom's taxonomy, design a lesson for a sixth-grade class that is learning about the complexities of human anatomy.

5. Discuss how you would integrate technology into a unit study on the food chain. Outline learner objectives and explain how you would assess student comprehension.

6. Explain how you would integrate math, language arts, fine arts, and social studies in the unit study on the solar system. In addition to the explanation, provide an example of one activity for each subject area mentioned.

7. The Constructivist Theory of education, formed by Piaget, enhances the study of science. Describe how this theory relates to the subject of science and explain the various activities that could be utilized in an elementary classroom based on the application of this theory.

8. A fourth-grade class is studying the Earth's four principle components: Atmosphere (air), Lithosphere (land), Hydrosphere (water), and Biosphere (life). Create and outline a cooperative learning activity to include a list of materials and how the activity will be assessed. Then identify how the teacher should address differentiated instruction in implementing this cooperative learning activity.

9. Healthy living is a concept related to health education that may have a lifelong impact on students. Identify five activities that an elementary teacher might use to engage and motivate students at the fifth-grade level to begin making healthy personal choices.

10. A student enrolls in your elementary classroom four months after the beginning of school. This student demonstrates both cultural and linguistic diversity. Outline and describe four instructional methods that should be utilized to help this student learn the science concepts that have already been covered and how to continue to engage this student.

Physical Education Curriculum, Instruction, and Assessment (0011)

The National Association of Sports and Physical Education (NASPE) recognizes the importance of physical fitness at the elementary level. They have developed national standards that place emphasis upon the learning of skills, knowledge, and behaviors that will enable children to be physically active throughout their lives.

- Enjoyment of activity
- Positive participation in both organized and informal activities
- Awareness of fitness concepts
- Development of skills and knowledge of meaningful physical activity

The Council on Physical Activity for Children (COPEC) has written guidelines suggesting that elementary aged children

- Should participate in 30–60 minutes of developmentally appropriate physical activities on all or most of the days of the week
- Are encouraged to have an additional 60 minutes or more of free play per day
- Should participate in daily activities that include 10–15 minutes of moderate to vigorous action with brief periods of rest and recovery

Developmentally Appropriate

As with any subject, children must utilize and practice skills to become proficient and to develop finely tuned abilities. Developmentally appropriate physical education acknowledges that children progress at a variety of rates and possess a multitude of abilities. The environment, when focused on being developmentally appropriate, is a crucial component in their motor skill development.

When designing curriculum in Physical Education, these three concepts must be considered:

1. Children develop motor skills at different rates; do not expect all children to be able to perform the same tasks with the same accuracy.
2. A child's age does not predict motor ability. Although some children may seem to be naturally skilled in athletics, motor skill is obtained not through heredity but through use and practice.
3. Children develop motor skills naturally through play; informal play helps motor skills develop as well as involvement in structured physical education programs or sports.

There are four levels in elementary appropriate activities.

Level	Activity
1	Involves large muscle skill development and movement Has little formal organization Includes lifestyle activities
2	Is aerobic (biking, swimming) and includes basic skills (swimming strokes) Includes recreation activities and formal sports Considered cardiovascular activities

Level	Activity
3	Reinforces fitness concepts of muscular strength and flexibility
	Improves development of specific skill exercises
4	Considered "quiet" time
	Includes rest and inactivity

The focus in the **K–5** grades should be placed upon spatial awareness, effort, and peer relationships. It is during this period that a strong foundation for physical activity should be developed through movement concepts and skill themes.

The focus in the **6–8** grades relies heavily upon the foundation that was set in the previous years. During these years, the focus now shifts to the use of skills and concepts in a multitude of movement techniques. Exploring the many possibilities of movement and activity is the main focus to stimulate interest in lifetime fitness.

Basic Concepts

The purpose of physical education is to steer children into the practice of becoming physically active throughout their lifetimes. Studies demonstrate that when additional physical activity is included in school curricula, students improve their academic achievement and their ability to gain knowledge.

Physical education and sports are essential for elementary students because these both help children build confidence and self-respect, increase social interactions and abilities, and prepare children to cooperate and function together. Schools are the primary place where students acquire the basic concepts about healthy habits, nutrition and gain the fundamental skills necessary for competing and participating in physical activities.

The basic concepts in physical education include motor development, body awareness, and social adjustments and interactions. Students gain fitness skills, knowledge about sports and games, and learn to work with others through physical education activities and programs.

Following are some Physical Education terms with which you should be familiar:

- **physical fitness**—The body's ability to function efficiently and effectively. This includes both during work and leisure, for the body to be healthy, to resist disease, and to function in emergency situations. Health-related fitness encompasses muscular strength, muscular endurance, flexibility, cardiovascular efficiency, and body composition.
- **muscular strength**—The amount of force that a muscle can produce.
- **muscular endurance**—How long (what duration of time) can a muscle produce force.
- **flexibility**—The ability of a joint to move through its range of motion; can be increased through stretching of muscles, ligaments, and tendons. Flexibility is unique and specific to each joint and will differ from person to person.
- **cardiovascular efficiency**—Describes the body's capacity to maintain vigorous physical activity for a period of time and is developed through activities that increase the heart rate for extended lengths of time.
- **body composition**—The determined amount of fat cells in comparison to the amount of lean cells within a person's body mass and can be measured by skin-fold thickness. Body fat percentage is determined by heredity, nutrition, and activity level.

Increased physical activity has been proven to aid in academic improvements, such as higher mathematics scores, increased concentration, enhanced memory, reduction of inappropriate behaviors, and improved reading and writing scores. Other specific areas that aid children during their daily lives and are a focus for physical education courses include locomotor skills, body management, social discipline, game/sport skills, and learning about healthy lifestyles.

Locomotor Skills

Locomotor skills aid the student in traveling or moving some distance. Locomotion is the foundation for participation in game/sports as well as a fundamental skill for accessing home, school, and community. Locomotion follows chronological stepping stones of development and progresses from beginner to mastery level. Elementary students must obtain these basic skills in order to progress to higher levels.

Locomotor skills at the elementary level include, in progression from low to high:

- Walking
- Running
- Hopping
- Leaping
- Sliding
- Galloping
- Skipping

Assessment of locomotor skills can include the following:

- Informal observation
- Authentic assessment
- Formal observation
- Testing

Body Management

This is the ability of a student to control his physical self, personal movements, recognize spatial conditions, and develop body-space relationships. Body management includes the following:

- Spatial awareness
- Concept of direction
- Concepts of levels
- Pathways
- Extensions in space

Social Discipline

This topic focuses on improving social skills through the use of appropriate behaviors. It entails having the entire class on the same task or activity while productively engaged and actively focused upon the task being taught. There are two branches essential to managing social discipline.

Proactive—Intended to be used prior to the occurrence of the inappropriate behavior.

- Positive interaction—The teacher communicates with the students using praise or compliments acceptable behaviors. (For example, the teacher states "I really like the way Haley is walking to line up at the door.")
- Eliminate differential treatment—Teacher does not single out students for either positive or negative reinforcement. (For example, instead of stating "Andrea, please be quiet" the teacher states "I will wait for the class to listen.")
- Prompting—Reminding students of expectations and behaviors in a positive manner. (For example, "Remember to place your equipment in the bin.")

Reactive—Intended to be used after the inappropriate behavior occurs.

- Ignore the behavior—The teacher does not engage in the student's inappropriate actions. (For example, Eric calls out an answer without raising his hand; his answer is ignored, and another child's whose hand is raised is called upon.)
- Non-verbal interactions—The teacher uses techniques such as proximity, specific signals, or redirection. (For example, Justin veers from the task at hand so the teacher walks over and stands near him for the rest of the instructional period.)
- Person-to-person dialogue—The teacher sets up a time outside of class to discuss behavior. (For example, Teacher asks a student to attend a lunch or after school meeting.)

Game and Sports Skills

Children must understand specific concepts in order to participate in games or sports. These skills can be taught by using four levels of assessment.

1. **Precontrol** (beginner)—The movement or equipment moves the child instead of the child being in control. (For example, in trying to catch a ball, a child misses the ball and must chase it.)

2. **Control** (advanced beginner)—The movement seems to be more controlled, and the skill seems to be repeated in a similar manner each time it is demonstrated. This level involves strong concentration on the part of the child. (For example, when shooting a basketball, the ball goes in the general direction of the hoop.)

3. **Utilization** (intermediate)—The movements and skills are carried out with intensified instinctive actions. (For example, a child learns to dribble a basketball against an opponent.)

4. **Proficiency** (advanced)—The movements or skills become natural and are completed without thought. (For example, when a football is overthrown, a student can quickly change directions, track the football path, and make a successful catch.)

Healthy Lifestyles

Incorporating physical activity at an early age increases the likelihood that the child will become a life-long lover of movement. Early physical activity also helps to decrease or eliminate the ill effects of a sedentary lifestyle. Children's nutrition and activity level also assist them in leading healthy lifestyles.

> **The 1996 Surgeon General's report concludes** "that people of all ages, both male and female, who are physically active derive many benefits; reduction in the risk of premature mortality, in general, and of coronary heart disease, hypertension, colon cancer, and diabetes mellitus, in particular. Consistent influences on physical activity patterns among adults and young people include confidence in one's ability to engage in regular physical activity, enjoyment of physical activity, and support from others, positive beliefs concerning the benefits of physical activity, and lack of perceived barriers to physical activity. Physical activity also appears to improve health-related quality of life by enhancing psychological well-being and by improving physical functioning in persons compromised by poor health" (Surgeon General Report, 1996, pg 4).

Curriculum

The curriculum used for physical education should have a set scope and sequence with goals that are appropriate for all children. Activities should result from this plan that are both meaningful and age appropriate and that include some relation to previous experiences. The program should reflect cognitive development and support diversity.

The **multi-activity curriculum approach** is most suitable for the elementary grades as it includes such a variety of content and activities for the students. Educators can develop team sports, small group functions, and activities for individuals. Teachers can also create adventure activities, fitness activities, and those activities that require specific skills (such as dance).

Many types of curricula are possible in physical education, although some have a stronger focus for older students. Types of physical education curricula include the following:

- **Movement education**—Students gain knowledge about human movement, such as dance, gymnastics, and games.
- **Fitness approach**—Students learn more about the physiological aspects of the body and focus activities on endurance, flexibility, strength, and so on.
- **Academic-discipline approach**—With this problem-solving approach, students learn about healthy lifestyles and how to maintain recreational activities in their lifetimes.
- **Social-developmental model**—Students focus on personal growth and social skills, as individuals.
- **Sports-education model**—Students build knowledge about sports and seasons, so working as a team and increasing specific skill areas are important, as well as learning that competition can be fun.

- **Adventure-education approach**—Students learn about outdoor recreation and safety, and develop lifelong interests.
- **Eclectic approach**—This approach includes a combination of the many types of curricula available depending on the school, the students, the location, and the physical education teacher.

Assessment of Physical Education

In order for physical education to be meaningful, it is important to be able to identify at what skill level the students are working. Physical education is different than most other subjects because physical education touches on all three domains: the psychomotor domain, the cognitive domain, and the affective domain. It is important to be able to address and assess all three domains in each lesson to have a clearer understanding of where each individual student falls in each area of the curriculum and to be able to address the needs of all students.

Following are examples of assessments:

- Teacher observation
- Exit/entrance slips
- Homework
- Peer observation
- Self assessment
- Event task
- Videotaping
- Student illustrations
- Student displays
- Portfolios

Fine Arts Curriculum, Instruction, and Assessment (0011)

There is a connection between the arts and academic achievement, particularly in mathematics, language arts, and science. The arts provide aspects critical to the development of the human mind and body. The vast array of disciplines in the arts nurtures human systems, which include the senses, cognition, emotions, social skills, and physical abilities.

Extensive research shows that using fine arts opportunities is the primary component in improving learning across all academic areas. Research in the cognitive sciences and brain studies confirm and recommend that the arts should be integrated across the curriculum, as it is essential for student success. Other studies have proven that offering the arts as part of the curriculum helps improve student attendance, behavior, motivation, interest, and self concept, which overall create individuals with a desire to learn. One study focused on students currently involved in arts programs found that these children demonstrated superior skills in critical thinking, problem solving, creative thinking, self-expression, and cooperation when compared to peers who were not in arts related programs.

However, even with the support of research and the organizations that announce the positive effects, the arts programs offered in schools diminish each year. Experts highly recommend arts integration into the core school curriculum across all subjects each and every day. It is evident that the skills and abilities required for the arts (complex cognitive skills and foundational skills) are the same that are required for success in other subject areas. So, whether there is a program for the arts at a school or not, the elementary classroom teacher should be prepared to integrate core knowledge by using the arts.

Following is a list that demonstrates the overall importance of the arts:

- Integrates other subjects and topics
- Promotes symbol systems similar to science and mathematics
- Improves language and literacy skills
- Uses higher order thinking skills
- Helps students make connections across academic disciplines
- Allows creative self-expression and develops the imagination
- Develops independence, self-concept, and self-confidence
- Encourages the use of personal strengths and talents
- Motivates students and generates more ambition
- Enhances cultural awareness and engages diverse learners
- Promotes arts appreciation
- Helps students achieve high standards

Standards

The arts are a common thread that connect other aspects of our society. The arts are based in the history of various cultures and should provide rich experiences for students that reflect the people and community of the greater society. Implementing activities that include the fine arts as an expansion of academic programs will substantially benefit students. The content should be based on academic standards and connect to the scope and sequence of each school's curricula.

Standards created by the Consortium of National Arts Education Associations with support from the National Association for Music Education (MENC) are divided into four categories by grade levels:

- Visual arts
- Music
- Theater
- Dance

The National Standards for Arts Education have outlined what is considered necessary for students upon completion of secondary school. They have identified two primary reasons for the standards of arts education: to help define what arts education should provide and to ensure that schools support the arts. In summary, the standards promote that students should be able to do the following:

- Communicate at a basic level in the four arts disciplines (dance, music, theatre, and visual arts).
- Communicate proficiently in at least one art form.
- Develop and present basic analysis of works of art.
- Have an informed acquaintance with exemplary works of art from a variety of cultural and historical periods.
- Relate various types of arts knowledge and skills within and across the arts disciplines.

Arts Integration

Research studies support the idea that integration of the arts promotes academic achievement and gains on standardized tests. These studies reveal that students learn better and improve when the arts are integrated into the core curriculum, connecting it with other subjects (literature, science, social studies, and math). Some believe that the inclusion of fine arts stimulates brain development and that similar cognitive skills are as necessary for art as for academic subject content. Further studies focused on the positive gains made by lower socio-economic groups and those at risk for school failure.

Standards that reflect the integrated arts are divided into three main categories with one primary goal for each of the categories. The various grade levels have a series of goals and objectives that pertain to the age and the content of that age level.

- **Creating arts**—Students know and apply the arts disciplines, techniques, and processes in original or interpretive work.
- **Arts as inquiry**—Students reflect upon concepts and themes, and assess the merits of their own work and the work of others.
- **Art in context**—Students analyze works of art from their own and other cultures and demonstrate how interrelated conditions (social, economic, political, historical) influence the development and reception of thoughts, ideas, and concepts in the arts.

A **parallel process** is blending an arts related activity with an academic subject activity. Examples of parallel processes for integration of the arts with academic areas include the following:

- Use journal writing with drawing pictures of the content.
- Read literature and observe the famous paintings mentioned.
- Learn fractions by using drama to act out the number of parts.
- Study and learn the dances of historical periods for social studies.
- Play simple keyboard passages or the recorder for poetry accompaniment.
- Incorporate the use of clay to create science structures (volcanoes, cells, and so on).

Curriculum

The curriculum used for the arts should be aligned with the scope, sequence, and academic goals appropriate for all children. Multiple art forms may be integrated throughout the curriculum to cultivate the special talents and interests embedded in all students. Using the added components of fine arts in a school curriculum complements the academic features of learning by adding the aesthetic focus. It is possible that additional materials, equipment, and possibly staff would be needed to integrate the visual and performing arts, but even at the elementary level, these will provide enrichment in all areas of the curriculum.

Adding an emphasis on the arts (drama, music, dance, visual arts) provides students with additional opportunities for personal and academic expression. This arts focus may be achieved through the integration of academic subject areas and by creating opportunities after school. The addition of arts in a school classroom also addresses the issue of providing differentiated instruction and should include field trips that deliver opportunities some children may not have otherwise.

Fine arts is the general subject area that encompasses art (drawing and other medium), music and movement, singing, and creative dance and drama. Including these forms of art at the elementary level will allow children a distinctive method to process information, to express themselves, and to gain academic success. The arts can help students develop skills, gain foundational skills, become innovative thinkers, and develop attitudes about the world that they may not acquire in other ways. They can actively participate in learning experiences, using the visual, auditory, and kinesthetic processes, when integrating arts into the curriculum.

Basic Concepts

The study of the arts is an indispensable topic for elementary students because they support children in their development and academic achievement. Children learn the basic concepts and skills related to the arts in school programs. Students may be more motivated to learn by integrating art with other content areas.

Schools should focus on the fundamental value of art experiences. The arts are useful to the study of literature, writing, learning mathematic concepts, understanding science, and learning about historical events. Educators must implement arts education into classroom practice to promote appreciation and to gain the multitude of skills that are related to the arts, yet applied to other subject areas. The purpose of arts education is to encourage children to become participants and observers, and to appreciate the arts throughout their lifetimes.

Visual Arts

Arts education, which is recommended as part of the general education program, is based on visual or tangible arts such as painting, using clay or pottery, designing sculptures, drawing, or using fabrics. Students may be involved in activities or select opportunities based on the standards that are related to or integrated into the core curriculum. These experiences should allow students to express themselves while showing appreciation of the art form.

Classroom activities must allow students to explore the visual arts and the varieties of materials. They should be encouraged to share their ideas through this form of expression, knowing that what they create is acceptable. Children gain a sense of accomplishment, as they control this form of creative expression, which instills self-confidence.

The environment is crucial for implementing the visual arts. There needs to be ample physical space, a variety of accessible materials, and support from the adults who refrain from correcting a child or changing the work. There are developmental stages related to the arts, and not all children will move through those stages at the same time. Art needs to be integrated with other subjects so it may be fully appreciated, and the students' products should be on display often.

Music

Music fills children's lives outside of school, but they may learn to appreciate it from the educational opportunities and experiences they receive in school. Music offers repetitive, sequential patterns, and an emotional connection to information. Music should be present in elementary classrooms not only for pleasure, but for learning about the rhyme, rhythm, and patterns it contains. Children should learn to sing, dance, and play instruments for musical variety. Use of music will help children grow in all five domains: cognitive, language/literacy, social-emotional, self-help/adaptive, and physical. Music, according to research, has a special connection to learning mathematics and developing literacy skills.

Music can provide students with integrated activities that promote the development of motor skills, physical health, coordination, social interactions, communication, and creativity. A classroom teacher might utilize learning centers for individual and small group instruction that incorporate music to enhance the study of math, language/literacy, science, and history. Even using background music in the classroom has a profound effect on individual learners.

Drama and Dance

Drama and dance engage children in movement activities, which help develop coordination and other physical skills. Students can use dance and drama to communicate their emotions, interpret a poem, share a historic moment, or tell a story. They may create a set routine to share or use interpretive and impromptu improvisational movements. Teachers may have music, costumes, props, and a small staging area available in the classroom. Students should learn to describe, interpret, and evaluate performances in order to learn how to appreciate these art forms.

Instruction

Implementation of the arts requires a variety of approaches and a host of strategies. Students gain competencies differently, as they enter programs with different skills, talents, and desires. In order for them to adequately learn the vocabulary, the concepts, and the perspectives and use the tools and techniques that are related to the various art forms, they must progress and build upon their abilities each year. The arts need to be included in successive years of schooling, from preschool to grade 12, in order for children to gain the most from the arts opportunities.

Instruction ought to acknowledge the varying abilities and be delivered using the developmentally appropriate approach. This method acknowledges that children develop at a variety of rates, possess an array of abilities, and confirms that the environment and materials are critical components to learning.

Academic achievement is broadly improved when arts instruction is included. There is evidence of improved

- Higher order thinking skills
- Concentration and memory
- Verbal expression
- Attention spans and retention rates
- Interpersonal and intrapersonal skills
- Self-discipline
- Teamwork and cooperation
- Intuition and reasoning
- Manual dexterity and physical health

Strategies

There are endless opportunities for delivering instruction in the arts and for combining this instruction into the existing curriculum across subject areas. Educators need to be aware of students' skills and abilities, as well as their interests as they incorporate the arts into their classroom. The materials needed and the training necessary to use the various mediums of the arts are essential for student success. Permitting students to participate in designing the assignments, allowing individual freedom of expression, and creating authentic learning situations will make learning memorable and enjoyable.

Examples of utilizing the arts in an integrated approach include the following:

- Re-enact historical events, math story problems, or literary works.
- Learn about the music and dance that reflect various cultures in history.
- Invite community artists to share their work.
- Participate in community events that feature the arts.
- Utilize visual arts to convey scientific processes.
- Use drama to communicate mathematics principle and concepts.

Pedagogy

The No Child Left Behind legislation describes the necessity of arts education and has included it as one of the core subject areas in school. However, NCLB also requires accountability, which is being met in states by use of standardized testing, but there is no standardized assessment for the arts. This becomes a current educational issue.

Several theories support arts in education:

- Discipline-based art education—Allows students to study western art and construct their own artwork based on themes and movements of art history.
- Visual culture art education—The teacher brings attention to the visual record of human experience within the art curriculum.
- Progressive education theory—John Dewey promoted the arts as aesthetic, and he believed that art objects and experiences of the local community culture should be studied.
- Multiple intelligences model—Addresses the various types of intelligences, specifically the musical intelligence, the visual intelligence, and the kinesthetic intelligence and has supported the rationale for the integrated arts models in teaching and learning.
- Metacognitive approach—Students transfer knowledge and skills across disciplines by controlling their own learning.
- Kodaly approach—Encouraged physical instruction with music instruction and tried to instill lifelong interest in music.

Two names worth mentioning in regards to arts education are Harry Broudy and Elliot Eisner. Broudy was an advocate for the arts, which he felt improved and developed the imagination, an essential component of learning. He promoted the integration of arts education into all subjects. Eisner believed that the arts were critical to cognition and that they help students understand the world on a broader and deeper level.

Assessment

Arts education should include ongoing evaluations, both formative and summative, incorporated within the core curriculum. Often, teachers use authentic or performance assessments to evaluate students on dance, music, drama, or visual arts work.

Students should have the opportunity for feedback on their performances and their work, even though these are personal forms of expression. Teachers may use oral feedback, written comments, and portfolios to indicate progress on specific work.

For other forms of art, teachers may select various assessment tools and methods. Students should know ahead of time upon what type of assessment their work will be based. They need to know the components of a rubric, a rating scale, or a checklist before they delve into composing their artwork. Observations may be conducted periodically during the class and length of the project, but it is best to organize an observation with a previously developed checklist or rating scale as a guide. Students will know what behaviors are appropriate for their performances and works and seek to achieve those as goals.

Performance Assessments	Forced Answer Tests
checklists	vocabulary
essays	completion
rubric scales	true-false
observations	multiple-choice
portfolios	matching
rating scales	

PART II

PRACTICE EXAMINATIONS WITH ANSWER EXPLANATIONS

Directions: Read the following multiple-choice questions and select the most appropriate answer. Mark the answer sheet accordingly.

1. What were the first civilizations called?

   A. Tigris
   B. Valley
   C. River-Valley
   D. Mesopotamia

2. What is the value of the x on the following number line?

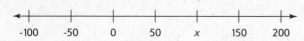

   A. 100
   B. 25
   C. 75
   D. 125

3. When a solid changes into a liquid, which of the following occurs?

   A. Pressure increases and energy increases.
   B. Pressure decreases and energy increases.
   C. Pressure increases and energy decreases.
   D. Pressure decreases and energy decreases.

4. A first-grade student reads a story about a dog lost in the woods. When he is finished reading, he states, "I was lost in a store and couldn't find my mommy. It was scary. The puppy must have been scared, too. He missed his mommy." The first grader is demonstrating which stage in the interpretation of literature?

   A. initial
   B. developing
   C. reflection-response
   D. critical analysis

5. The Earth's magnetic field originates in this thick, viscous part called the

   A. crust
   B. mantle
   C. inner core
   D. outer core

6. Which of the following was developed prior to the twentieth century?

   A. radio
   B. airplane
   C. firearms
   D. electronic refrigeration

7. The algorithm used in addition and subtraction both fall into which category?

   A. carrying
   B. borrowing
   C. regrouping
   D. consigning

8. The limited omniscient point of view is when the story is told by

   A. a narrator who is detached from the story and tells about the actions and dialogue
   B. a narrator whose knowledge is contained to knowing all inner thoughts and feelings of one character
   C. a narrator who knows everything about every character including all inner thoughts and feelings
   D. a narrator who is directly involved in the story and action and may or may not be trusted

GO ON TO THE NEXT PAGE

9. The exposition of a narrative accomplishes which of the following tasks?

    A. tells the events of a story
    B. triggers the central conflict of a story
    C. concludes the events in a story
    D. introduces the characters, setting, and tone of a story

10. Which of the following did classical civilization contribute to present day?

    A. writing, trade, wheel
    B. time measurement, alphabet, art
    C. social cohesion, religions, agricultural options
    D. monotheistic belief, democratic rule, family structure

11. A third-grade student demonstrates the use of which algorithm when he writes:

13×7 is one 10 and 3 ones taken 7 times, and the product is equal to 9 tens plus 1 unit.

    A. whole multiplication
    B. regrouping multiplication
    C. long multiplication
    D. distributive multiplication

12. A ball that is resting on the top of an incline plane is said to have what type of energy?

    A. inertia
    B. kinetic energy
    C. potential energy
    D. conserved energy

13. Which of the following non-European civilizations brought forth the concept of present day irrigation, road systems, and military organizations?

    A. Incas
    B. Islams
    C. Mayans
    D. Mongolians

14. The law that states the effort force times the distance the effort moves is equal to the resistance times the distance the resistance moves is

    A. the Law of Simple Machines
    B. the Law of Conservation of Matter
    C. the Law of Conservation of Energy
    D. the Law of Energy, Mass, and Substance

15. User manuals are an example of what type of literature?

    A. poetry
    B. nonfiction
    C. fiction
    D. research

16. What is the missing number in the number pattern below?

5, 15, 45, _____ , 405, 1215

    A. 130
    B. 135
    C. 205
    D. 235

17. When using maps to teach distances between continents, one limitation to take into consideration is that they

    A. show land masses without distortion
    B. are used to analyze spatial organization
    C. depict the most precise representation of the Earth
    D. cannot accurately represent a sphere on a flat surface without distortion

18. The preceding illustration represents which number?

    A. 1048
    B. 481
    C. 841
    D. 148

19. The following is an example of what poetic device?

The rain falls mainly on the plains of Spain.

    A. alliteration
    B. assonance
    C. consonance
    D. repetition

20. When a student adds one drop of food coloring to a warm cup of water without stirring, but observes the food coloring changing the water into one solid well-mixed color, he is witnessing

    A. melting
    B. diffusion
    C. evaporation
    D. vaporization

21. Which type of map would be BEST used when teaching a sixth-grade class about tectonic plates and fault lines?

    A. outline map
    B. physical map
    C. conformal map
    D. topographical map

22. The best characteristics to define sound are

    A. pitch, amplitude, quality
    B. wave, rare fraction, amplitude
    C. pitch, wave length, compression
    D. compression, wave length, quality

23. Which is a true statement of equivalence?

    A. one fourth equals six twenty-fourths
    B. one fourth equals two sixths
    C. one fourth equals twenty six one hundredths
    D. one fourth equals twenty percent

24. Geographically, the largest continent is

    A. Asia
    B. Africa
    C. Europe
    D. North America

25. Mutant genes can cause a disruption within the DNA of an organism that usually results in

    A. an aborted egg
    B. unneeded eggs
    C. a fertilized egg
    D. non-fertilized eggs

GO ON TO THE NEXT PAGE

Use the following poem to answer questions 26–28.

JABBERWOCKY

– Lewis Carroll

'Twas brillig, and the slithy toves
Did gyre and gimble in the wade;
All mimsy were the borogoves,
And the mome raths outgrabe.

"Beware the Jabberwock, my son!
The jaws that bite, the claws that catch!
Beware the Jubjub bird, and shun
The frumious Bandersnatch!"

He took his vorpal sword in hand:
Long time the manxome foe he sought —
So rested he by the Tumtum tree.
And stood awhile in thought.

And as in uffish thought he stood,
The Jabberwock, with eyes of flame,
Came wiffling through the tulgey wood,
And burbled as it came!

One, two! One, two! And through and through
The vorpal blade went snicker-snack!
He left it dead, and with its head
He went galumphing back.

"And hast thou slain the Jabberwock?
Come to my arms, my beamish boy!
O frabjous day! Callooh! Callay!"
He chortled in his joy.

'Twas brillig, and the slithy toves
Did gyre and gimble in the wabe;
All mimsy were the borogoves,
And the mome raths outgrabe.

26. This poem is an example of what common stanza?

    A. quatrain
    B. sestet
    C. octane
    D. triplet

27. The rhyme scheme of this poem is best represented by which of the following patterns?

    A. aa bb cc dd ee ff gg hh
    B. aaba bbcb ccdc dded
    C. abab cdcd efef ghgh
    D. aaaa bbbb cccc dddd

28. The figurative language device employed in this poem is

    A. onomatopoeia
    B. imagery
    C. metaphor
    D. personification

29. Eleven is a factor of which one of these three digit numbers?

    A. 680
    B. 892
    C. 736
    D. 583

30. A cartographer is defined as which of the following?

    A. a person who writes the history of the Earth
    B. a person who studies the Earth's composition
    C. a person who designs, describes, and develops maps
    D. a person who studies the science or practice of map drawing

31. The ratio of girls to boys in sixth grade is 5:4, and there are 64 boys. How many girls are there?

    A. 69 girls
    B. 75 girls
    C. 80 girls
    D. 16 girls

32. Natural selection is BEST described as which of the following?

    A. the basic principle of biological evolution
    B. the survival of offspring with recessive traits
    C. the dying out of mutant genes so the organism cannot reproduce
    D. the process in which individuals with favorable traits survive and reproduce

33. If a basketball player shoots 77% from the free-throw line and during a game she is at the line 16 times, how many shots did she make? (Round to the nearest whole number.)

    A. 12
    B. 4
    C. 13
    D. 20

34. The following is an example of which type of sonnet?

Weary with toil, I haste me to my bed,
The dear repose for limbs with travel tired,
But then begins a journey in my head
To work my mind when body's work's expired;
For then my thoughts, from far where I abide,
Intend a zealous pilgrimage to thee,
And keep my drooping eyelids open wide,
Looking on darkness which the blind do see;
Save that my soul's imaginary sight
Presents thy shadow to my sightless view,
Which, like a jewel hung in ghastly night,
Makes black night beauteous and her old face new.
Lo, thus, by day my limbs, by night my mind,
For thee and for myself no quiet find.

- **A.** German sonnet
- **B.** Shakespearean sonnet
- **C.** Petrarchan sonnet
- **D.** Italian sonnet

35. When defining a region or place in the world, the two types of characteristics used are

- **A.** physical and human
- **B.** human and regional
- **C.** physical and regional
- **D.** human and geological

36. Within a garden ecosystem, if all the earth worms were to be removed, this changes the balance by

- **A.** interrupting the food cycle within the ecosystem
- **B.** changing the supply of energy within the ecosystem
- **C.** producing a natural phenomenon within the ecosystem
- **D.** disrupting the organic matter and nutrients recycled within the ecosystem

37. When tectonic plates collide, the result is the

- **A.** formation of new crust
- **B.** formation of mountains
- **C.** occurrence of volcanoes
- **D.** occurrence of earthquakes

38. A survey is an example of which kind of source?

- **A.** written
- **B.** secondary
- **C.** observational
- **D.** primary

39. Haley makes 6 peanut butter and jelly sandwiches more than Gill. Gill makes 2 sandwiches less than Tzvia. If Tzvia makes 15 peanut butter and jelly sandwiches, how many does Haley make?

- **A.** 13
- **B.** 19
- **C.** 21
- **D.** 23

40. Which of the following BEST defines a biome?

- **A.** a large geographical area of distinctive plant life and animal life groups that have adapted to a specific environment
- **B.** a large geographical area of non-distinct plant life and animal life groups that have adapted to a specific environment
- **C.** a small geographical area of distinctive plant life and animal life groups that have adapted to a specific environment
- **D.** a small geographical area of non-distinct plant life and animal life groups that have yet to adapt to a specific environment

41. A student brings in a rock with obvious layers and tells you it is a piece of marble. The type of rock he most likely has is

- **A.** striated
- **B.** igneous
- **C.** sedimentary
- **D.** metamorphic

42. A pattern of organization used in nonfiction is

- **A.** story and plot
- **B.** metaphor and simile
- **C.** compare and contrast
- **D.** theme and meaning

GO ON TO THE NEXT PAGE

43. Which equation represents the statement, "2 times a number decreased by 6 distributed equally 5 times."?

    A. $(2A - 6)5$
    B. $(2A + 6)5$
    C. $(2A - 6) \div 5$
    D. $(2A + 6) \div 5$

44. Which physical process includes rock formation, soil formation, plate tectonics, and erosion?

    A. biosphere
    B. lithosphere
    C. atmosphere
    D. hydrosphere

45. The consumption of natural resources from one area to be used in another area does what to the earth?

    A. depletes the ozone
    B. changes natural patterns
    C. increases resource demands
    D. helps produce more resources

46. A kindergarten teacher reads a picture book aloud to her class every day. Before she begins the story each day, she discusses parts of the book (the front cover, the title, the author, the illustrator, and the back cover) with her students. The teacher is demonstrating which foundation of literacy?

    A. print concepts
    B. word identification
    C. alphabetic principle
    D. comprehension

47. The three most contributing factors of weather are

    A. solar radiation, wind patterns, and the seasons
    B. the Water Cycle, wind patterns, and the seasons
    C. the Earth's movement, the Water Cycle, and wind patterns
    D. solar radiation, the Earth's movement, and the Water Cycle

48. Which of the following is an example of the associative property?

    A. $(5 + 3) + 10 = 5 + (3 + 10)$
    B. $(5 - 3) - 10 = 5 - (3 - 10)$
    C. $(5 * 3) + 10 = 5 + (3 * 10)$
    D. $(5 * 3) - 10 = 5 - (3 * 10)$

49. The multiplicative inverse for 0.2 is

    A. -0.2
    B. 5
    C. -5
    D. $1/2$

50. Which of the following did *early* civilizations contribute?

    A. culture
    B. science
    C. petroglyphs
    D. alphabetic writing

51. The Law of Superposition is best defined as

    A. the scientific law that governs the Earth today is the same scientific law that has governed the Earth since the beginning of time
    B. the law that proposes that the Earth and its life forms developed slowly over a long period of time
    C. the oldest rocks and events are found at the bottom of formations while the youngest are found at the top
    D. the youngest rocks and events are found at the bottom of formations as they overtake any existing oldest rocks or events

52. A third-grade student is reading a story about a sloth. When he reaches an unknown word, *unobtrusive*, he sees that he recognizes the prefix (*un-*) and the root word (*obtrusive*) and is able to decipher the meaning. Which word recognition strategy is he displaying?

    A. context clues
    B. semantic clues
    C. analogy clues
    D. word structure clues

53. A fourth-grade child is presented with the following number pattern. Using all previous knowledge and number sense, the student is able to figure out the next value in the pattern is 13 and is able to write an equation to explain the pattern. What equation does he write?

1, 3, 5, 7, 9, 11, ___ , 15, 17, 19

A. $2n + 2$
B. $2n$
C. $2n - 1$
D. $n - 1$

54. The three classical civilizations are

A. India, Greece and Rome, Japan
B. China, Greece and Rome, India
C. China, Japan, Greece and Rome
D. Britain, Greece and Rome, Russia

55. The BEST description of the solar system is

A. the sun and the planets
B. the sun, the stars, and the planets
C. the sun, the comets, and the planets
D. the sun and all bodies that revolve around it

56. While reading a story about a high school baseball player, a second-grade student may use which of the following two context clues to determine the missing words of the following sentence: The young baseball player was good at

A. semantic and symbolic clues
B. symbolic and syntactic clues
C. syntactic and semantic clues
D. sequential and symbolic clues

57. When a fourth-grader reads with expression and her reading flows smoothly, she is demonstrating

A. comprehension
B. fluency
C. word identification
D. phonemic awareness

58. Solve: $(6^2)(6^4)$

A. 7,776
B. 46,656
C. 1,296
D. 279,936

59. Which of the following BEST describes the Townshend Act of 1767?

A. the first land tax placed on the colonies
B. a tax placed on all media that required stamps
C. a tax on essential goods like paper, glass, and tea
D. a tax imposed by the East India Trading Company

60. When the sun lights the back of the moon, we are experiencing a

A. Full Moon
B. New Moon
C. Solar Eclipse
D. Lunar Eclipse

61. Solve: 4532 divided by 6

A. 755
B. 755.4
C. 755 1/3
D. 756

62. When a second-grade student sees the word "giraffe" and states "that is the big yellow and black animal with a really long neck in Africa," she is demonstrating which foundation of literacy?

A. word identification
B. alphabetic principle
C. print concept
D. comprehension

63. The six basic processes of science are

A. observation, classification, experimentation, prediction, hypothesis, methods
B. observation, communication, data, hypothesis, measurement, experimentation
C. observation, classification, communication, measurement, prediction, inference
D. observation, communication, inference, classification, experimentation, hypothesis

GO ON TO THE NEXT PAGE

64. Which of the following was a direct result of the War of 1812?

    A. Slavery was abolished.

    B. The national anthem was written.

    C. Four governments were overthrown.

    D. Boundaries were drawn between the North and South.

65. The Mayflower Compact was signed en route to the New World and established which of the following?

    A. rights of the monarch over the Pilgrims

    B. housing, communities, and schools for the Pilgrims

    C. the separation of the 13 colonies from Great Britain

    D. temporary majority rule government for the Pilgrims

66. Find the slope of the line segment joining the points (3,5) and (6,4).

    A. 1/3

    B. −1

    C. −1/3

    D. 3

67. Words that are high-frequency and should be learned to be recognized instantly are called

    A. sight words

    B. instant recognition words

    C. dolch words

    D. fluency words

68. When a 10-year-old student watches a baby bird struggling to fly from a nest and states "the bird will fall but begin to flap its wings before it hits the ground," she is using the scientific processes of observation and

    A. inference

    B. prediction

    C. measurement

    D. communication

69. The Earth and other planets each revolve around the sun in a shape that most resembles

    A. a circle

    B. a sphere

    C. an ovoid

    D. an ellipse

70. The proclamation of 1763 restricted American movement across the Appalachian Mountains but was ignored, which led to expansion

    A. eastward

    B. westward

    C. northward

    D. southward

71. A fifth-grade student reads a text about Jamestown, Virginia. After reading about the settling of the colony, he remarks how difficult it must have been for the colonists to leave everything that was familiar to them in England and make a long journey to the New World. He concludes that the move must have been particularly difficult for children. He is demonstrating which comprehension strategy?

    A. think and read

    B. inferential reading

    C. metacognition

    D. summarizing

72. Which of the following is a plane figure?

    A. rhombus

    B. pyramid

    C. cylinder

    D. ovoid

73. The reasons that formal governments are established are to

    A. create laws, order, and security

    B. establish rule, control, and protection

    C. join together people, cultures, and rights

    D. protect individual liberties, properties, and lives

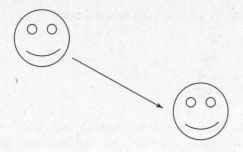

74. The preceding illustration represents what type of transformation?

A. rotation
B. translation
C. reflection
D. mutation

75. Concept books and pattern books are examples of which type of children's literature?

A. traditional
B. fiction
C. nonfiction
D. early childhood

76. The water cycle is a natural process in which water

A. precipitates, dissipates, accumulates
B. evaporates, condensates, precipitates
C. accumulates, evaporates, precipitates
D. condensates, accumulates, dissipates

77. The best explanation for the function of animals is that they are on the Earth to grow, reproduce, and

A. die
B. adapt
C. interact with humans
D. interact with the environment

78. A second-grade student is struggling to read the word "complementary." She draws a connection between a word she already knows, "elementary," and is able to determine the pronunciation of the word. She has used which word recognition strategy?

A. word structure clues
B. context clues
C. analogy clues
D. phonemic clues

79. How many centimeters are in 47 kilometers?

A. 470 cm
B. 4,700 cm
C. 4,700,000 cm
D. 470,000 cm

80. An oligarchy is a form of government in which

A. no one rules
B. a majority rules
C. a minority rules
D. a monarch rules

Use the graph to answer questions 81 and 82.

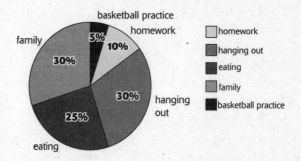

Use of Time on Saturday
Total time: 18 hours

81. How much time was spent completing homework?

A. 2 hrs.
B. 1.8 hrs.
C. 3 hrs.
D. 1.6 hrs.

GO ON TO THE NEXT PAGE

82. Which of the following is closest to the fraction of the total time spent with family and eating?

    A. 2/5
    B. 3/4
    C. 1/2
    D. 1/3

83. The legislative branch of the U.S. government is comprised of

    A. the court systems
    B. the president and his cabinet
    C. the primary government contractors
    D. the Senate and the House of Representatives

84. The part of a plant that houses the reproductive organs is the

    A. root
    B. fruit
    C. leaves
    D. flower

85. Copper is a metal that allows electric current to flow through it, which is an example of

    A. a circuit
    B. a conductor
    C. an insulator
    D. an accumulator

86. Which of the following is the correct way to write "volcano" in the plural form?

    A. volcanos
    B. volcano's
    C. volcanos'
    D. volcanoes

87. What noun type is underlined in this sentence:

    The park is a great <u>place</u> to have a picnic.

    A. predicate noun
    B. subject noun
    C. object noun
    D. possessive noun

88. Which Amendment abolished slavery?

    A. 9th
    B. 10th
    C. 12th
    D. 13th

89. The Declaration of Independence led to the development of which two important documents?

    A. Bill of Rights and Gettysburg Address
    B. Articles of Confederation and Constitution
    C. Constitutional Amendments and Preamble
    D. Magna Carta and Articles of the Union

90. When you slide across a tile floor in your socks and come to a gradual stop, you are experiencing which force?

    A. inertia
    B. friction
    C. centrifugal
    D. momentum

91. The past tense of "lay" is

    A. lay
    B. lain
    C. lie
    D. laid

Question 92 refers to the following diagram.

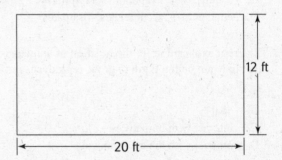

92. Mabel plans to place a wood floor in her living room. If each square foot of wood costs $12.25 how much will Mabel spend on her new wooden floor?

    A. $294.00
    B. $240.00
    C. $2880.00
    D. $2940.00

93. Which of the following figures is the greatest in value?

    A. 30% of 80

    B. 13% of 120

    C. 10% of 100

    D. 5% of 600

94. When comparing two tribes of Native Americans, if the class studies how food is obtained, they are using what type of Anthropology?

    A. cultural

    B. physical

    C. economic

    D. behavioral

95. The particles inside an ice cream shake are moving

    A. slowly

    B. rapidly

    C. sporadically

    D. not at all

96. Which of the following is the most specific category in the biological taxonomy?

    A. class

    B. species

    C. kingdom

    D. phylum

97. What is the mean of 68, 45, 32, 90, 15?

    A. 40

    B. 45

    C. 50

    D. 55

98. Which of the following sentences is an example of a verbal gerund?

    A. She was hitting the boy.

    B. I am hitting the wall.

    C. Hitting is not an acceptable behavior.

    D. He was grounded for hitting others.

99. In the sentence, "That boy is smart when he wants to be," the word "that" is categorized as what type of adjective?

    A. demonstrative adjective

    B. compound adjective

    C. indefinite adjective

    D. predicate adjective

100. What is the volume of a pyramid that has a base of 12.5 in. and a height of 16 in.?

    A. 66 2/3 in.

    B. 9 1/2 in.

    C. 64 in.

    D. 200 in.

101. A society that has a strict free-market with no government involvement can be said to have which economy?

    A. socialist

    B. anarchist

    C. capitalist

    D. laissez-faire

102. The three components of citizenship education are

    A. content, values, processes

    B. rights, concern, community

    C. democracy, equality, patriotism

    D. responsibilities, relationships, justice

GO ON TO THE NEXT PAGE

103. Which of the diagrams best depicts the structure of a lunar eclipse?

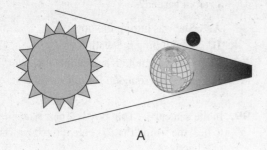

A

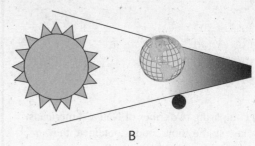

B

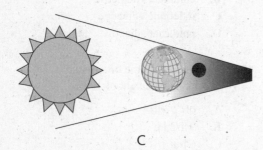

C

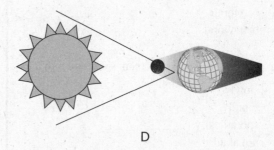

D

104. In the following sentence, what part of speech is the word "often?"

He often practices the electric guitar.

   A. noun
   B. adjective
   C. preposition
   D. adverb

105. Which of the following is a complementary angle for an angle measuring 40°?

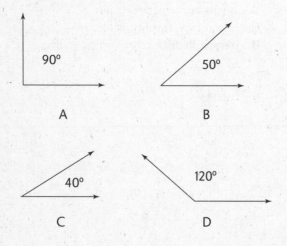

106. Justin puts his CDs on shuffle mode. The CD player holds 16 CDs at one time and shuffles the discs at random. He puts 4 country, 6 punk, 2 folk, and 4 rock into the machine. What is the probability that a punk CD will play?

   A. 3/8
   B. 5/8
   C. 1 in 6
   D. 60%

107. Advances in technology have helped economies by

   A. increasing the sales of computers
   B. bringing manufacturing costs down
   C. balancing social and economic gains
   D. creating a broader, more accessible market

108. Which of the following tectonic illustrations best represents the formation of new rock for the Earth's surface?

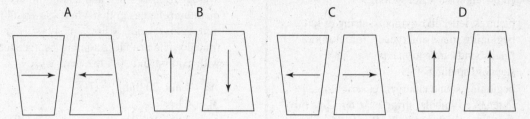

A   B   C   D

109. A free-market economy is based on which of the following?

 A. production and services
 B. population and resources
 C. businesses and development
 D. competition through supply and demand

110. An atoll is best described as a

 A. chain or group of islands in a sea or ocean
 B. body of land that is surrounded by water on three sides
 C. ring or partial ring of coral that forms an island in a sea or ocean
 D. narrow pointed piece of land that juts out from a coastline into a body of water

111. In the typical animal cell, what structure functions as a canal or tube to transport material to the nucleus through to cytoplasm?

 A. ribosomes
 B. mitochondria
 C. Golgi apparatus
 D. endoplasmic reticulum

112. Which of the following is the world's coldest and driest biome?

 A. Taiga
 B. Alpine
 C. Tundra
 D. Chaparral

113. Which of the following structures are found in a typical plant cell, but not in a typical animal cell?

 A. ribosomes, vacuoles
 B. plastids, chloroplasts
 C. mitochondria, nucleus
 D. reticulum, Golgi apparatus

114. What is the complete predicate in the following sentence?

The caged, restless, Siberian tiger roars loudly at the crowd of people.

 A. Siberian tiger roars
 B. roars loudly
 C. roars loudly at the crowd of people
 D. The caged, restless, Siberian tiger roars

115. Which of the following illustrations demonstrates a first-class lever?

1   2   3   4

 A. 1
 B. 2
 C. 3
 D. 4

GO ON TO THE NEXT PAGE

116. Which of the following is the correct progression through the eight stages of writing?

   A. pictures, letter-like symbols, string of letters, beginning sound emergence, initial-middle-final sounds, transitional phases, and standard spelling

   B. beginning sound emergence, scribbling, letter-like symbols, string of letters, inventive spelling, initial-middle-final sounds, transitional phases, and standard spelling

   C. scribbling, letter-like symbols, string of letters, beginning sound emergence, consonants represent words, initial-middle-final sounds, transitional phases, and standard spelling

   D. letter-like symbols, scribbling, string of letters, beginning sound emergence, vowels represent words, initial-middle-final sounds, transitional phases, and standard spelling

117. Accurate listening comprehension is dependent upon the following three components?

   A. hearing, understanding, and judging

   B. visual contact, understanding, and a lack of distractions

   C. hearing, speaker, and occasion

   D. attention span, posture, and understanding

118. How many different groups of three t-shirts can be chosen from a selection of ten shirts?

   A. 3,600

   B. 120

   C. 1,200

   D. 30

119. Eric is a marathon runner. He wants to maintain an average time of 4 hrs. and 20 min. In his last 5 marathons he has gotten 4 hrs. 45 min., 4 hrs. 55 min., 5 hrs. 5 min., 4 hrs., and 4 hrs. 15 min. What time does he need to get in his last race to finish with a 4 hrs. and 20 min. average?

   A. 4 hrs. 20 min.

   B. 4 hrs.

   C. 3 hrs. 10 min.

   D. 3 hrs.

120. Transitional spelling is

   A. when symbols are used to represent the alphabet, and letters and sounds do not correspond

   B. when letters and sounds begin to correspond, and single letters are used to represent words, sounds, or syllables

   C. when every sound heard is represented by a letter or group of letters

   D. when conventions and rules of spelling are learned and all letters are present in a word, although the letters may not be in the correct order

Answer Key

1. C	36. D	71. B	106. A
2. A	37. B	72. A	107. D
3. B	38. D	73. D	108. C
4. C	39. B	74. B	109. D
5. D	40. A	75. D	110. C
6. C	41. D	76. B	111. D
7. C	42. C	77. D	112. C
8. B	43. C	78. C	113. B
9. D	44. B	79. C	114. C
10. C	45. B	80. C	115. A
11. C	46. A	81. B	116. C
12. C	47. D	82. C	117. A
13. A	48. A	83. D	118. B
14. A	49. B	84. D	119. D
15. B	50. D	85. B	120. D
16. B	51. C	86. D	
17. D	52. D	87. A	
18. D	53. C	88. D	
19. B	54. B	89. B	
20. B	55. D	90. B	
21. B	56. C	91. D	
22. A	57. B	92. D	
23. A	58. B	93. D	
24. A	59. C	94. A	
25. D	60. B	95. A	
26. A	61. C	96. B	
27. C	62. D	97. C	
28. B	63. C	98. C	
29. D	64. B	99. A	
30. D	65. D	100. A	
31. C	66. C	101. D	
32. D	67. A	102. A	
33. A	68. B	103. C	
34. B	69. D	104. D	
35. A	70. B	105. B	

Answer Explanations

1. **C.** First civilizations were developed alongside rivers for agricultural production and called River-Valleys.

2. **A.** Based on number sense, the value of "*x*" is 100 since the number line is divided into segments of 50.

3. **B.** For a solid to become a liquid it must incur a decrease in pressure to allow the molecules more free movement along with an increase in energy as the molecules begin to move more quickly.

4. **C.** When a reader uses text knowledge to reflect upon personal knowledge and draw connections between text and personal experience, they are in the *reflection-response stage*. The first grader is relating his personal experience and knowledge of feelings when he was lost to that of the lost puppy in the story. The *initial stage* is when the reader has first contact with the tone, characters, and content. The *developing stage* is the extending stage in which the reader takes in the information and begins to ask questions about the text. During *critical analysis,* the reader reflects and reacts to the content by judging, evaluating, and examining the text.

5. **D.** The outer core is a thick viscous liquid that is rich in iron and produces the Earth's magnetic field.

6. **C.** Guns and the use of gunpowder began in the ninth century with Chinese alchemists who were searching for an elixir of immortality and happened upon the combination of the explosive mixture of sulfur, charcoal, and potassium nitrate. The radio, airplane, and electric refrigeration were not developed until the twentieth century.

7. **C.** Regrouping is used in both operations of addition and subtraction. In addition it is called "carrying," and in subtraction it is referred to as "borrowing."

8. **B.** *Limited omniscient* point of view is when a narrator knows everything about only one character (major or minor). The reader must draw conclusions about other characters through this one point of view and setting and dialogue to get the complete picture and meaning of the story. The *objective* point of view is when the narrator is a detached observer and tells only the dialogue and actions so that the reader must infer all inner thoughts and feelings. *Omniscient* point of view is when the narrator knows all feelings and inner thoughts of all characters. *First person* point of view is when the narrator is directly involved in the story and may or may not be a reliable source for the reader.

9. **D.** The *exposition* is the initial understanding of a story, in which the characters, setting, tone, and initial understanding of the story are presented to the reader. The *plot* tells the events of a story; the *inciting force* tells the events that lead to the central conflict; and the *conclusion* ends the story by wrapping up all actions.

10. **C.** Classical civilizations developed many structures and institutions that are still present today. The three recognized classical civilizations contributed the following: expansion of trade, new and various religions, increased agricultural options, extended territories, and social cohesian, integrating people and societies.

11. **C.** Long multiplication, sometimes called elementary multiplication, is when the multiplication problem is broken down into its components (multiplicand and multiplier) and then added together to reach the product. Long multiplication is the algorithm used in multiplication.

12. **C.** The ball has potential energy because it possesses the ability to have energy even though it is at rest.

13. **A.** The Incas are considered a non-European civilization and are credited with contributing artistic pottery and clothing, metallurgy, architecture, irrigation, road systems, supreme military organization, and agriculture to present day societies.

14. **A.** The Law of Simple Machines states that whatever force is exerted times the distance moved is equal to the output force of the machine times the distance the output force moves.

15. **B.** Nonfiction is writing in which information is presented as fact or truth. A user's manual explains how to operate something in a factual manner. Poetry is a creative form of writing that is organized into stanzas and uses poetic devices. Fiction is a story that follows certain elements and is not true. Research is not a type of literature but is a material used to evaluate something.

16. B. This is a geometrical sequence in which the value is multiplied by three each time. 5×3, 15×3, 45×3, and so on. The missing value is the product of 45×3, which is 135.

17. D. Flat maps distort size, distance, direction, and the shape of the objects on the Earth.

18. D. Place value works on a base-10 system. Using manipulatives or diagrams to demonstrate this aids in student comprehension. The square is equal to 100, the bar is 10, and the single squares are equal to one. Therefore, the number represented is 148.

19. B. Because the vowel sound "ai" is repeated throughout the line, the correct answer is assonance. *Assonance* is the repetition of a vowel sound. *Alliteration* is the repetition of a beginning consonant sound. *Consonance* is the repetition of consonant sounds anywhere within the words. *Repetition* is the stating of a word or phrase more than once.

20. B. Diffusion is the movement of particles from a high concentration (the drop of food coloring) to an area of low concentration (plain water) until all areas are in a state of equilibrium (the same color).

21. B. Physical maps reveal the features of actual geographical surfaces, like mountains or rivers and the underlying geological structures, such as rocks or fault lines.

22. A. *Pitch* is how high or low a sound is made, *amplitude* is the volume of the sound, and *quality* shows the source of the sound.

23. A. The equivalence to 1/4 is 2/8, 3/12, 4/16, 5/20, 6/24, and so on. An equivalence is when numbers are equal in value. 6/24 can be reduced to 1/4 by dividing both the numerator and denominator by 6.

24. A. Asia is the largest continent in geographical terms. The following then by size are Africa, North America, South America, Antarctica, Europe, and Australia.

25. D. Mutant genes most commonly result in a non-fertilized egg because DNA strands cannot be fully developed.

26. A. Stanzas are how poems are broken up into lines and sections. A *quatrain* breaks lines into groups of four. This poem has seven quatrains. A *sestet* has six lines, an *octane* has eight lines, and a *triplet* has three lines.

27. C. The poem has end rhyme, which follows the rhyme pattern of line 1 and 3 (denoted by the letter 'a'), 2 and 4 (denoted by the letter 'b'), 5 and 7 (denoted by the letter 'c'), 6 and 8 (denoted by the letter 'd'), and so on. The rhyme scheme is therefore written abab cdcd and so on.

28. B. *Imagery* is language that appeals to the five senses and to the imagination of the reader. The most prolific types of imagery found in the poem "Jabberwocky" are visual and auditory. Even though most of the words are made up by Carroll, they provoke visual images in the reader's mind ("All mimsy were the borogroves" and "The Jabberwock, with eyes of flame"). Carroll also uses auditory imagery in the lines "Came wiffling through the tulgey wood/And burbled as it came!" as well as "The vorpal blade went snicker-snack!". *Personification* is attributing human qualities to objects, animals, or places; *onomatopoeia* is when a word sound relates to its meaning; *metaphor* is a comparison of two unrelated objects without using the words "like " or "as."

29. D. 11 is a factor of a three-digit number if the sum of the first and third digit is equal to the middle digit. In 583, $5 + 3 = 8$ so 11 is a factor.

30. D. A cartographer is someone who studies the science or practice of map drawing.

31. C. It is helpful to set up a proportion to solve this problem. $5:4 = x:64$ (let x represent the unknown value of girls). Write the proportion in fraction form and solve using cross-multiplication.

$$5/4 = x/64$$

$$320 = 4x$$

$$80 = x$$

32. D. Natural selection states that individuals become better adapted to survive environments through favorable adaptation and traits; those without such traits perish and do not reproduce.

33. A. Set up a proportion using percentages.

$77/100 = x/16$

$1232 = 100x$

$12.32 = x$

Round your answer to 12; since 3 is not large enough to round up, you round the value down.

34. B. Sonnets are a 14-lined poem that states the poet's personal feelings. This sonnet is a *Shakespearean* sonnet (English), because it is set in quatrains, ending in a rhymed couplet. It has a rhyme scheme of abab cdcd efef gg. A *Petrarchan* sonnet is also called an *Italian* sonnet and has an octave and a sestet with a rhyme scheme of abbaabba and cdecde, cdccdc, or cdedce.

35. A. Physical characteristics include water systems, plant/animal life, landforms, and climate. Human characteristics include values, religions, languages, political, and economic factors. Human and physical characteristics both act together to define a region or place.

36. D. Earthworms, although part of the food chain, play a vital role in the breakdown of organic matter within an ecosystem. Removal of those creatures would cause nutrients to build up and disrupt the balance.

37. B. When plates collide, they force the crust upward, forming mountains.

38. D. A survey is a questionnaire used to help gather opinions and preferences firsthand. A *primary* source is when resources/research is gathered from an original source in order to give the reader direct, firsthand knowledge.

39. B. Using representational terms you can organize your data to solve the problem. Let H = Haley, G = Gill, and T = Tzvia.

$H = G + 6$ $G = T - 2$ $T = 15$

Now substitute Tzvia into Gill's equation to solve for Gill: $15 - 2 = 13$ (Gill makes 13 sandwiches). Lastly, substitute Gill into Haley's equation and solve for Haley: $13 + 6 = 19$. Haley makes 19 sandwiches.

40. A. A biome is defined as a large geographical area of distinctive plant life and animal life groups, which have adapted to a specific environment. A biome includes two entities (animal and plant) living together and modifying themselves to live in a certain environment. Biomes are determined by climate and geography.

41. D. Metamorphic rock forms through heat and pressure of igneous and sedimentary rocks, resulting in layers. Marble is a type of metamorphic rock.

42. C. Literature is structured and organized in patterns so that authors can convey their message to the reader. Nonfiction is structured differently than poetry and also fiction. Nonfiction follows a formula of description and details, main idea and supporting details (introduction of the subject and the support to prove it), compare and contrast, chronological order (time pattern), cause and effect (situations/events and the reasons it occurs), and process (describes how an event happens).

43. C. The key terms to focus on are times (multiply), decreased by (subtract), and distributed (divide). Therefore, $(2A - 6) \div 5$ is the correct answer.

44. B. The lithosphere is the ground and surface, atmosphere is air, hydrosphere is water, and biosphere is life. Therefore, rock formation, soil formation, plate tectonics, and erosion, which are part of the Earth's surface, are included in the lithosphere.

45. B. Natural physical patterns are changed when natural resources are consumed. Meeting resource demands across the world places great stress upon the planet's physical systems, forcing changes in natural patterns to occur.

46. A. When the teacher goes over the structure of a book and repeats the same vocabulary each time ("a book by," "illustrated by") she is demonstrating that letters have sounds, and they form words which is the foundation of print concepts. *Word identification* decodes words by sound, *alphabetic principle* shows letters represent speech, and *comprehension* is the processing of the content read.

47. D. Solar radiation causes heat, Earth movement causes seasons/wind, and the Water Cycle determines precipitation, thus resulting in weather conditions.

48. A. The associative property states that numbers can be grouped or regrouped without changing the outcome. "A" is the only equation that remains true as the numbers are regrouped:

$$8 + 10 = 5 + 13$$

$$18 = 18$$

49. B. The multiplicative inverse for a number is the reciprocal. When 0.2 is converted to a fraction, it is equivalent to 1/5. In order to find the multiplicative inverse of a fraction, invert the fraction. In this case, this procedure would yield 5 (1/5 = 5/1). −0.2 is the additive inverse, −5 yields a −1, and 1/2 produces a 0.1.

50. D. Early civilizations developed the following: basic achievements (wheel, math, time measurement), art and architecture, alphabetic writing, defined religion, commonality, and diversity.

51. C. The Law of Superposition is a geologic law that states the past will hold the position at the bottom, and the present will hold the position on the top.

52. D. When recognizing frequent letter groupings, prefixes, suffixes, and inflectional endings, a reader is using *word structure clues* to deconstruct the unknown word and construct a meaning from the parts known. The student has broken the word into parts he recognizes and knows and then reconstructed the unknown word to obtain its meaning. *Context clues* is using words, meaning, and content to extract meaning of the unknown; *semantic clues* are a type of context clue in which the reader uses the meaning of the text to decipher unknown meanings; and *analogy clues* are used to draw connections between known words and unknown words.

53. C. The student recognized the repeating pattern as an increasing odd repetition. The equation he wrote explains the pattern by taking any numeral and multiplying it by 2 and then subtracting 1 to obtain the odd number. For example: (1*2) − 1 = 1 the first number in the sequence. To obtain the fifth number in the sequence: (5*2) − 1 = 9.

54. B. The Civilization of China (1029 B.C.E.), the Civilization of Greece and Rome (800 B.C.E.), and the Civilization of India (600 B.C.E.) are the three recognized classical civilizations.

55. D. The solar system encompasses all the bodies that revolve around the sun (planets, stars, comets, meteorites, and so on) and also the sun itself.

56. C. The reader uses the meaning of the text and the word order of the sentence to determine the appropriate words for the blank. *Semantic clues* are based upon the content read and help the reader determine reasonable vocabulary associated with the content. *Syntactic clues* are based upon the order and structure of the words in the sentence and help the reader determine meaning based upon grammar rules.

57. B. A reader is *fluent* when she reads with expression and automatically without unwarranted pauses or mistakes. *Comprehension* is when the reader uses critical thinking to process the information read. *Word identification* is when a reader uses word recognition strategies to pronounce or to determine word meaning. *Phonemic awareness* is when a reader is able to break words into the individual sounds (phonemes).

58. B. The law of exponents tells you to combine the like terms and add their exponents:

$$6^{2+4}$$

$$6^6$$

$$6*6*6*6*6*6$$

59. C. The Townshend Act of 1767 was a tax on essential goods like paper, glass, and tea. These taxes were placed upon the American colonies by the British in order to exercise control and authority of the newly formed world.

60. B. A New Moon occurs when the sun is behind the moon, thus lighting the back of the moon and giving us what looks like no moon at all or a New Moon.

61. C. Using long division, the answer gained is 755.33 (with a repeating decimal). The repeating decimal of 0.33 is equivalent to 1/3. The problem does not ask you to round your answer.

$$
\begin{array}{r}
755.333 \\
6\overline{)\,4532.000} \\
42 \\
\overline{33} \\
-30 \\
\overline{32} \\
-30 \\
\overline{20} \\
-18 \\
\overline{20} \\
-18 \\
\end{array}
$$

62. D. The student is processing the meaning of word she has seen by using prior knowledge to describe the animal which the word refers to. *Comprehension* is when readers use critical thinking and are able to process the information and words they have read. *Print concept* is when the reader sees that letters have sounds and they form words, *alphabetic principle* shows letters represent speech, and *word identification* is when a reader uses word recognition strategies to pronounce or to determine word meaning.

63. C. *Observation* uses the five senses to take in the world around; *classification* uses commonalities of objects for grouping; *communication* allows someone to share findings and results; *measurement* promotes the ability to use appropriate tools; *prediction* taps into prior knowledge and experience to foresee what may occur; *inference* utilizes prior knowledge and experience to explain why something occurs.

64. B. The War of 1812 increased national patriotism, united the states into one nation, built confidence in the military strength, and brought forth the *Star Spangled Banner,* which later became the national anthem of the United States.

65. D. In 1620, the Mayflower Compact was signed to set up a temporary government for the Pilgrims, which operated on the majority rule basis and was the beginning of our democratic republic.

66. C. Use the slope formula:

$$ m = \frac{y_2 - y_1}{x_2 - x_1} $$

$$ m = \frac{4 - 5}{6 - 3} $$

$$ m = \frac{-1}{3} $$

67. A. *Sight words* are words that should be known as soon as they are seen. These words are seen so frequently that they make up 50% of what is read by both adults and children (for example, said, the, read, these, what, when, she, have, and so on).

68. B. The student is watching (observation) the bird and making an educated guess based on prior knowledge as to what may occur next (prediction).

69. D. The nine planets revolve around the sun in an elliptical pattern.

70. B. The proclamation of 1763 was ignored by colonists who then traveled westward across North America, leading to the expansion of the United States and further migration of the colonists.

71. B. The student is drawing conclusions and making inferences based upon his prior knowledge and the details of the story. *Inferential reading* is when the reader makes conclusions based upon the provided information and their prior knowledge. *Think and read* is done prior to reading when the reader asks himself what he knows about the subject already. *Metacognition* is when the reader thinks about thinking, monitors his own understanding, and identifies difficulties he is having. *Summarizing* is when the reader identifies the main ideas and recalls what he has read.

72. **A.** A rhombus is a two-dimensional figure containing four edges, four vertices, and four angles. A pyramid, cylinder, and ovoid are all solid figures (3-D) containing edges, faces, and vertices.

73. **D.** Formal governments have been around for more than 5,000 years and have maintained the same functions throughout time. Governments were established to protect individual liberties, properties, and lives.

74. **B.** A translation is when the shape or object moves by sliding to another area in the plane. Reflection is a mirror image and rotation is when the shape turns on a 360° axis.

75. **D.** The *early childhood* category encompasses picture books, concept books, pattern books, and wordless books. There are six basic categories in children's literature. The *traditional* category includes myths, fables, tales, folk songs, and legends. *Fiction* includes fantasy, historical, and contemporary. *Nonfiction* encompasses reference books, encyclopedias, almanacs, and historical books.

76. **B.** The water cycle involves evaporation (liquid turning into a gas), condensation (gas turning into a liquid), and precipitation (the falling of the liquid or solid) of water.

77. **D.** In order to survive as a species, animals must grow, reproduce, and interact with their environment. Maintaining survival is essential to Earth's biomes, ecosystems, and food chains.

78. **C.** The student is able to recognize patterns in the unknown word that she has seen before in other words. She compares the unknown word to the word she knows in order to determine sounds, which is the foundation of *analogy clues*.

79. **C.** There are 100 cm in a meter and 1000 m in a kilometer. To solve, multiply 100 times 1000 times 47.

80. **C.** An oligarchy is the type of rule in which the minority rules, such as in Sparta, Greece, and some African tribes.

81. **B.** Homework was done 10% of the time. The total time was 18 hours. Multiply 18 by 10% to obtain the answer. 18 * 0.1 = 1.8 hrs.

82. **C.** The total time spent with family and eating is 55%. The closest fraction is 1/2, which is equal to 50%. 2/5 is equal to 40%; 3/4 is equal to 75%; and 1/3 is 33%—all of which do not come close to 55%.

83. **D.** The legislative branch contains Congress and other government support agencies. Congress incorporates both the Senate and the House of Representatives. Congress has the power to create laws (legislation), which is the main function of the legislative branch.

84. **D.** The flower is the sexual reproduction site of the plant, as it contains the stamen, the pistil, the stigma, and the ovaries.

85. **B.** Conductors are materials that permit electrical current to run through them. Gold, copper, aluminum, and silver are examples of conductors.

86. **D.** If a word ends in "o" with a consonant right before it, you must add "es" to make it plural. Apostrophe "s" is used to indicate singular possession, and the "s" apostrophe is used to indicate plural possession.

87. **A.** A *predicate noun* is when a noun repeats or renames the subject. Since the word "place" renames the word "park," it is classified as a predicate noun. A *subject noun* is when a noun is being talked about within a sentence; *possessive nouns* show ownership; and *object nouns* are nouns used as the direct object, indirect object, or object of the preposition.

88. **D.** The 13th Amendment to the U.S. Constitution was passed in 1865, under the presidency of Abraham Lincoln, and abolished slavery in this country.

89. **B.** After the Revolutionary War, the 13 colonies wrote the Articles of Confederation to establish a federalist government. After the *Founding Fathers* realized the Articles left the nation too separated and distant, they wrote the Constitution of the United States to create a stronger unified government.

90. **B.** Friction is the force between two objects that come into contact with one another. When someone slides on a tile floor wearing socks, the reason the person comes to a gradual stop is due to the interaction between the tile and the fabric of the socks and the opposing force.

91. D. "Lay" is an irregular verb, which does not follow a distinct pattern. "Laid" is both the past and future tense of "lay." "Lain" in the future tense of "lie," and "lay" is the past tense of "lie."

92. D. Use the area formula to determine how many square feet of wood Mabel will need to purchase.

$$A_{rect} = lw$$

$$A_{rect} = 20 \text{ ft} * 12 \text{ ft}$$

$$A_{rect} = 240 \text{ ft}^2$$

After the total area is found, multiply the cost per square foot by the total area.

Total cost = 240 * 12.25.

Total cost = $2,940.00.

93. D. Divide each percent by 100 to obtain the decimal form and then multiply with the value "out of."

$$0.3 * 80 = 24$$

$$0.13 * 120 = 15.6$$

$$0.1 * 100 = 10$$

$$0.05 * 600 = 30$$

94. A. Cultural anthropology is the study and comparison of ancient and modern cultures and groups of people that include food getting, economic systems, social stratification, patterns of residence, political organization, religion, and arts.

95. A. The cooler a substance, the slower the particles move. When a substance is warm or hot, the particles move more rapidly.

96. B. Species is the last biological classification and the most specific in the order: kingdom, phylum, class, order, family, genius, species.

97. C. The mean of a set of numbers is the average. To find the mean, add up all values and divide by the number of values in the set.

$$68 + 45 + 32 + 90 + 15 = 250$$

$$250 \div 5 = 50$$

98. C. A gerund is when a verb ends in "ing" and is used as the subject of a sentence. In the sentence *Hitting is not an acceptable behavior*, the word "hitting" is the noun and also the subject and not treated as a verb.

99. A. A *demonstrative* adjective singles out a specific noun ("that boy"). A *compound* adjective is made up of two or more words and is hyphenated; an *indefinite* adjective gives approximate information (some, few); and a *predicate* adjective follows a linking verb and describes the subject.

100. A. Use the pyramid volume formula, $1/3 * b * h$, where b = base and h = height.

$$V = 1/3 * 12.5 * 16$$

$$V = 1/3 * 200$$

$$V = 66 \; 2/3$$

101. D. Laissez-faire is an economy in which the government does not interfere or become involved, and it operates solely as a free-market system.

102. A. Citizenship is the way we act and live out our lives within society. It includes how individuals make decisions and demonstrate concern for the community and nation. Three components important to citizenship education are content (knowledge), values (standards of behavior), and processes (practicing).

103. C. A lunar eclipse is when the moon passes through the Earth's shadow (sun-Earth-moon).

104. D. *Adverbs* are used in a variety of ways: time adverbs, place adverbs, manner adverbs, and degree adverbs. In the sentence, the word "often" is used to tell how frequently something occurs which makes it a time adverb.

105. B. The figure shows an angle measuring 50°. Complementary angles, when measured, have the sum of their degrees equal to 90°. 50° + 40° = 90°.

106. A. The favorable outcome is a punk CD, of which there are 6 and the total number of possibilities is 16 CDs. The probability formula is $P_{event} = \dfrac{\text{number of favorable outcomes}}{\text{number of possible outcomes}}$.

Therefore, $P_{punk} = \dfrac{6}{16}$ and when reduced, $\dfrac{3}{8}$ or 3 in 8 or 37.5%.

107. D. Technology such as the telephone and computers (Internet) has allowed markets to expand and reach a larger audience. This improvement in communication has enabled products and services to be more widely distributed.

108. C. This illustration shows the separation of the tectonic plates and the cooling of rising magma, which creates new rock or new crust.

109. D. A free market economy, like that of the United States, is based on the two premises of competition: supply and demand. This allows the businesses and consumers to decide what should be produced, what employees should be paid, how much product or service should cost, and how much should be provided for the population.

110. C. An *atoll* is a ring of coral that forms an island. An *archipelago* is a chain of islands. A *cape* is a narrow piece of land jutting out from a coastline. A *peninsula* is a body of land surrounded by water on three sides.

111. D. The endoplasmic reticulum (ER) connects the cell membrane to the nucleus and is the transport tube for the materials to the nucleus.

112. C. Tundra has cold, dark winters with a soggy, warm summer. It is a vast and treeless area covering the Northern part of the world from latitude 55° to 70°. The ground is permanently frozen, and trees cannot grow there.

113. B. Only plants have plastids (tiny colored structures that give the plant color and are used for storage) and chloroplasts (plastids that contain chlorophyll).

114. C. A predicate is the part of the sentence that tells what the subject is doing or what the subject is. It adds the action to the sentence. The complete predicate includes the verb and all the modifiers.

115. A. A first-class lever has the fulcrum (pivot) between the effort and the load, best illustrated by scissors.

116. C. Writers progress through specific phases. While children frequently draw pictures, this is not part of the writing process. The first stage is *scribbling* in which the random marks placed throughout the page hold meaning to the child. Writers then progress to *letter-like symbols*. The next phase is *strings of letters,* then *beginning sound emergence.* The use of vowels to represent words is not a specific stage though which writers progress. Inventive spelling is a part of the initial, middle, and final sounds stage and not a stage itself. After beginning sound emergence, writers progress through the stage in which *consonants represent words.* The final three stages in which writers progress are *initial-middle-final sounds, transitional phases,* and *standard spelling.*

117. A. Because listening is a dynamic procedure, the most vital components are *hearing* so that the listener can retain what was heard, *understanding* so that the listener can understand the information heard in addition to asking significant questions and forming suitable responses, and *judging* so that the listener can create opinions and scrutinize the information stated.

118. B. Use the formula for finding combinations since the problem does not require the objects be in a specific order.

$$_nC_r = \frac{n!}{(n-r)!r!}$$

Solve using $n = 10$ and $r = 3$.

$$_nC_r = \frac{10!}{(7)!3!}$$

$$_nC_r = \frac{3628800}{(5040)(6)}$$

$$_nC_r = \frac{3628800}{6048}$$

$$_nC_r = 600$$

119. D. Let "x" represent the unknown value needed. It is easier to change the values into minutes in order to solve the problem. Set up an equation, using minutes:

$$\frac{x + 285 + 295 + 305 + 240 + 255}{6} = 260$$

$$\frac{x + 1380}{6} = 260$$

$$x + 1380 = 1560$$

$$x = 180 \text{ min.}$$

$$x = 180 \text{ min.} \div 60 \text{ min.} = 3 \text{ hrs.}$$

120. D. Transitional spelling is the final stage of spelling before accurate spelling occurs. At this stage spellers begin to use rules of spelling to construct words. It is at this time that vowels appear in each syllable.

Directions: Read the following multiple-choice questions and select the most appropriate answer. Mark the answer sheet accordingly.

1. Read the following passage:

   The hikers prepared for a five-day trip into the canyon. They expected perfect weather with no hint of winds or rains. They were surprised when the storm came and flooded their camp the first night. *Nevertheless*, they continued on their morning journey and successfully made it to the planned destination.

   The word *nevertheless* in this passage is an example of a

   A. cohesive tie
   B. expository text
   C. figurative language
   D. comprehension link

2. A third-grade teacher selects a book about the oceans of the world for her students. Prior to reading, she asks the students what they know about the ocean and its creatures and then asks what else they want to know about sea life. When they are done reading, she asks what they learned about the ocean and the creatures. Following these procedures is a reading strategy used at the elementary level. What is this method called?

   A. metacognition
   B. K-W-L strategy
   C. reciprocal teaching
   D. literal comprehension

3. A first-grade student can step with the opposite foot while throwing a ball. A classmate steps with the same foot as his throwing hand. This is an example of motor

   A. ability through heredity
   B. ability delineated by age
   C. skill development of variable rates
   D. skill development through informal play

4. The two main types of standardized tests can sometimes be interrelated. The primary difference between an aptitude test and an achievement test is

   A. The aptitude test is more reliable than an achievement test.
   B. The aptitude test has a scoring rubric; the achievement test uses stanine scores.
   C. The aptitude test predicts a student's ability; the achievement test measures mastery.
   D. The aptitude test shows outcomes through the validity of a score, and an achievement test uses the variability of a score.

5. Which answer best completes the following statement?

   Instructional activities should address federal and state standards while also meeting

   A. the goals addressed in the textbook
   B. the outline of the yearly curriculum
   C. the individual needs of the students
   D. the specific policies of the district

6. A component that is necessary for improving students' reading skills is the use of *imagery*. A recommended activity for teaching the use of imagery is

   A. the use of poetry and art
   B. memorizing new vocabulary
   C. reading and rereading passages
   D. incorporating science and history

GO ON TO THE NEXT PAGE

7. Look at the color wheel. There are three categories of colors represented. The instructional concept about color relationships can be difficult for elementary children. Which of the following is the most appropriate method for teaching the concept of color and the vocabulary that includes hues, values, and intensity, as well as primary, secondary, and tertiary?

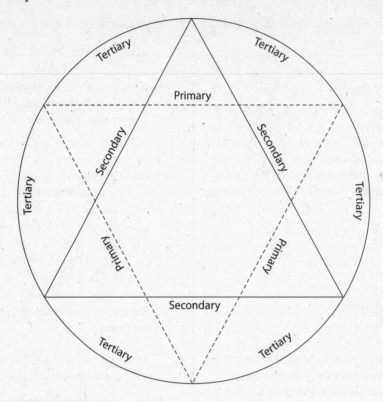

A. science—mixing colored liquids
B. social studies—designing a kaleidoscope
C. math—teaching proper three-part vocabulary
D. language arts—reading books about rainbows

8. A kindergarten teacher uses nursery rhymes, songs, and fingerplays on a daily basis to instill reading ability and language development. What specific skill does this confirm for students?

A. phonetics
B. phoneme addition
C. phonemic awareness
D. phonetic demonstration

9. One exemplar method used to instruct students in estimation is the use of

A. a set of tens frames
B. simple graphs and tables
C. situations that resemble real life
D. specially designed manipulatives

10. Educators believe that teaching the _____ of science are more important than teaching the products.

A. laws
B. formats
C. equations
D. processes

11. When a third-grade teacher suggests that students should organize their seats, theatre-style, for a brief lecture on plant and animal structures, she is using an instructional method best described as

A. discovery
B. integration
C. expository
D. guided-inquiry

12. In order for a student to be able to use decoding skills, he must have adequate instruction in the areas of print concepts, letter knowledge, and

 A. reading fluency
 B. classical literature
 C. word comprehension
 D. the alphabetic principle

13. A theory exists that promotes that a child's very basic needs must be met before the child may partake in an educational experience which will be meaningful and permit learning to occur. These basic needs, at Level I on this hierarchy, include food, water, rest, and shelter. Who was the master behind this theory of human development?

 A. Freud
 B. Piaget
 C. Skinner
 D. Maslow

14. When teachers select children's literature and trade books in a leveled format to teach reading, they are implementing a reading approach called

 A. linguistics
 B. basal reading
 C. language experience
 D. literature-based reading

15. The most important reason for elementary students to obtain locomotor skills is to

 A. be able to compete in sports
 B. increase cardiovascular efficiency
 C. progress in development of physical fitness
 D. build a strong foundation for the access of their environment

16. A third-grade teacher plans to assess the students on a social studies project involving the music and dance of other cultures. She wants to be sure students are prepared for the final exam, which is a forced answer exam, on this unit of historical information. Which of the following might she use in preparation for their studies?

 A. Conduct a vocabulary test.
 B. Request the performance of a dance.
 C. Observe a cooperative learning activity.
 D. Use a checklist of the students' responses.

17. The transmission model in teaching citizenship is

 A. the acquisition of open-minded thoughts, values, and ideals.
 B. the analyzing of information, forming opinions, and acting upon it.
 C. the learning of government functions and following government rules.
 D. the following of laws, study of implications, and acknowledgement of rights.

18. A kindergarten teacher uses buttons to instill the concept of classification, a critical mathematical skill. This type of math manipulative may be identified as

 A. reflective
 B. inflective
 C. structured
 D. unstructured

19. A kindergarten teacher says /p/ /i/ /g/ to her students and asks them what she is saying. She suggests they do the same and sound out the hidden word. This is an example of

 A. phoneme identity
 B. phoneme addition
 C. phoneme blending
 D. phoneme segmentation

20. A third-grade teacher notices that one of her students is playing with equipment when she is trying to provide instructions to the class. The best type of social discipline to use would be to

 A. move closer to the student in order to enable him to hear the lesson better.
 B. ask the student to remain after class so she may ask the student about the disruption.
 C. continue instruction, using the equipment the student has to demonstrate the next activity.
 D. stop the entire class to point out how the student is disrupting the class, causing other students to lose time for the activity.

GO ON TO THE NEXT PAGE

21. A third-grade teacher has determined that the new student just placed in her class is somewhat behind the others in the area of math, primarily because the student's previous learning experiences did not cover the same principles and standards. In order for this student to catch up with the other students, the teacher has decided which of the following strategies would be most beneficial?

    A. retention
    B. prompting
    C. peer tutoring
    D. modifications

22. A fourth-grade class is examining the family structure of the Maori tribe of New Zealand. This falls under which of the following social sciences?

    A. sociology
    B. economics
    C. psychology
    D. anthropology

23. Educators need to prepare students for the new millennium and the additional reading and writing skills necessary to comprehend and use technology. In using the traditional reading and writing of texts, students are exposed to the linear format. The new technology requires that students be exposed simultaneously to _____ format of materials.

    A. advanced
    B. interactive
    C. culturally rich
    D. multidimensional

24. Music education at the elementary level is supported by extensive research about its benefits. Which of the following subject areas demonstrate substantial improvement when students have the opportunity to be exposed to music through school experiences and activities?

    A. mathematics and art
    B. mathematics and literacy
    C. science and social studies
    D. science and physical education

25. During a writing assignment, the teacher roams around the classroom making observations of the students' generalizations and use of skills. He makes notes about each of the students as they use grammar and spelling in their writing. The notes are used to make adjustments to the instruction for the next writing period or to address a specific skill with a particular student. This type of informal assessment is referred to as

    A. a running record
    B. a notation record
    C. an anecdotal record
    D. an observational record

26. Which of the following is the best example of an activity that promotes phonemic awareness?

    A. singing a song
    B. writing a story
    C. reading a letter
    D. talking to someone

27. A fifth-grade teacher focuses science study on the solar system. Students learned the composition of the planets and compared them to the Earth. The teacher has divided the class into cooperative learning groups and assigned a project based on this topic. The project given to the students is to identify the planet they believe could sustain a life form and describe how this creature would differ from humans in order to live on the planet. This is an example of which of the following stages of Bloom's taxonomy?

    A. synthesis
    B. knowledge
    C. application
    D. comprehension

28. To help students learn _____ an elementary teacher created a set of cards that look like

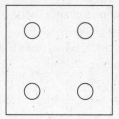

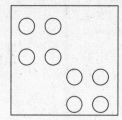

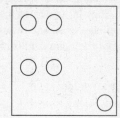

Four   Eight (4 and 4)   Five (4 and 1 more)

A. grouping sets
B. anchor numbers
C. counting objects
D. spatial relationships

29. A writing assignment has been given to a fifth-grade class of students. The students are to construct a written report on one of the inventions of the twentieth century that was studied during a unit on inventors. One of the students went to the library to gather some books on Thomas Edison. The student also began to list some words that seemed important to the report: light bulb, electricity, watts. Then the student designed a web of Edison's life. What stage of the writing process is this student in?

A. editing
B. revising
C. rough draft
D. prewriting

30. Which of the following is the most emphasized pedagogy in elementary science education and related to inquiry based learning?

A. behavioral
B. sociological
C. constructivist
D. psychodynamic

31. The use of which of the following is a procedure that is often used to aid students in learning how to gain information from text?

A. expository texts
B. content exercises
C. literature readings
D. reciprocal teaching

32. A key principle of No Child Left Behind (NCLB), the federal law mandated in 2002, is the

A. school accountability of adequate yearly progress.
B. inclusion of student's with disabilities in classrooms.
C. provision for detailed scope and sequence in curricula.
D. involvement of parents in hiring highly qualified teachers.

33. The skills that a child acquires in language are based on his exposure to which of the following?

A. procedures and strategies
B. education and motivation
C. instruction and assessment
D. environment and experiences

GO ON TO THE NEXT PAGE

Practice Exam (0011)

34. A first-grade teacher uses product containers, newspapers, and small signs to share new words with students. They have learned the words exit, stop, florist, cereal, beans, and theatre in just one week. The use of these items falls under the category of

    A. instructional guide

    B. appositives sources

    C. environmental print

    D. classified groupings

35. When students learn to measure the *weight* of an object, they are learning to

    A. determine when something may begin

    B. compare the mass of one object to another

    C. analyze the degree to which something changes

    D. figure the quantity of three-dimensional objects and figures

36. Which of the following learning theories supports the philosophy that students should build, design, and create their own art work?

    A. ecological

    B. behavioral

    C. sociological

    D. constructivist

37. What is the highest level of Bloom's Taxonomy reached when a fifth-grade student diagrams the consequences a new law will have upon a local community?

    A. analysis

    B. synthesis

    C. knowledge

    D. understanding

38. An elementary teacher is reading *The Very Hungry Caterpillar* by Eric Carle. She is using dialogic reading to seek answers to questions such as:

Who has seen a caterpillar before?

Have you ever eaten an apple?

What does a caterpillar change into?

By conducting a reading session in this manner, what is the teacher trying to establish for the students?

    A. using prior knowledge to make connections to the text

    B. preparing for an assessment by learning the vocabulary

    C. providing a chance to use oral language with a large group

    D. allowing time for individuals to review the pictures in the book

39. If a student is able to dribble a basketball against an opponent, what sport skill level has she reached?

    A. control

    B. utilization

    C. precontrol

    D. proficiency

40. A second-grade teacher has given one of her leveled reading groups a book titled, "The Princess and the Horse Who Could Fly," and asked them to think about the name of the book. One of the students stated, "I think this book is about a young girl who lives in a kingdom with a very special horse. The girl loves her horse, and they have some fun adventures." What skill group is this student building upon?

    A. interpreting and predicting

    B. prereading and identifying

    C. imagery and understanding

    D. comprehending and translating

41. A sixth-grade teacher uses peer assessment for her physical education class to identify the level of mastery of the volleyball skills each student possesses. Which answer is an example that best describes peer assessment?

    A. Two students take turns observing each other to determine their volleyball skill level.

    B. Students submit displays and essays on what they believe are their volleyball skill levels.

    C. The teacher walks around the class and observes students practicing their volleyball skills.

    D. The teacher videotapes the class to watch it later in order to determine the students' volleyball skill levels.

42. Read the following excerpt from a second-grade writer.

> Won dey my mudr and my fadr tok me to the park.
> We saw sum duks. We fed thm bred. The duks wer green
> and blu. We had fun.

What does this child's writing reflect to the teacher?

A. The child should work on vowel sounds.

B. The child needs remedial spelling instruction.

C. The child uses invented spelling to deliver a message.

D. The child will gain knowledge about sentence structure later.

43. For students who are capable of participating in extended instruction or gaining additional information on a topic, the teacher might offer tiered lessons, or learning centers. These are examples of which of the following strategies?

A. motivation

B. assessment

C. enrichment

D. intervention

44. When a teacher observes a student who demonstrates difficulty remembering some of the letters in a word that is not only familiar, but easy to read, this may indicate that the student

A. does not apply context clues

B. has not learned the correct spelling

C. is not clear on the consonant-vowel rules

D. lacks knowledge of letter-sound correspondence

45. Models in science are useful to students as they can learn spatial relationships and meet mathematical challenges through these

A. inquiry assessments

B. alternative activities

C. simplified structures

D. visual representations

46. Which of the following is considered a parallel process related to arts education?

A. Take a test on the music terms.

B. Read about artists to improve literacy.

C. Construct a model of a cell for science.

D. Visit a museum and write a story about it.

47. As an elementary teacher, you are teaching a unit on map skills, and you want to address all learning intelligences. Which of the following would satisfy the needs of a kinesthetic learner?

A. singing a song about the different map components

B. reading a passage about the different map components

C. using manipulatives to learn the different map components

D. moving physically around the areas as the different map components

48. What is one of the best methods for teaching a student silent letters or letter patterns in words to help with memorization of more regular spelling?

A. Practice writing words multiple times until the student is able to write the word without a cue.

B. Compare different types of words and word endings to help the student choose the proper spelling.

C. Conduct regular assessments on students' abilities to spell the words in the weekly reading passages.

D. Point out words that have the same silent letters or patterns, especially in those words the student may already know.

GO ON TO THE NEXT PAGE

49. An elementary teacher who is teaching the properties of geometric objects and makes this statement, "If all four angles are right angles, the shape must be a rectangle. If it is a square, all angles are right angles. If it is a square, it must be a rectangle." This *if-then* reasoning reflects which of the following theories?

   A. van Hiele—informal deduction
   B. Gardner Theory—logical intelligence
   C. Van de Walle Approach—developmental teaching
   D. Piaget Constructivist Approach—"hands on learning"

50. Piaget is responsible for describing and promoting which of the following theories of learning?

   A. cognitive
   B. ecological
   C. behavioral
   D. sociological

51. A fourth-grade teacher prefers to divide his students into heterogeneous groups to conduct experiments. Which of the following is the name of this instructional format?

   A. control groups
   B. guided activities
   C. unifying presentations
   D. cooperative learning process

52. While studying the U.S. Constitution, as the elementary teacher, you take your class on a field trip to the National Archives to see the Constitution document. This is an example of which instructional strategy?

   A. scaffolding
   B. cooperative learning
   C. fiction incorporation
   D. primary source utilization

53. A fifth-grade student is recently demonstrating undesirable behaviors during the social studies lessons. The class is studying the cultures around the world. The teacher has incorporated the study of languages, foods, dances, dress, and customs by asking students to give presentations. Based on this information, what may be the cause (antecedent) of this student's inappropriate behaviors?

   A. afraid of other students
   B. not sure about the assignment
   C. unable to read the information
   D. embarrassed to perform in class

54. Multiplication can be a complex operation to learn. An elementary teacher places the following example on the board to teach a specific multiplication strategy related to another formal operation, addition. Which of the following specific strategies of multiplication is identified in this example?

   Example: $2 * 4 = 8$ $4 + 4 = 8$

   A. fact families
   B. part-part-whole
   C. doubles equivalency
   D. whole number computation

55. A first-grade teacher reads the story of *The Three Bears* to the class. When he rereads the story, he points out the initial consonants of the main vocabulary words of the week and asks students to predict what the word is: bears, porridge, house, and bed. This is a strategy used to promote which type of knowledge?

   A. writing
   B. reading
   C. spelling
   D. phonics

56. Health education has become a component of science education at the elementary level. Its primary purpose is to

   A. instill healthy lifestyles
   B. minimize at-risk behaviors
   C. motivate parents in proper nutrition
   D. demonstrate proper grooming routines

57. One of the critical issues that teachers face related to high-stakes testing is the

   A. scores only reflect last year's skills
   B. amount of time students need to study
   C. parent outrage at the content in the exam
   D. "dumbing down" of curriculum and teaching to the test

58. Under the theory of multiple intelligences, the one most closely tied to reading and language arts is

    A. verbal

    B. logical

    C. existential

    D. kinesthetic

59. Look at this computation:

$$\begin{array}{r} 19 \\ 4\overline{)436} \\ \underline{4} \\ 036 \\ \underline{36} \\ 0 \end{array}$$

This error is an example of a student who has not adequately learned how to use

    A. decimals

    B. place values

    C. division operations

    D. 3-digit multiplication

60. A third-grade teacher instructs students on the five Great Lakes. To help the students remember the names of the lakes, he uses the word "HOMES." Which of the following is the name of this instructional strategy?

    A. chunking

    B. prompting

    C. mnemonics

    D. task analysis

61. A critical design element of a curriculum is the _____, which includes decisions and planning about the information to be taught as well as an outline of the grade levels at which the sequential skills and concepts are taught.

    A. scope and sequence

    B. pedagogical practices

    C. instructional objectives

    D. extension and remediation techniques

62. Students should learn how to record collected data using charts, tables, or graphs. A graph is a visual format of expressing and exploring numbers and information. Using a graph may be introduced at the

    A. 1st grade

    B. 2nd grade

    C. 4th grade

    D. 5th grade

63. Which theory encompasses the following scenario? A child relates newly learned knowledge about the technology of the twentieth century to that of her prior knowledge on classical civilization developments.

    A. cognitive

    B. sociological

    C. constructivist

    D. psychodynamic

64. The domain of science that includes the properties of objects, materials, and matter is

    A. earth science

    B. energy science

    C. natural science

    D. physical science

65. A third-grade teacher has assigned a cooperative learning activity for the study of haiku poetry. She has based the student groupings on the performance in the poetry unit. Students are to work together in separate groups to develop a haiku, create an illustration, and present the haiku to the class using actions and props.

This activity is an example of

    A. integrating fine arts

    B. using written expression

    C. utilizing authentic assessment

    D. diagnosing post learning goals

66. When students are active in their education because they enjoy learning and they want to succeed and gain skills or knowledge in a particular subject, they are considered to have which of the following types of motivation?

    A. explicit

    B. implicit

    C. intrinsic

    D. extrinsic

GO ON TO THE NEXT PAGE

67. Students have been asked to study four different plants that the teacher has brought into the classroom. They are to carefully examine the structure, identify the parts, and compare their properties. After they have gathered this specific information, students are to proceed with developing a generalization based on their knowledge of the plant kingdom to determine the habitat in which each plant must exist and how each plant may affect its environment. This is a form of which of the following teaching styles?

   A. inductive
   B. deductive
   C. reflective
   D. inflective

68. Using the trade book, *Silly Sally* by Audrey Wood, in a reading aloud activity, a kindergarten teacher shares the pictures with the students as the story is read. He asks students to predict what will happen next as they read the text on each page and look at the pictures. In reference to Bloom's taxonomy, which level does this refer?

   A. analysis
   B. synthesis
   C. application
   D. comprehension

69. A fifth-grade teacher presents a unit on the three branches of government. She asks her students to give five examples for each branch, paraphrases the textbook, and expounds upon ideas the students have. What integration strategy is she utilizing?

   A. debriefing
   B. scaffolding
   C. whole class
   D. cooperative learning

70. A worksheet of fractions is given as homework with directions to chose the larger of the two and write the reason.

   #1. 3/8 or 4/10

   #2. 8/9 or 7/8

   #3. 7/13 or 4/13

Which concept related to fractions is the teacher reinforcing?

   A. ordering
   B. reducing
   C. expanding
   D. comparing

71. A third-grade teacher has just completed a thematic unit of study on the ocean. Which of the following types of assessment would be the most beneficial in planning instruction for the next unit?

   A. formative
   B. alternative
   C. summative
   D. observation

72. Scientific experiments follow certain steps in order to comply with scientific inquiry and discovery. Students are instructed on these steps prior to being permitted to conduct independent or small group experiments. The primary steps include state the question, _____, describe the variables, and collect the data.

   A. gather the materials
   B. formulate a hypothesis
   C. organize the correlations
   D. establish the environment

73. A strategy that promotes listening and speaking skills in a classroom is

   A. mnemonics
   B. oral language
   C. guided practice
   D. choral responding

74. The anticipatory set that an elementary teacher could use to engage a second-grade class while teaching citizenship would be

   A. to give a short quiz on citizenship terms
   B. to have the students create a diorama on citizenship
   C. to deliver a speech or lecture about the basics of citizenship
   D. to act out a scene from the playground that demonstrates citizenship

75. As the anticipatory set, if a teacher writes these examples on the board for students to discuss, what math concept is he planning to introduce?

It will be cloudy tomorrow.
A fish will die if it does not live in water.
Andrea and Justin will see a movie at 7:00 P.M.
A storm will begin on July 28.
Mabel will be about 6 years old next year.

    A.   number lines
    B.   algebraic equations
    C.   primes and composites
    D.   probability and estimation

76. One of the standards of assessment in science for elementary children established by the NSES is the evaluation of

    A.   attitude
    B.   equipment
    C.   experiments
    D.   comprehension

77. A fourth-grade teacher has developed a consistent method of behavior management that includes modeling the desired behaviors and shaping the behaviors through a system of rewards and consequences. He is using the model for behavior management developed by

    A.   Jones
    B.   Canter
    C.   Kounin
    D.   Skinner

78. A fifth-grade teacher has created a unit on famous authors and as an end of unit assessment, students are required to research the life of an author and write a report using the skills of writing acquired during the unit study. This demonstrates the use of which of the following types of assessment?

    A.   explicit
    B.   implicit
    C.   formative
    D.   summative

79. A third-grade student whose parents are concerned about his abilities to keep up with the math content want regular contact with the teacher about the child's mathematics progress. The

teacher would like to accommodate the parents and provide them with solid information. Which of the following assessment types would be best used to illustrate the student's progress over time?

    A.   an aptitude test
    B.   dynamic assessment
    C.   a portfolio assessment
    D.   a norm-referenced test

80. If a teacher asks his class "Why did the Revolutionary War occur?" and waits 1–3 minutes for a response, he is demonstrating

    A.   scaffolding
    B.   processing time
    C.   instructional pacing
    D.   student response technique

81. The instructional model created by Hunter that improves academic achievement by supporting diverse learners and structuring a sequence for learning is called

    A.   inquiry learning
    B.   mastery learning
    C.   direct instruction
    D.   traditional approach

82. A fourth-grade teacher is preparing to introduce the concept of decimals to the class, as they are learning about the U.S. monetary system, which is based on the decimal system. However, she is unsure whether all of the students are ready to learn this mathematics concept. What area of math should she assess her students on prior to teaching decimals?

    A.   fractions
    B.   operations
    C.   percentages
    D.   whole numbers

83. Which of the following formal measures should a teacher use to assess student progress on the terminology of the poetry unit?

    A.   dynamic assessment
    B.   criterion-referenced test
    C.   ecological based assessment
    D.   performance based assessment

GO ON TO THE NEXT PAGE

84. An elementary student writes the following, making a consistent error.

> This summer my family went to a palce in Canada. We went to a lake to go fishing. We stayed at a palce on the edge of the lake in a small cabin. Then we went to another palce in Oregon to go camping. We had lots of fun!

Which of the following stages of spelling development does this passage demonstrate?

- **A.** phonetic
- **B.** transitional
- **C.** semiphonic
- **D.** precommunicative

85. One of the six principles established for school mathematics by the National Council for Teachers of Mathematics is

- **A.** equity
- **B.** diversity
- **C.** equivalency
- **D.** objective thinking

86. When evaluating a student's performance assessment, the best strategy is to use a prepared and predetermined _____ that establishes criteria and expectations on which performance will be judged.

- **A.** stanine index
- **B.** grading scale
- **C.** scoring rubric
- **D.** percentage chart

87. A fifth-grade student has been demonstrating some behavior problems in class and could use a structured program of intervention. Of the following, which would offer the student the most involvement in learning to self-manage his off-task behaviors?

- **A.** modeling
- **B.** contingency contract
- **C.** implied consequences
- **D.** negative reinforcement

88. When a student writes the word, "house" in the following manner, it is an example of which of these developmental stages of writing?

⊥O(|s4

- **A.** scribbling
- **B.** transitional
- **C.** letter-like symbols
- **D.** beginning sound emergence

89. A first-grade teacher has asked her students to explain several of the basic math facts as a way of checking their skills. Which of the following level of Bloom's taxonomy is this activity an example of?

- **A.** synthesis
- **B.** knowledge
- **C.** application
- **D.** comprehension

90. When an assignment or skill is broken down into smaller sequential steps and each of those steps are taught, one at a time, this strategy is known as

    A. chunking
    B. task analysis
    C. cloze procedure
    D. scaffolded lessons

91. In order to determine a student's reading strengths and needs, which of the following might the teacher conduct?

    A. reader profile
    B. parent interview
    C. curriculum survey
    D. teacher observation

92. A fourth-grade teacher is designing the lessons for mathematics based on great diversity in his classroom. He has students with cultural and linguistic diversity, some students who are also placed in special education, and some who receive services as gifted or talented students. What is the best way for him to accommodate all these learning needs?

    A. Request an assistant.
    B. Simplify the materials.
    C. Develop tiered lessons.
    D. Increase the assessments.

93. Students need to be assured that they are performing appropriately in math, and develop a strong self-concept and competence that inspires their attitude for the future in math classes. Which of the following strategies will help students develop a positive attitude and desire to learn math?

    A. skill drill
    B. time trials
    C. strategic instruction
    D. systematic feedback

94. An elementary teacher writes the following word parts on the board and assigns the students to blend the words and recite them to a partner. Then each student must write them as practice for both spelling and for familiarity. What are these two collective forms called?

    tr-   ack   bl-   ack

    tr-   ain   bl-   and

    tr-   am   bl-   eak

    tr-   ash   bl-   end

    A. onsets and rimes
    B. blends and rhymes
    C. segments and words
    D. prefixes and suffixes

95. The implementation of reading strategies has a different impact on the various abilities of student readers. Which of the following is the most comfortable for less proficient readers?

    A. choral reading
    B. guided reading
    C. reader's theatre
    D. round robin reading

96. Which of the following teaching styles offers the most autonomy to the learners?

    A. delegator
    B. facilitator
    C. demonstrator
    D. formal authority

97. A second-grade teacher requires each student to complete a five-page research paper at the end of the second semester for the study of literature. Students have had difficulty achieving mastery of this assignment. The principal of the school has received numerous complaints from parents and peer educators about the complexity and use of this assignment. What did the principal determine was the reason the teacher should eliminate this requirement from this class?

    A. It was not developmentally appropriate.
    B. It did not adequately measure yearly progress.
    C. Not all of the students have access to resources.
    D. It was taking parents too much time from their schedules.

GO ON TO THE NEXT PAGE

98. There are 10 general national academic standards for mathematics instruction. They are divided into two groups with the first set of five standards relating to number and operations, algebra, geometry, measurement, and

    A. reasoning and proof

    B. data analysis and probability

    C. connections and representation

    D. the processes of problem solving

99. A fifth-grade teacher works with a student to brainstorm some ideas for writing assignments and writes down some key words. The student orally states some of the sentences before writing them down. Then the student begins to write the sentences, and the teacher encourages rereading and revision. This is an example of instruction using the practice of

    A. drafting

    B. dictation

    C. guided writing

    D. repeated writing

100. To assess a reader's comprehension and use of reading skills and strategies, a teacher may present a passage using the following format. This is an example of _____.

    Rabbit and tortoise ran a _____. They each decided to _____ at their own speed. Rabbit could run very _____ and tortoise was very _____. But tortoise was wise. _____ was foolish and careless.

    A. context clues

    B. cloze procedures

    C. word recognition

    D. phonemic awareness

101. Which of the following equations is the BEST example of the basic facts of mathematics?

    A. $5 + 3 = 8$

    B. $24 \div 12 = 2$

    C. $44 - 11 = 33$

    D. $20 * 11 = 220$

102. In a third-grade classroom, during small group instruction, a student is having trouble reading the word "canyon" as the group reads about areas of the southwest. Which of the following skills might show the area the student is having the most difficulty with?

    A. content clues

    B. context clues

    C. phonetic clues

    D. phonemic clues

103. The primary reason that elementary teachers should use manipulatives to teach mathematics is because they enable students to

    A. visualize concepts

    B. be more motivated

    C. learn at their own rate

    D. maintain concentration

104. An elementary teacher is preparing to introduce geometry and shape relationships, which is a new concept for the class. She should consider which of the following strategies to more appropriately help the students in acquiring the proper skills related to this topic?

    A. response cards

    B. triad grouping

    C. choral responding

    D. scaffolded instruction

105. An elementary teacher receives the following paragraph from a student on an assignment about a favorite animal. This passage demonstrates that the student is having difficulty with which of the following?

> Katz kin be fun at hom. I lick to play iwth mi dog and berd too. Mi kat has a purple kolar. Mi dog kin run fast. Mi muder wil walk wit the dog but not the kat. Mi bab sistr wans a frog to play with. I lik to feed mi dog good food.

    A.   conventions
    B.   word choice
    C.   organization
    D.   sentence fluency

106. The following is an example of

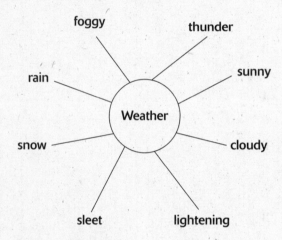

    A.   key scaling
    B.   expository text
    C.   semantic webbing
    D.   background information

107. A key component to effective classroom management when instructing in the subject of mathematics is to ensure that the lessons, activities, and assessments

    A.   offer self-paced instruction
    B.   demonstrate ability groupings
    C.   are developmentally appropriate
    D.   are designed for independent learners

108. Which of the following is the most preferred theory to implement in elementary mathematics education?

    A.   ecological
    B.   behavioral
    C.   constructivist
    D.   psychoanalytic

109. The recommended method of teaching grammar to elementary students is to use

    A.   an authentic and meaningful approach
    B.   a system of direct instruction and practice
    C.   familiar rules and guidelines
    D.   periodic evaluations and altered instruction

110. A third-grade student, excited about learning new words, wanted to practice writing some words at home. Even though there was no homework assigned, he wanted to share his word list with the teacher. Based on this list that he created, what stage of spelling development is he in?

> parkd   char (chair)
> fishd   jragin (dragon)
> changd   chrane (train)

    A.   phonetic
    B.   semphonic
    C.   transitional
    D.   precommunicative

GO ON TO THE NEXT PAGE

Answer Key

1. A	36. D	71. C	106. C
2. B	37. A	72. B	107. C
3. C	38. A	73. D	108. C
4. C	39. B	74. D	109. A
5. C	40. A	75. D	110. A
6. A	41. A	76. A	
7. A	42. C	77. D	
8. C	43. C	78. D	
9. C	44. D	79. C	
10. D	45. D	80. B	
11. C	46. C	81. C	
12. D	47. D	82. A	
13. D	48. D	83. B	
14. D	49. A	84. B	
15. D	50. A	85. A	
16. A	51. D	86. C	
17. C	52. D	87. B	
18. D	53. D	88. C	
19. C	54. C	89. D	
20. C	55. D	90. B	
21. C	56. A	91. A	
22. A	57. D	92. C	
23. D	58. A	93. D	
24. B	59. B	94. A	
25. C	60. C	95. A	
26. A	61. A	96. A	
27. A	62. B	97. A	
28. D	63. A	98. B	
29. D	64. D	99. C	
30. C	65. A	100. B	
31. D	66. C	101. A	
32. A	67. A	102. B	
33. D	68. D	103. A	
34. C	69. B	104. D	
35. B	70. D	105. C	

Answer Explanations

1. **A.** A word or phrase that creates a link between sentences or between a sentence and its content to make a connection for the reader is called a *cohesive tie*.

2. **B.** The K-W-L strategy is used to promote students' active thinking as they read passages. It stands for K-what do you *know*, W-*what* else you want to learn, and L what did you *learn* from the reading.

3. **C.** Even though both students are first graders, skill development will vary from individual to individual. Expecting children to develop the same skills at the same time is unrealistic. Age and heredity is not a predictor of motor ability. Skill must be developed from use and practice.

4. **C.** An aptitude test is designed to predict how well a student will learn a skill or gain knowledge in a topic area, whereas an achievement test is used to measure what the student has already learned or to identify the skills the student has mastered.

5. **C.** It is critical to meet the needs of all students as lessons are presented and taught to ensure comprehension of the materials and competencies of the content. Some students will need accommodations, and others may need enrichment. The other answers are areas a teacher should review, but none of these will separately guarantee that students will have what they need.

6. **A.** Teachers should read descriptive poetry lines to students and ask them to create a picture in their mind or ask students to write poetry that depicts a scene. They may also use art such as drawing pictures or making a collage to help teach imagery.

7. **A.** Having students mix colored liquids in science is the best selection, as the concept is visual and will be imprinted in their minds as they perform the activity. It is a positive method for integrating art into a subject area and using the vocabulary as it is appropriate to the activity. The other options are related to color relationships, but would not offer the depth and concept development of the science lesson.

8. **C.** At a young age, students should be exposed to phonemic awareness, which is matching the sounds of a word given orally to the knowledge that a word exists. This may be accomplished by using songs and rhymes to "play" with word and syllable sounds.

9. **C.** Estimation is an important life-long skill that is used in figuring measurements and figuring the quantities of objects. Teaching students by using typical daily situations will be more meaningful to understanding this concept.

10. **D.** Students are better able to learn the laws, the facts, and the content of science if they first understand the processes. Knowing the processes will aid students in better grasping the concepts of science and pursuing the inquiry of science.

11. **C.** The expository method of instruction is based on teacher-dominated activities, such as conducting a lecture (as in the stem), reading stories, showing videos, or demonstrating an activity.

12. **D.** The alphabetic principle is the concept that written language is comprised of letters that represent sounds in spoken words. This is essential to knowing how to decode.

13. **D.** Maslow's Theory of Hierarchy of Needs was created to show the various levels through which humans develop to become a self-actualized person who is capable of managing himself in society. The first level consists of basic needs, and Maslow believed that these must be met first for the person to continue up the hierarchy to more advanced stages where they may learn to be independent.

14. **D.** The literature-based reading approach supports children through various literature selections and a variety of trade books. These are chosen through the use of specific criteria that relates to grade levels. Research finds that this approach encourages children to read as they are motivated and gain interest through the materials.

15. **D.** Children must obtain locomotor skills so that they may gain better access of their home, school, and community environments. While locomotor skills are required for participation in sports, aid in physical fitness and improve the cardiovascular system, they are more importantly linked to a student's ability to navigate the world around them.

16. **A.** The teacher should conduct a vocabulary test to check student comprehension of the music terms, the dances taught, and the cultural aspects of the study. Although the other choices have potential for evaluating student progress, they are all performance-based assessments and not forced answer assessments.

17. **C.** The two different models recommended in the teaching of citizenship are transmission and transformation. Transmission is the learning of government function and following the rules. There are two perspectives in the transmission model: legalistic and assimilationist.

18. **D.** A mathematics manipulative considered unstructured is one that has various uses and may be applied to more than one concept in learning math. Buttons can be used to teach classification, ordered sets, math operations, and a variety of other concepts.

19. **C.** Phoneme blending is the strategy of providing a sequence of spoken phonemes and then using them to sound out and form a word. Examples include /t/ /a/ /p/ is tap, /m/ /o/ /m/ is mom, /d/ /e/ /n/ is den.

20. **C.** The best social discipline technique to use in this situation is one of a reactive nature since the distraction is already taking place. Nonverbal teacher instruction in which the teacher uses the equipment the student is playing with to teach the next lesson can be effective in reducing the inappropriate behavior without stopping the class.

21. **C.** For a new student who has yet to be introduced to the concepts and needs to be caught up to the other students in the class, the most beneficial strategy would be peer tutoring. The use of this strategy would allow the teacher time to observe the new student and allow the student to become comfortable in the class, while not feeling incompetent. Peer tutoring is conducted under the guidance of a teacher in which a student who needs assistance in an academic area works with a student who is more competent or knowledgeable in that particular area.

22. **A.** The social science sociology is the study of human behavior and society specifically related to institutions, groups, social changes, communications, and relationships among people. Anthropology encompasses the study of physical characteristics of people and cultural traits. Psychology is the study of human behavior and society but is also focused upon perceptions and behaviors, individual differences, and emotions. Economics is considered a social structure of a society.

23. **D.** In the new literacies of technology, students must be able to act upon information immediately. The skills required are more complex and different. Students must address multidimensional formats of information through a variety of technology tools. Students will need to interact with the materials and deliver concise and clear information to others in the world. Teachers will need to be uniquely trained in addressing these skills.

24. **B.** Research studies confirm that when students are exposed to music in structured standards-based educational opportunities, and it is integrated into the curriculum, students reap the benefits in academic areas, particularly mathematics and literacy.

25. **C.** An anecdotal record kept during a writing assignment is helpful to a teacher in planning for future instruction in this area. It includes a description of meaningful information observed by the teacher and collected as notes so the teacher may interpret the information. The teacher may then modify and adjust instruction for individual students.

26. **A.** Phonemic awareness is the understanding that oral sounds in the language become words and that blending the sounds in a word make it possible to say the word.

27. **A.** Synthesis is the step in which students demonstrate the capability of combining the information they already know into creating something new and unique. Taking what they have learned in this example of the solar system, students can work together to identify a planet and create a life form capable of inhabiting it.

28. **D.** Children understand how to recognize the amount in sets of objects when given patterned arrangements. Using cards such as those in the example help in teaching and grasping the concept of spatial relationships.

29. **D.** In the stage of prewriting, students generate ideas for their writing piece and gather details. They do so through reading literature, creating maps or webs of the information, developing word banks or determining the audience for the piece.

30. **C.** The constructivist theory is based on Piaget's developmental stages and related to how children construct their own knowledge based on prior experience and investigation. The focus in elementary science education is inquiry-based learning in which children utilize hands-on learning to discovery the principles and concepts of science.

31. **D.** Students need practice in extracting information from texts in preparation for reading expository texts at the higher grade levels. The use of reciprocal teaching helps students learn how to read expository texts. A set process for implementing reciprocal teaching is important and includes predicting, reading, questioning, clarifying, summarizing, and predicting.

32. **A.** Under the law NCLB, states are required to create a system of accountability to ensure that all students are making adequate annual progress in prime subject areas. There is a measurement system in place that determines the school's adequate yearly progress and each state establishes a system for remediation of schools.

33. **D.** A child's environment and experiences at an early age contribute to the development of the language domain and impacts future success specifically in reading, and language arts, and overall in school.

34. **C.** Environmental text has shown to be beneficial in literacy development. Sharing words from a child's daily world, such as those on product containers, in newspapers, ads, or small signs contribute to rich vocabulary development.

35. **B.** The concept of weight measurement compares the mass of one object to another and is one of the first measurement concepts taught. Students may use informal units of measure such as their hands to determine mass when first learning this concept.

36. **D.** The constructivist theory, regarded by Piaget's work, suggests that children learn best when they participate in hands-on learning, which is an appropriate selection for the area of arts education.

37. **A.** Analysis is the fourth level in the taxonomy in which students recognize patterns, organize parts, identify components, conclude, and clarify. Questions found at this level include "how" and "what."

38. **A.** The teacher is establishing background for all students by seeking answers to simple questions that relate to the book and to student lives and experiences. This aids students in using their prior knowledge to make connections to the text.

39. **B.** In the stage of *utilization* students are able to carry out movements and skills with more autonomy, and there is a purpose for each intentional movement or skill.

40. **A.** Interpreting and predicting are complex cognitive skills and important reading skills. *Interpreting* is the ability of a reader to use inference and apply literal information to his life. In this instance, the student must have some familiarity with horses and like them. *Predicting* is also the use of inference in making a deduction about what may happen next or what ideas are present. In this illustration, the student is imagining that there will be fun adventures, perhaps based on experiences she has had with horses or wishes she had.

41. **A.** Peer assessment is best described as two students who observe each other to determine whether they are each able to complete the predetermined skills on which they are being assessed. They must use a rubric for scoring created by the physical education teacher. Peer assessment is a positive assessment technique to provide information to the teacher on individual student skill levels and supports the affective domain by having students work together to reach a goal.

42. **C.** The child is using invented spelling in this passage, which is an early strategy for young children. They guess on how a word might be spelled according to what they hear and the spelling skills and knowledge they have. Children should be allowed to use invented spelling, and as they are exposed to more standard spelling instruction, they will improve.

43. **C.** Enrichment is an instructional method used for extending a lesson or unit for those students who are able to grasp more of the topic and need additional participation in the learning situation. Many of the students who require enrichment activities are found to be gifted or talented.

44. **D.** A student who shows problems with remembering some of the letters in a word that he can easily read, he may not have a complete understanding of letter-sound correspondences, so the word becomes difficult to remember.

45. **D.** Building models in science offer concrete, visual representations of things that cannot easily be seen due to the size of the actual object. Models require skill in spatial relationships and mathematics to accurately build them.

46. **C.** Using art to create a model of something studied in science offers the best selection for a parallel process, which is the blending of an arts related activity with an academic subject.

47. **D.** A bodily-kinesthetic learner acquires knowledge through body movements and physical activity; therefore, having the students physically move about an area to learn the map components would best meet the needs of these learners.

48. **D.** Showing the student some lists of other words with the same silent letters or letter patterns from words that the student already knows aids in memorization of these regular spellings. For example, right, bright, tight, fight.

49. **A.** Level 2 of the van Hiele Theory of Geometry is the informal deduction approach. It promotes the idea related to the properties of shapes and the relationships among the properties of geometric objects.

50. **A.** Piaget believed that individuals construct new knowledge based on prior knowledge, and there are distinct stages of learning. He promoted the cognitive theory, which encompasses the constructivist approach to learning, often used in science.

51. **D.** Group activity using homogeneous or heterogeneous combinations of students, selected by the teacher is considered cooperative learning as the students work collaboratively to derive outcomes. The cooperative learning process aids students in gaining problem-solving, communication, and critical-thinking skills.

52. **D.** Primary source utilization is one of the three essential types of lessons used for social studies. It includes actual items from the period or the place into the studies (for example, original documents, artifacts, maps, photos, clothing, music and tools).

53. **D.** Based on the information provided, this student may be embarrassed about performing a dance, the languages, or using dress in class. Teachers must take into account student abilities and interests when creating lessons. This student may need an accommodation for this assignment and asking the student about preferences and desires may help to promote trust and understanding, thus encouraging participation.

54. **C.** This example is the multiplication strategy of *doubles that are equivalent* to doubles in addition problems.

55. **D.** When a teacher points out the initial consonants in a story to help students begin to predict a word, it encourages phonics skills.

56. **A.** Health education has become a timely and important topic in the science curriculum. The primary goal is for students to attain and maintain a healthy lifestyle, and while in school, good health impacts student learning and achievement.

57. **D.** Individuals believe that the high-stakes tests promote the "dumbing down" (a focus on lower order skills) of the school curriculum by implementing rote memorization strategies in learning key concepts rather than emphasizing critical thinking skills and other more complex cognitive skills.

58. **A.** The verbal intelligence is most closely related to the subject area of reading and language arts, as it is the ability to express oneself orally or in writing.

59. **B.** This error shows a student who has forgotten to record the zeros (0). Using column lines between numbers with place values in division will help students learn this concept.

60. **C.** Mnemonics is a strategy that enhances student memory by using key words, acronyms, or acrostics to highlight the information. "HOMES" stands for the following Great Lakes: Huron, Ontario, Michigan, Erie, and Superior.

61. **A.** Scope and sequence is an essential design component of a curriculum. It includes the planning of learning sequences and an outline of the sequential development of skills and concepts of the content.

62. **B.** Recording small amounts of data plotted on a simple graph is a skill that is reasonably introduced at the second-grade level.

63. **A.** Cognitive theorists believe that an individual constructs the acquisition of new information and skills based upon prior knowledge. The internal mental processes included in this theory are problem solving, memory, and language.

64. **D.** The study of science is divided into specific domains, one of which is physical science. It includes the study of the tangible and material world, such as properties of objects, materials and matter, motion and force, light, heat, electricity, magnetism, and energy.

65. **A.** This is an example of integrating fine arts into the reading and language arts content area. Having students compose an original piece and then creating an illustration (art) and performing before peers (drama) is one way to incorporate two or more subjects and meet additional goals and standards.

66. **C.** Students who participate in learning activities for the pleasure of doing so and complete assignments or participate in activities because they want to successfully master a subject or skill have intrinsic motivation, which comes from within the individual.

67. **A.** Inductive instruction is the process of moving from more specific to more generalized information. Students study detailed information on which to base a broad conclusion. In this example, students study specific plants and the details of each, which will lead them to a generalized statement about where the plants must live and their purpose for being there.

68. **D.** This is an example of the level *comprehension,* as students are asked to predict which demonstrates an understanding of the information, and the ability to interpret the material.

69. **B.** Scaffolding provides a temporary support for a learner who is not ready to perform the task alone. The teacher is giving needed support at the beginning of her lesson by paraphrasing the textbook, asking questions and exploring ideas. She will gradually decrease it as the students become more independent and gain higher order thinking skills.

70. **D.** Through this activity, students are learning more about the top and bottom numbers and the relative sizes, which is the concept of comparing.

71. **C.** A summative assessment is the best choice for an assessment at the completion of a unit to identify the future needs of learners and make decisions to support student achievement.

72. **B.** The second most important step in conducting an experiment is to determine the hypothesis based on the first step of stating the question. The hypothesis is an educated guess as to the answer to the proposed question. The hypothesis is the basis for proceeding with the experiment and the concept to be proved or disproved.

73. **D.** Choral responding is an excellent strategy to use in the classroom to promote listening and speaking. Choral responding is the oral response of a class of students to a question that is presented by the teacher. Students must listen to the question, interpret the meaning, conjure an answer, and respond orally (speaking).

74. **D.** The purpose of an anticipatory set, one of the essential skills, is to engage students and grab their attention, getting them motivated and interested in the subject matter. If you were to act out a playground scene depicting citizenship, it would link student's prior knowledge to current learning.

75. **D.** Using meaningful content as a discussion prior to introducing a new concept should be motivating to the students. If they discuss whether these sentences are true, impossible or possible, it will support their understanding of the new concept to be introduced: probability and estimation.

76. **A.** It is important to establish the appropriate attitudes surrounding science at an early age so children will continue to pursue this subject area, regardless of gender or culture. Elementary teachers should evaluate student attitudes and enhance their curriculum to address this area.

77. **D.** The Neo-Skinnerian Model, developed by Skinner, is described as the shaping and modeling of desired behaviors through the use of consistent rewards and consequences.

78. **D.** A summative assessment is the type of evaluation used at the end of a unit of study to check a particular skill or concept. The method of obtaining data may be left to the teacher and, in this instance, the delivery of the report may be used as an authentic assessment and scored using a rubric.

79. **C.** A portfolio assessment is a collection of student work that may be selected by both the student and the teacher to demonstrate strengths, progress, skills, and completed assignments. It is a recommended method of assessment for use with parents, as it demonstrates ongoing progress, acquisition of skills, and actual performance on tasks.

80. **B.** Allowing learners the appropriate time between instruction/task presentation and responding to a question posed is called processing time, wait time, or think time. Time to pause and think should be based upon the difficulty of the task and the age of the students.

81. **C.** Madeline Hunter is well known for her approach of Direct Instruction which includes an instructional sequence for any subject and grade level, considering the diversity of learners. Students move along a sequence, supported by the educator, reviewing previous concepts and moving to the next step after mastery of the skills is complete.

82. **A.** The U.S. monetary system as well as the system of scientific measures are based on decimals. Students must have a solid grasp of fractions before beginning the study of decimals as these are related, not separate concepts. The teacher should assess the students' understanding of fractions.

83. **B.** A criterion-referenced test is a formal measure that may be used to evaluate students on the specific information of the poetry unit by having students answer specific questions, such as those about terminology.

84. **B.** This passage is an example of the transitional stage of writing in which all letters are present in the word, but they may not be in the correct order.

85. **A.** One of the six primary topics created by the NCTM for mathematics in the schools is **equity,** which focuses on the expectations and support that should be available to students. Its premise is that every student should have the same goals, support, materials, and instruction in math in order for each to reach the highest potential.

86. **C.** A scoring rubric offers several viable components in grading a performance assessment. It is a predetermined outline of how the product will be scored. It sets the criteria to be used to judge the performance, the range of quality that is acceptable, and the value of the score. Students know ahead of completing the performance assessment the outline of the rubric.

87. **B.** A contingency contract is a written agreement that is developed by the student and the teacher. It describes the expected performance and the kinds of reinforcers that should be used. The steps and procedures are discussed with one another, giving the student an active role in learning to self-manage behaviors.

88. **C.** The word "house" in this example suggests the student is in the phase of *letter-like symbols*, which shows writing in which letters begin to emerge although still randomly placed with numbers mixed throughout.

89. **D.** Comprehension is the level that is best described as understanding the information, where students are able to explain, discuss, review, and summarize the information.

90. **B.** Task analysis involves creating a set of sequential steps to learn a specific skill, which helps students move to a preferred level of skills.

91. **A.** A reader profile may include a student interview of reading preferences, a miscue analysis, and a retelling and discussion of the materials. This is a beneficial tool in determining a student's reading strengths and needs.

92. **C.** Developing tiered lessons would be the best solution, as these provide accommodations for various learners, both at the lower end of the bell curve and those at the higher end of the academic curve.

93. **D.** Systematic feedback provides regular positive reinforcement and confirms for the learner that he is performing adequately which improves learning. In mathematics education, students need consistent and constant feedback so they know that they are performing the tasks appropriately, which helps them improve their skills.

94. **A.** Onsets and rimes are parts of words in the spoken language that are smaller than syllables. An **onset** is the initial consonant sound of a syllable and a **rime** is the portion of the syllable with the vowel and is the remainder of the word.

95. **A.** Choral reading is used to involve several readers taking different parts as a specific selection is read aloud. These parts are rehearsed and since more than one student reads the part at the same time, readers with less proficiency will feel more comfortable.

96. **A.** The delegator style of teaching is the choice that encourages greater autonomy in learners and makes the educator available as a consultative resource. It would be useful with older age groups, who are more responsible.

97. A. When creating assignments for students in a class, teachers should refer to developmentally appropriate practices, which consider the level at which each student is presently functioning. The assignments selected should meet the expectations for the age group and the ability of the group.

98. B. Data analysis and probability are identified in the first five standards, and the other options given are all connected to the second set of five in the ten general standards.

99. C. Guided writing is the use of instruction that scaffolds the writing process for a student. As the teacher works with and models the steps in the writing process, the student will gain mastery and reach independence.

100. B. The cloze procedure omits about every fifth word in a passage and requires that the student supply the missing word to make sense of the passage.

101. A. Basic facts means the addends and the factors in addition and multiplication problems that are less than 10. In subtraction and division, it means that the facts related to addition and multiplication and both parts equal less than 10.

102. B. The use of context clues should allow students to determine words that they have heard before, but may not know in print. If a student has trouble reading a word, he may lack the ability to use context clues.

103. A. Using manipulatives to teach mathematics provides practice in visualizing the concepts, which helps students acquire math skills and retain the information.

104. D. Scaffolding is a teaching strategy that provides temporary support to the learner who is not yet ready to perform a task independently. The use of this strategy delivers support in the beginning, then gradually decreases the teacher participation as the student becomes more competent, and ends with independent practice as the student masters the skill. This is especially helpful when students are learning new concepts and must perform tasks related to those concepts.

105. C. Lack of organization is evident in this sample. This student needs additional training in how to organize ideas and compose a proper structure for a paragraph.

106. C. Graphic displays often aid students in learning new vocabulary words. Using semantic webbing can support a main concept and relate the new words to some a student already knows. In this example, the main concept is *weather* and some of the eight vocabulary words may be known by the student. If a student knows the word rainy, then new words such as sleet or snowy will be easier to relate to.

107. C. Essential to the positive attitude students will gain regarding mathematics is that the lessons and activities, as well as the assessments are developmentally appropriate for the students. If these are too difficult or too easy for the students, the interest and ability to achieve will decrease.

108. C. The Constructivist Theory, based on Piaget's work, relates to how children construct their own knowledge based on prior experiences and investigations. The emphasis for elementary mathematics education is based on hands-on learning so students may discover the principles and concepts of math and relate them to what they already know.

109. A. The recommended method of instruction for students to learn proper grammar and its use is to provide authentic and meaningful lessons to students. Demonstrating grammar through the design of poetry and other narratives will aid students' use of correct grammar in the context of reading, writing, and speaking.

110. A. This student shows evidence of being in the phonetic stage of spelling development. He is attempting to write a letter for each sound that is heard. However, some of the endings, such as –ed may become 'd' or 't' in some words and blends are substituted in some words.

For each essay, recommendations are provided for considering the key information and primary points that the examinee should include. Since each examinee composes and answers essay questions in a different manner, based on prior knowledge and previous experiences, the answers for this practice exam provide only an outline and some suggestions for potential answers on the actual exam.

Read each of the following essay questions and complete a detailed and supportive written answer. These answers will be scored according to a standard rubric.

Essay 1

1. An elementary teacher is planning a unit for a fifth-grade class about explorers. Write three learner goals that demonstrate the integration of the subjects of social studies, science, and mathematics in this unit. Then develop and compose an activity using the format of Bloom's taxonomy that demonstrates the integration of two or more of these subjects with reading and language arts.

Examinees should be fully aware and clear about the meaning of "integration" prior to composing an answer to this question. For study purposes, the definition as well as the benefits of integration have been included here, although neither would be required as part of the written answer. This information should help an examinee study and prepare for the composition of a written answer to this question.

Definition of Integration

Integration literally means "to combine into a whole," which helps to clarify the meaning when used in elementary education. When integrating subjects in the curricula, the focus is on comprehensive and whole understanding of concepts and topics rather than the individual topics. Integration means to help students gain comprehensive understanding across various disciplines. It is the act of instructing concepts that cross disciplines and subjects, such as teaching mathematics through science activities, and literature through social studies.

Benefits of Integration

- When appropriate and done properly, integration helps supply students with an understanding of the relationships of all the individual parts to the whole.
- Integration helps students to take ownership of their own learning and creates autonomy.
- Integration aids in social relationships and cooperation among students.
- Integration increases knowledge in all subject areas.
- Integration cultivates appreciation for all areas of study.

In writing the answer for this question, examinees should include information based on the definition, the benefits, and purpose of integration. Although the question only requires three learner goals, a number of them are included for further consideration.

Learner Goals

For social studies, the following should be considered appropriate learner goals:

- Compare and contrast the differences of ideas, values, behaviors, personalities, and institutions.
- Hypothesize about some of the greatest influences of the past.

- Explain cause and effect of historical actions.
- Create time lines to show the significant achievements in history, math, and science.
- Identify problems or dilemmas of the past.
- Propose alternative choices for addressing problems.
- Evaluate the consequences of decisions made by explorers that influence areas of science or math.

For math, the following should be considered appropriate learner goals:

- Measure using techniques of the past.
- Carry out conversions to standard measurement.
- Create and use representations to organize, record, and communicate mathematical ideas.
- Use representations to model and interpret physical, social, and math phenomena.

For science, the following should be considered appropriate learner goals:

- Recognize the impact humans have upon the environment (irrigation, roads, cities, and so on).
- Identify environmental changes caused by living things.
- Predict the effects of human actions and/or natural disasters during this period in history on the environment.
- Determine the importance of crops and farming over this period in history.
- Recognize the impact of society's use of nonrenewable resources over time.

Bloom's Taxonomy

As review, the examinee should be knowledgeable about Bloom's Taxonomy in order to clearly state activities that may reflect this philosophy. Benjamin Bloom was an educational psychologist who developed a classification of levels of intellectual behavior important in learning. These levels should be incorporated into lessons, and the educator should strive to progress the students into the upper levels (analysis, synthesis, and evaluation).

- Knowledge—Recall or recognition of facts (arrange, define, label, list, name, order, repeat, relate, recall)
- Understanding (comprehension)—Grasping the meaning (classify, describe, discuss, explain, identify, indicate, locate, recognize, report, select, translate)
- Application—Use of previously learned information in new situations to solve problems (apply, choose, demonstrate, employ, illustrate, operate, practice, sketch, solve, use, write)
- Analysis—Breaking down of whole into parts to identify causes, make inferences, or find evidence to support (analyze, calculate, compare, contrast, criticize, discriminate, distinguish, examine, question, test)
- Synthesis—Creatively applying prior knowledge and skill to produce a new whole (arrange, assemble, collect, compose, construct, create, design, develop, formulate, manage, organize, plan, report)
- Evaluation—Judging the value of material based upon individual values and producing a final product (appraise, argue, assess, attach, compare, estimate, judge, predict, rate, select, support, value, evaluate)

Activities

A multitude of activities could impart knowledge to the students, but activities that encourage active learning should be promoted in order to reach the stages of application, analysis, and synthesis.

- Students study parts of a map and write a user's manual on map reading (social studies, language arts/reading) *application & synthesis.*
- Students study the parts of a map: compass rose, legend, and so on and create a map of the school using the parts studied (language arts/reading, math, social studies) *understanding & application & synthesis.*

GO ON TO THE NEXT PAGE

- Students map a specific explorer's course across his expedition using precise measurement, appropriate time, geographic entities, major landforms, and label each part of the map (social studies, math, and language) *understanding & application & synthesis*.

- Students study travel media and then create a travel brochure to an explored region; include climate, landforms, historical significance, and colorful, descriptive language to entice tourists (science, social studies, language arts/reading) *understanding & application & synthesis*.

- Students study North American explorers and make a timeline of exploration, including illustrations (language arts, social studies, mathematics) *knowledge & application & synthesis*.

- Students keep a journal as if they are the explorer themselves, complete with illustrations, dated entries, miles traveled, and comments on major discoveries (language arts/reading, social studies, mathematics) *application & analysis & synthesis*.

- Students study explorer ships and then create their own ship of exploration, thinking about what size it must be, how to scale the size down into a model, the shape it must be, what supplies may be needed for a voyage, what tools may be needed, the size of the crew, and so on. Students will draw "blueprints" for the ship and then construct it (social studies, mathematics, language arts/reading, science) *understanding & application & analysis & synthesis*.

- Students will study an explorer, his contributions to society and his negative effects upon society and write a report or give a presentation based on this information (language arts/reading, social studies, science) *understanding & application & analysis & synthesis & evaluation*.

Essay 2

2. The first-grade team, of which you are a member, has designed a 6-week social studies unit on community helpers. The principal has asked for a copy of the assessment plan for this unit. Outline a plan for assessment during this 6-week unit that includes both summative and formative assessments. Describe five different types of student assessments that will be used and explain how each will specifically be used. Then describe what the teacher will be evaluating in this unit.

Define Assessment

Many forms and types of assessments are within the realm of determining student comprehension. Summative assessment is an assessment that is given periodically to gauge students' comprehension of a particular skill at a particular point in time and includes standardized tests, end-of-chapter exams, and semester finals. Formative assessments are assessments that occur during the learning process so that the teacher may adjust and revamp teaching techniques and include portfolios, student record keeping, observations, and student-led conferences. Assessments allow learners to identify what they need to learn and what they want to learn. It also provides learners with the insight to their strengths and weaknesses. Assessments allow learners to see what they have learned, what they have retained, and how they have grown. It gives students the chance to understand individual capabilities so that they may assess tasks and projects for themselves. It is also an opportunity for students to gain a sense of what strategies work best for them personally and why these are effective.

Choosing Assessments

Assessments utilized should not only be connected to learner backgrounds and interests but should be matched to the appropriate tasks and skills measured. Teachers must consider these points when selecting the proper assessment:

- A combination of assessments should be chosen
  - Some assessments focus on skills, some on strategies, some on the acquisition of knowledge
  - It is important that authentic assessments concentrate on the application of skills in learners' daily lives
- Learners should participate in the decision of which tasks they need to work on and also in the kinds of assessments they want to select to evaluate their skills (especially important in the older grades).
  - Self–assessment, conferencing, and reflections should be implemented at an early age in all subjects and disciplines to promote ownership of learning.

Type of Assessments Implemented

Memory matrix is a sheet of paper with rows and columns (as many as are needed), and only the headings of each row are filled in. It is a formative assessment used to advance the organization of ideas and the illustration of relationships.

For the first grader learning about community helpers, it may be as simple as placing the community helper in the appropriate row. (For example, *helps people* column would include firefighter, policeman, teacher; *provides a service* column would include mail carrier, baker, butcher.)

Word journal is a notebook of words that the learner keeps, which are associated with the task at hand. The words are placed in alphabetical order (similar to a dictionary), and meanings are written. It is a formative assessment used to examine the depth of comprehension and the ability to summarize information.

For the first grader learning about community helpers, it would be used to keep new or complex words associated with the unit. (For example, hydrant, veterinarian, canine, feline, community, cooperation, language, and so on.)

Writing task is an activity in which the student is asked to write something on a given topic to gauge comprehension. It is a formative assessment used to analyze student understanding and synthesis of the content learned.

For the first grader learning about community helpers, it may be a functional writing assessment in which he writes about a day in the life of a specific community helper, writes a job description of a community helper, writes a song or poem about a community helper, illustrates the job of a community helper, and so on. The student could also paint a picture of the community helper.

Test could be constructed in the format of true/false, multiple choice, essay, matching, or fill in the blank. It is a summative assessment used at the conclusion of a unit or given time frame.

For the first grade student learning about community helpers, the test may have pictures of community jobs and pictures of the community helper that the student must match or words that relate to specific community helpers that must be placed under the appropriate community member.

Oral presentation would be a researched and planned presentation given on a specific topic. It is a formative assessment used to evaluate student understanding, analysis, synthesis, and application of skills and content learned.

For the first grader learning about community helpers, the presentation may be a brief discussion about which community helper he would most like to be when he grows up. This could be assessed through simple one-on-one conversations with the teacher or through peer interviews. The teacher could use a simple rubric in assessing knowledge during this time.

Essay 3

3. Measurement is a basic mathematics concept and necessary in daily life. Using Hunter's guide for the *essential elements of instruction*, write a lesson plan at the third-grade level for the instruction of standard customary liquid measures.

Introduction to Lesson Plan

Measurement knowledge is an essential skill, and the concept of measurement is complex. Students should be able to use the units, systems, and processes of measurement throughout their lifetimes. Using the proper tools, techniques, and formulas to determine measurement should be included in the instruction.

In third grade, students may learn about volume/capacity and the proper measurement tools or containers. Measuring volume and capacity relates to three-dimensional objects and figures. The standard units of measurement utilized for volume include ounces, cups, pints, quarts, and gallons. Students may also use containers to check the amount being measured, such as cups, boxes, and bowls.

GO ON TO THE NEXT PAGE

Summary of Lesson Plan Using Essential Elements of Instruction (Hunter)

Examinee will include more details and explanations. This is a sample of a lesson outline, as all lessons written for this question will be clearly different.

Standards-expectations Objectives	The students will be able to identify the various measurement tools used for measuring volume and capacity. The students will be able to compare the capacity of different containers used for measuring liquids.
Anticipatory set	Clear containers (cup, pint, quart) are set up on a center table as students gather for lesson. The teacher has a pitcher of water and a set of food coloring. Water is poured into the cup and a few drops of coloring added. That is poured into the pint container to compare the amount. More is added to the cup which is then added to the pint. The same is done for the quart, so students may not only compare the amounts in each container, but see how the colors change by the amount added.
Instruction	Teacher provides direct information: Provides names of containers and comparison of amounts. Demonstrates how various liquids and amounts can be measured. Uses question and answer period to determine student understanding.
Guided practice	Cooperative groups are created to practice measuring amounts and charting what the different containers can hold.
Closure	Teacher plays a quick trivia game with students to check knowledge.
Independent practice	Learning center is created with measuring tools and various liquids. Students may practice measurements, comparisons, and conversions.

Essay 4

4. The National Reading Council and reading research suggest five primary core skills that are factors that contribute to the success of readers. These include phonemic awareness, phonics, fluency, vocabulary, and comprehension of text.

Define each of these skills and describe how each skill relates to reading instruction. Write an activity for elementary students at grades pre-K to 2 that will promote each of these predictor skills in young children (a total of five activities).

Definitions

These may be written in more detail, but should include the main points as follows.

- *Phonemic awareness*—The knowledge that speech sounds are found in the letters of the alphabet and that blending sounds can create words
- *Phonics*—The relationship between the sounds in spoken language with the letters that represent the sounds when written
- *Fluency*—When reading is done accurately and automatically with expression and a consistent rate
- *Vocabulary*—The words that are either being learned or already known and used
- *Comprehension of text*—Specific strategies used such as critical thinking in the processing of reading to understand the content

Activities

Examinee should describe an activity for each of the five core skills listed in this question. The following are provided as suggestions for the purpose on which to base an activity for students.

Activities for **phonemic awareness** could include the following:

- Use of nursery rhymes.
- Exposure to poetry, jingles, or rhyming phrases.
- Utilize songs with rhyme and rhythm.
- Play games with nonsense syllables.

Activities for **phonics** could include the following:

- Sight reading new words.
- Compare new words to those with similar patterns.
- Practice blending words through onsets and rimes.
- Create word banks.
- Recite poetry and rhymes.

Activities for **fluency** could include the following:

- Practice oral reading periods.
- Use reader's theatre opportunities.
- Provide a chance for choral readings.
- Use listening center, read alouds and models.
- Use sustained reading periods.

Activities for **vocabulary** could include the following:

- Use games and puzzles.
- Create word books.
- Instruct use of dictionary.
- Improve oral vocabulary usage.
- Compare types of words, such as homographs or homophones or homonyms.
- Instruct use of prefixes or suffixes and root words.
- Teach context clues strategies.
- Use descriptive words in speaking and writing.

Activities for **comprehension of text** could include the following:

- Practice with inferences.
- Use imagery.
- Learn to make connections.
- Understand question-answer relationships.
- Use of K-W-L strategy.
- Practice with summarizing what is read.

Historical Timeline

Year	Event
12,000 B.C.E.	Asians migrated over Bering Strait into North America.
100 C.E.	Hopewell Culture established large trading network.
300 C.E.	Mayan city of Tikal established.
800 C.E.	Mayan cities collapsed.
1325	Aztecs built Tenochtitlan (Mexico City).
1585	Roanoke Island colony established on the Virginia coast and then disappears.
1607	Jamestown Colony founded.
1620	Plymouth Colony founded.
1630	Massachusetts Bay Colony founded.
1681	Pennsylvania established by William Penn.
1754	French and Indian War began.
1763	Pontiacs revolted. Treaty of Paris signed.
1764	Sugar Act; Currency Act
1765	Stamp Act; Sons of Liberty form.
1770	Boston Massacre
1773	Tea Act; Boston Tea Party
1774	Intolerable Acts; First Continental Congress convened.
1775	American Revolution began. Battle of Bunker Hill
1776	Declaration of Independence signed.
1780	French Army landed in Connecticut
1781	Articles of Confederation
1783	Treaty of Paris ended war.
1787	New territories prohibited slavery. Constitutional Convention held in Philadelphia.
1788	Federalist Papers published. Constitution ratified and made the law of the land.
1789	Federal Court system established (Judiciary Act).
1791	Bill of Rights approved.
1794	Whiskey Rebellion
1802	Louisiana Purchase
1804	Lewis and Clark expedition
1812	Congress declared war on Britain (War of 1812).
1814	British burned Washington D.C.; Treaty of Ghent ended War of 1812.
1820	Missouri Compromise
1823	Monroe Doctrine
1846	United States declared war on Mexico. Oregon Treaty
1848	Gold discovered in California. Treaty of Guadalupe Hildalgo
1849	California Gold Rush

(continued)

Year	Event
1850	Compromise of 1850
1860	South Carolina succeeded from the Republic.
1861	Confederacy formed and Civil War Began. First Battle of Bull Run
1863	Battle of Gettysburg
1865	Civil War ends. 13th Amendment ended slavery. Lincoln assassinated.
1867	Alaska purchased from Russia.
1869	Transcontinental Railroad completed.
1877	Custer defeated by the Sioux at Little Big Horn (Custer's Last Stand).
1890	Wounded Knee Massacre
1898	Spanish-American War began
1899	Treaty of Paris ended Spanish-American War.
1914	Panama Canal opened. World War I began. Arizona became a state.
1917	United States declares war on Germany.
1919	Treaty of Versailles
1920	19th Amendment (Woman's Suffrage)
1931	Star Spangled Banner designated national anthem by an Act of Congress.
1939	World War II began.
1941	Japan attacked Pearl Harbor.
1945	Atomic bombs are dropped. Japan and Germany surrendered. WWII ends.
1947	Cold War began between United States and USSR.
1950	Korean War began.
1955	Montgomery Bus Boycott
1956	Vietnam War began
1957	Sputnik; Civil Rights Act
1961	Bay of Pigs, Cuba
1962	Cuban Missile Crisis
1963	Kennedy assassinated and Johnson becomes President.
1968	Robert Kennedy and Martin Luther King both assassinated.
1969	First man landed on the moon (Neil Armstrong).
1973	United States withdrew from Vietnam.
1983	Reagan started the Strategic Defense Initiative.
1990	Iraqi forces invaded Kuwait.
1991	The Persian Gulf War began. Kuwait is liberated. United States and Allies defeated Iraq.
1992	United States and Russia signed the Treaty to officially end the Cold War
1994	Republican Party wins majority in both Senate and House for first time in 40 years.
1998	Two American embassies in Eastern Africa destroyed by terrorists. U.S. forces launched air strikes in Iraq.
1999	Panama gain control of the Panama Canal.
2001	September 11, Terrorists attacked World Trade Center and Pentagon.
2003	United States led forces invaded Iraq.

CUT HERE